DATE

The Teaching for Social Justice Series

William Ayers—Series Editor
Therese Quinn—Associate Series Editor

Editorial Board: Hal Adams, Barbara Bowman, Lisa Delpit, Michelle Fine, Maxine Greene, Caroline Heller, Annette Henry, Asa Hilliard (1933–2007), Rashid Khalidi, Kevin Kumashiro, Gloria Ladson-Billings, Charles Payne, Mark Perry, Luis Rodriguez, Jonathan Silin, William Watkins

TEACH FREEDOM

Education for Liberation in the African-American Tradition

Edited by
CHARLES M. PAYNE
CAROL SILLS STRICKLAND

Foreword by Charles E. Cobb, Jr.

Teachers College, Columbia University
New York and London

Teach Freedom: Education for Liberation in the African-American Tradition is published with support from the Spencer Foundation.

Published by Teachers College Press, 1234 Amsterdam Avenue, New York, NY 10027

Library of Congress Cataloging-in-Publication Data

Teach freedom : education for liberation in the African-American tradition / edited by Charles M. Payne and Carol Sills Strickland.
    p. cm.
  Includes bibliographical references and index.
  ISBN 978-0-8077-4872-5 (pbk. : alk. paper)—ISBN 978-0-8077-4873-2 (hardcover : alk. paper)
  1. African Americans—Education—History.   2. African Americans—Civil rights—History.   3. Popular education—United States.   4. United States—Race relations.   I. Payne, Charles M. II. Strickland, Carol Sills.
  LC2741.T43 2008
  370.89'96073—dc22
                                                          2007044711

ISBN 978-0-8077-4872-5 (paper)
ISBN 978-0-8077-4873-2 (hardcover)

Printed on acid-free paper
Manufactured in the United States of America

15   14   13   12   11   10   09   08   8   7   6   5   4   3   2   1

It is not given to us to complete the task. Nor may we remove our hands from the plow.

—The Talmud

Be a lamp,
or a lifeboat,
or a ladder.
Help someone's soul heal.
Walk out of your house like a shepherd.
—*The Diwan of Shams of Tabriz* by Jalaluddin Rumi

I want to tell you about Mrs. Hazel Palmer, who is a lady who works with the Freedom Democratic Party in Mississippi. She was working for ten, fifteen dollars a week as a maid most of her life. She stopped and changed last summer. And if you want to write her, and I suggest you do—a lot of you—drop her a line. . . . Ask her, "What did you use to do? What do you do now? How come you changed? What gave you the courage to do that? What makes you think that instead of being a cook in somebody's kitchen you could help run a political party? Where did you go to learn how to do that? Did you go to school?

—Bob Moses, Student Nonviolent Coordinating Committee

Contents

Foreword: Full Circle

It was puzzling to me at first during my earliest days as a SNCC (Student Nonviolent Coordinators Committee) field secretary doing organizing work in the Mississippi Delta in 1962: Because before I arrived in the state my mental image of Mississippi was of Emmett Till and shacks, when I saw the many obviously new schools that had been built for the Black community, the sight of them was totally unexpected. I soon learned, however, that these schools were post–1954 Supreme Court decision shells built to hide the fact that the so-called separate but equal education being offered to the students who attended them was still "sharecropper education." Many of these schools shut down, and the students closed their books and went to the fields when cotton needed to be picked. Test tubes and microscopes were scarce in school laboratories. Many library shelves were empty. And despite the heroic efforts of more than a few teachers to encourage the idea that life could be about more than subservience to White power, the driving assumption of these state institutions was that young Black people did not need much education beyond that necessary for picking cotton, nursing babies, and preparing meals. Essential English grammar boiled down to "yes, sir" and "yes, ma'am" in the minds of school authorities.

"The more things change, the more things stay the same," goes an old sardonic French saying that nonetheless contains some truth along with its cynicism. Consider schools today. The expressed commitment to education so often and so loudly offered by local and national public figures is hardly confirmed by the reality one encounters in cities and many rural communities. For the most part, public schools that serve African Americans, other minorities, and the poor offer a 21st-century version of the sharecropper education I encountered in Mississippi 45 years ago. In my hometown, Washington, DC, the typical public school 12th grader graduates able to read and calculate at an eighth-grade level. These students are no better equipped to function in a high-tech society than the sharecroppers we encountered on Mississippi plantations were equipped to function in an industrial society requiring reading and writing literacy, and, in some ways, are worse off than their 20th-century counterparts. We see many of today's sharecroppers behind the lunch counters of fast-food chains and behind prison walls—the new plantations, complete with "darkies" singing in the yard.

Although there is a rough consensus that inner-city public schools in particular do not educate, there is no consensus on fixing these schools. Rather, school systems offer flight as a response to their failed institutions— moving some students, abandoning a great many more. Among the methods used to duck the issued of fixing public schools are magnet schools, charter schools, vouchers for private schools, and, especially in the South, "academies." And although I am willing to acknowledge that these all can have some merit as part of a school "system," they become harmful when used as instruments—excuses—not to tackle fixing our public schools.

This is not simply a matter of reading, writing, and arithmetic. There has always been a link between education and citizenship. African slaves in the antebellum and Confederate South recognized this. And one of the great accomplishments of the Reconstruction Era that followed the Civil War— driven by newly freed and politically enfranchised former slaves—was entrenching public education in the popular culture. Literally every state in the now reunified nation followed the South in making public education mandatory and free for the first 16 years of a child's life. When Reconstruction was abandoned, public education for Blacks became an immediate target of the restored Southern Confederacy. In the South that I knew as a SNCC field secretary, Black illiteracy created by deliberate state policy was used as a rationale and method for denying voting rights to the victims of that policy.

But beyond the tactics and politics of denying voting rights to Blacks, a deeper, more insidious issue related to how Blacks were being educated came into sharper focus as we organized voter registration and other civil rights campaigns. And it, too, resonates with what we encounter in public schools today. Blacks were being taught to believe in their own inferiority, to believe that their—our—race itself justified denial of full citizenship rights. To do this, thought itself had to be stifled in schools, and we were encouraged by the state to do it to ourselves—not to allow ourselves to think, for thought generates the one word that threatens any system, whether that system is constructed around White supremacy at home or the conquest and occupation of foreign lands: "Why?"

The White-only power structure in Mississippi where I worked, and also across the South, recognized that an educated population, a population raised from unconsciousness to consciousness, is a dangerous population. A whole way of life can become unraveled when people begin thinking. This is one of the great lessons found in the life of Mrs. Fannie Lou Hamer, who, when asked years later how despite knowing what the consequences in violence and reprisal could be, she still attempted to register to vote, responded by saying that she *thought* about it and decided that it was the right thing to do: "I thought on that. I could see that it was right and I was raised to do what was right so I went." The education of Mrs. Hamer took place, in part, in the few churches that gave us space to meet. The key word here is *space*—comfortable space that by all rights should have been part of civics education in public schools but was not. The roots of the Mississippi freedom schools of the summer of 1964 are lodged here in this idea of creating comfortable space for the expression and exploration of ideas. In short, the idea of a liberating education, which also defined freedom schools, grew out of the political and intellectual ferment of the civil rights movement. I think of this as I consider public schools today, which, insofar as I have observed them in inner cities, seem to be doing little more than creating 21st-century sharecroppers who are illiterate and unprepared for the demands of this new century.

It cannot be stressed enough how significant it was that in Mississippi and across the 1960s South we had political movement. What characterized that movement was that the very people who had been written off as apathetic and too primitive and backward for citizenship found their voice and refuted with words and action all of the assumptions about what they were satisfied with and wanted. Long-silent voices at the grassroots level began making demands, began demanding what society said they did not want or even care about. We need to hear similar voices today when expressed in words that are eerily reminiscent of what we heard 4 decades ago, we hear said of students in inner-city schools and rural areas of the South where public schools are largely populated by minorities and the poor: "They don't want to learn"; "You can't teach them!" "They act like savages!" Public schools will get better and actually educate the children who attend them when, as occurred with the civil rights movement, the people at the bottom, those who have been written off, begin to make demands.

But there has to be more than demanding that something be given to you. We have to demand something of ourselves, for that, too, was critical to civil rights struggle—perhaps its most crucial element. In this regard, it is impossible not to make some reference to Ella Baker, as several of the essays in this book do. It was this kind of challenge—to ourselves and to our community—that she always insisted was a crucial component in the making of social change. All of her work—pioneering work that helped shape a half-century of civil rights struggle—reflected this. Indeed, in organizing NAACP chapters across the South in the 1940s, midwifing the birth of SCLC in the 1950s and becoming that organization's first executive secretary, and playing an instrumental role in the formation of SNCC, becoming, in fact, the political godmother of that organization of young people, Baker really was laying down a challenge for us to accept or reject: "Make a demand; make a struggle." Her challenge still seems relevant today. The freedom schools, for example, were not just a reaction to poor education; they were an affirmation that anything we put our mind(s) to is possible. This is exactly what is missing from public education today. And the results are all around us, voiced far too often by young people whose minds are being wasted. Why else has it become so easy to hear coming from the mouths of our young people that wanting a good education is trying to "be White"? At least in Mississippi when folks warned me to be careful because, in trying to get people registered to vote I was fooling around with "White folks' business," they knew that getting registered to vote was important. Civil rights legislation notwithstanding, I cannot help but feel that in some important ways we have moved backward, especially in public schools.

So, as we seem to say every decade, "Where do we go from here?" I think my former SNCC colleague, Bob Moses, with whom I coauthored the book *Radical Equations*, is on the right track in launching a campaign for quality public education as a civil right. At this beginning stage, the shape of Bob Moses's campaign is not completely formed, but important questions and issues are at last being put on the table: Just what is quality public education? Can we start a national conversation on this? If quality education is a civil right, how do we claim it? What will be the base of such a movement? One direction for such an effort that Moses proposes taking is to campaign for an amendment to the U.S. Constitution that will guarantee quality public education for every child in the United States.

It remains to be seen whether such an idea will catch on, but one of the basic lessons of the Southern civil rights movement is that you cannot predict what spark will light a fire.

Charles E. Cobb, Jr.
December 28, 2005

Acknowledgments

We wish to acknowledge the support of the Spencer Foundation, which provided support for this project in several forms, including the time and space for Charles Payne to work on it. We also acknowledge the support of the Lewis-Sebring Family Foundation. We are grateful to Michelle Fine and Theresa Perry for their supportive and insightful comments on an earlier draft. We are endebted to Connie Blackmore for cheerful logistical support.

Introduction

Charles M. Payne

During his time in Detroit, C.L.R. James, the Pan-Africanist author and activist, used to invite young people to his home on Sundays, asking each of them to bring a newspaper from a different country. He wanted them to see how any event was seen differently when filtered through different national lenses. As simple an exercise as it was, he was teaching one of the most profoundly liberating of all lessons, a lesson about the partiality of viewpoints and about the way social perspectives are inevitably embedded in all ideas. Until one gets that straight, thinking with any depth about social issues is all but impossible.

In 1929, Charles Hamilton Houston (Phi Beta Kappa at Amherst and the first Black man to serve on the *Harvard Law Review*) became dean of Howard University's law school. He immediately set about making it an instrument of struggle. A lawyer, he liked to say, is either a social engineer or parasite. He fired faculty who could not keep up and flunked out students in droves. Thurgood Marshall came in with a class of 30, but graduated with a class less than half that size. Houston's motto was "No tea for the feeble, no crepe for the dead." He brought in Supreme Court justices for his students to argue before. Houston angered many people, but the cohort of lawyers who would lead the assault on the legal edifice of White supremacy was trained largely at Howard Law.

The self-conscious use of education as an instrument of liberation among African Americans is exactly as old as education among African Americans. Education for liberation can be something as simple and intellectually elegant as what James did or something as involved as the long-term institution-building that was Charlie Houston's lifework. It can be a direct assault on the citadels of privilege, or it can focus on the self-development of individuals in the hope, as Ella Baker put it, that strong people don't need strong leaders.

This book is about education for liberation among African Americans, those forms of education intended to help people think more critically about the social forces shaping their lives and think more confidently about their ability to react against those forces. We are concerned with the variety of forms it takes, from the shadow of slavery to the contradictions of hip-hop, with its evolution and impact, with its enduring contradictions and tensions, with its interconnections with other social currents, with the role played by people not of African descent, with the difficulties organizers encounter trying to start or sustain programs, with the lessons of the past for the present moment. One of the tragedies of Black civic culture of the last several decades has been the paucity of formal opportunities for young Black people to learn to think critically about social issues. It is as if Black adults somehow decided, yes, the society is racist, but, no, Black youngsters don't need any particular guidance to learn how to negotiate and understand that society. Let them work it out. Arguably, Black America did a better job of racial socialization in the years after World War II, when NAACP youth chapters were flourishing, when segregated institutions, even when not overtly political, provided space for critical reflection and individual growth. Indeed, given the simultaneous decline of Black institutional patterns and the rise of pervasive mass media, the latter half of the 20th century probably represents something of a low point in the ability of Black Americans to create counternarrative for the next generation.

In the last several years, however, there has been a sharp upturn of interest. The Children's Defense Fund Freedom Schools have experienced steady growth, challenging the organization's capacity to meet demand. One of the ironic consequences of the small school–charter school movement is that it has opened up space in public schools for curricula that are explicitly liberatory in intent. By fall 2006, Chicago had at least 10 schools and New York had 17 schools that identified themselves as having some kind of social justice focus, most of them less than 5 years old, most serving children of color. A website devoted to the civil rights movement now gets 130,000 page views a month during the school year (www.crmvet.org). It is still too soon to say where all of this is headed, but there is clearly more interest in emancipatory education, among African Americans and others, than has been the case since the early 1970s.

Education for African Americans has always had particular political and moral resonances. "For the slaves," Theresa Perry writes, "literacy was more than a symbol of freedom; it was freedom. It affirmed their humanity, their personhood" (Perry, 2003, 13). After the Civil War, "They rushed not to the grog shop but to the schoolroom," wrote Harriet Beecher Stowe in 1879. "They cried for the spelling-book as bread, and pleaded for teachers as a necessity of life." Booker T. Washington observed that "Few people who were not right in the midst of the scenes can form any exact idea of the intense desire which the people of my race showed for education. It was a whole race trying to go to school. Few were too young, and none too old, to make the attempt to learn" (Anderson, 1988, p. 5).

In Chapter 1 of this volume, Steven Hahn says that after slavery, Black women seem to have played a particularly active part in advancing the cause of education. The same might be said of the 20th century, from Mary McLeod Bethune to the women who ran Black Panther liberation schools. Perhaps no one did more to shape an African American pedagogy of the oppressed than Septima Clark and Ella Baker.

Clark's Citizenship Schools are paradigmatic in many ways. One of the enduring themes of education for liberation is its tendency to encourage people to play roles that they would ordinarily be prevented—by their youth, their race, gender, poverty, education, or by social convention—from playing. Clark, for example, didn't want traditionally credentialed teachers:

> I sat down and wrote out a flyer saying that the teachers we need in a Citizenship School should be people who are respected by the members of the community, who can read well aloud, and who can write their names in cursive writing. These are the ones that we looked for. . . . We were trying to make teachers out of these people who could barely read and write. But they could teach. (Brown, 1986, pp. 63–64)

In Chapter 3, David Levine notes that when one woman began speaking back to male leadership, Clark took that to be a positive benchmark, and when the leader in question learned that it was his function to encourage that kind of challenge, that was an even more important benchmark.

Emancipatory education is also intended to be transformative, which is one of the reasons shattering traditional role definitions is so important. The Citizenship Schools were intended not merely to prepare people to register to vote but to develop community leaders, people we might call "critical citizens," following Adam Green's usage (Payne and Green, 2003). The evaluation form in use in Mississippi in 1963 asked whether the graduate had been instrumental in getting others to vote, but it also asked whether he or she had signed petitions, attended community meetings, engaged in demonstrations, become more effective in community action, worked for any unselfish cause, or rendered more help to his or her neighbors. In other words, the form asked whether we had transformed this person. Farmers and laborers who had difficulty holding a pencil wound up opening credit unions and health centers and preschools.

Another of the enduring themes of liberatory education has been respect for the students with whom one is working, what David Levine, in Chapter 3, calls the radical affirmation of students' dignity. One of the reasons it is important to have students involved in decision making is precisely that it shows respect for them. Septima Clark found that her willingness to really listen to poor people gave her an advantage over even supposedly radical and sophisticated male colleagues.

One of Ella Baker's biographers, Barbara Ransby, calls Baker a radical humanist. That description would work for Clark as well. The Lakota would have called them Shirtwearers, people whose lives reflected the values and traditions of the tribe with special fidelity. Baker typically explained the development of her own politics in terms of the communal, quasi-socialist setting in which she had grown up. Clark described some of her formative influences similarly:

> There are three things I felt I learned from my father. One was that he wanted you to always be truthful. Next, he wanted you not to exalt yourself, but to look at the culture of others and see whether or not you could strengthen their weaknesses and try to investigate how you could improve yourself toward them. Then, too, he talked about having Christ in your life. This is one thing that helps you to understand people better. If you can get the spirit of Christ into your life, you will learn to see others as Christ saw them and be able to live with them and help them to live with themselves. I feel that sitting around that pot-bellied stove he really gave us three very good things to look forward to— being truthful, strengthening other people's weaknesses, and seeing that there is something fine and noble in everybody. (Brown, 1986, pp. 97–98)

From their family and community backgrounds, Clark and Baker both took a deep capacity for identifying with others, a sense that our differences are not that important, that the flaws of others are no greater than our own, that people have potentials that are ordinarily hidden. No doubt, this life-affirming humanism is a part of the reason both Clark and Baker had such an impact on so many of the people with whom they worked.

The Freedom Schools established by the Student Nonviolent Coordinating Committee (SNCC) in Mississippi during the summer of 1964 were directly affected by the work of Clark and Baker. Short-lived in their original form, they became one of the most influential models for generations of subsequent organizers and educators.

SNCC entered Mississippi in the summer of 1961, and shortly thereafter, helped form the Council of Federated Organizations (COFO), a coalition of civil rights organizations. From 1961 to 1964, SNCC-COFO waged a valiant campaign for the right to vote. The defenders of White supremacy responded with violence, sometimes lethal, against individual civil rights workers and their local allies, with constant police harassment and with wholesale firings and evictions of people thought to be associated with the movement. The federal government pretty much shrugged. For some in SNCC, the last straw was the January 1964 murder of Louis Allen. Allen had earlier witnessed the slaying of NAACP member Herbert Lee, which probably led to his own killing. At the time Allen was killed, SNCC-COFO was in the midst of discussing the possibility of bringing large numbers of White students into the state for the subsequent summer, partly because they had noticed that when White students had been in the state, the movement got more attention from the press and the FBI. In the context of the killing of Allen and several others, something had to be done to make the federal government take a larger hand (Dittmer, 1994; Payne, 1995).

That something turned out to be the Mississippi Summer Project, bringing nearly 1,000 young people to the state, mostly White and well-to-do, the kind of people, Ella Baker noted, who could bring the concern of the nation with them. "Until the killing of black mothers' sons is as important as the killing of white mothers' sons," she would say famously, "we who believe in freedom cannot rest" (Ransby, 2003, p. 335). The volunteers would be the kind of people the federal government deemed important and, in protecting them, they would also be offering some measure of protection to the activists based in the state. The volunteers were expected to run voter registration campaigns, operate community centers, and conduct Freedom Schools.

When Charlie Cobb is referred to as the inventor of the Mississippi Freedom Schools, he typically demurs, which honors the SNCC norm that although important ideas may be expressed through individuals, in fact they are ordinarily developed through group process. In this case, though, the rest of the group seems unanimous that Cobb, a Howard University student who had been in Mississippi since 1962, gave shape to the idea. Cobb's thinking was affected by the experience the SNCC had had a year earlier when it organized Nonviolent High in Pike County, Mississippi, for students kicked out of school there, by Septima Clark's citizenship schools, which were playing an important role developing leaders in some of the Delta counties where Cobb worked and by Ella Baker herself—just her style and the way she worked with the SNCC young people. During one of the early planning sessions for the summer, Cobb proposed that the Summer Project do something to address the impoverished nature of the education typically offered to Black students in Mississippi. He wrote:

> Repression is the law; oppression a way of life. . . . Here, an idea of your own is a subversion that must be squelched; for each bit of intellectual initiative represents the threat of a probe into the why of denial. Learning here means only learning to stay in your place. . . . There is hope and there is dissatisfaction. . . . This is the generation that has silently made the vow of no more raped mothers, no more castrated fathers; that looks for an alternative to a lifetime of bent, burnt, and broken backs, minds and souls. Their creativity must be molded from the rhythm of a muttered "white son-of-a-bitch;" from the roar of a hunger bloated belly and from the stench of rain and mudwashed shacks.

. . . What they must see is the link between a rotting shack and a rotting America. (Quoted in Howe, 1984, p. 9)

Cobb wanted a component in the Summer Project that would "make it possible for them to challenge the myths of our society, to perceive more clearly its realities and to find alternatives and ultimately, new directions for action" (Cobb, 1991, p. 36).

Getting students to see the connection "between a rotting shack and a rotting America" reflects one of the strongest themes in education for liberation, an insistence on a structural analysis of society. It is similar to what sociologists call the sociological imagination, the ability to see the connection between history and biography. As Cobb and many others in SNCC understood it, it is not just a matter of being able to critique social structures. One needs to be able to see how those structures are implicated in one's own life, how they internalize themselves in one's own behavior and thinking, how we ourselves contribute to our own oppression.

Frank Lopez Gonzalez (2004), the 2004 valedictorian of New York's El Puente Academy for Peace and Justice, said in his graduation address:

We unconsciously carry the burdens of our past. We bear the remnants of years of oppression and the backlash of society as we tried to change the social fabric of this country. These burdens have restricted us for decades, but as we try to push ourselves forward, to cure this disease, we must confront the barriers implanted in our hearts and minds.

This is very much the sense of struggle in Cobb's essay on organizing Freedom Schools (Chapter 7): "Every step in the fight against racism and discrimination was preceded by a deeper and more profound struggle that involved confronting oneself." One suspects that the psychological health of movements depends significantly on the degree to which participants can keep the two struggles in balance.

The idea of Freedom Summer was an intensely controversial one among movement veterans before it happened. Some people didn't want a bunch of outsiders, especially White outsiders, coming down at all. Some didn't think much of the Freedom School idea and joked about the schools being a place to dump some outsiders where they wouldn't get in the way. (This emphatically did not include the local people, who took the schools to heart from the very first [Adickes, 2005]). By all accounts, what happened in most schools that summer was transformative, exceeding the expectations of proponents and critics alike (Adickes, 2005; Belfrage, 1965; Howe, 1984; Rothschild, 1982; Sutherland, 1965). Within a few years, some of the people who had not been particularly high on the idea were running Freedom School–like projects of their own.

In Washington, DC, in 1968, Charlie Cobb and other SNCC members, including Ivanhoe Donaldson, Courtland Cox, and Jennifer Lawson, founded the Drum and Spear Bookstore, as much a library and community center as a bookstore, offering free classes for community youth and adults. In Atlanta, Vincent Harding, a longtime SNCC supporter who had been involved in training volunteers for the Mississippi Summer Project, and Bill Strickland, who headed a branch of SNCC called the Northern Student Movement, were among the central figures in the creation of the Institute of the Black World, which brought together intellectuals from across the African diaspora who shared an interest in using scholarship as a tool of struggle (Ward, 2001). Many members of the SNCC were involved in the national movement to establish Black Studies departments.

It is ironic that charter schools—publicly supported schools freed of many centralized restrictions—are now widely understood as a conservative initiative, if not a conservative plot to undermine public education. Had the same opportunities existed 40 years ago, the Black Panther Party would have dotted the ghetto with liberation schools. Politically left communities are no longer sufficiently well organized to take advantage of the opportunity these schools could represent (although, again, that seems to be changing; see, e.g., Chapter 17). Contrary to some expectations, Chapter 10 shows that Oakland's Black Panther school worked very hard to broaden the social experience of its children, to expose them to things that weren't a part of growing up in inner-city Oakland. This, too, is a recurring theme in the history of liberatory education. According to Bob Moses:

> Part of what the Movement did was just expose people to a lot. I mean it was exposing people to all different kinds of people who were coming in and out of Mississippi. Exposing people to people by taking them out of Mississippi, traveling, and meeting people elsewhere. And the people that they're meeting are all people who are somehow part of this Movement culture. They share in certain values and [are] talking about certain things. (Lawson & Payne, 2006, p. 173)

One can think of a place like the Highlander Center as specializing in giving people kinds of social experiences that are not available in their home communities. (And for many Southerners, the experience of interracial living at Highlander had as much impact as anything that was actually taught.) Many programs teach pride in one's origins, no matter how humble or despised, while encouraging students not to be limited by those origins.

Contemporary expressions of education for liberation face all the issues their predecessors have faced in the past, but with some changes, too. After 40 years, nearly all of the curriculum from the Freedom Schools (for the curriculum, see www.educationanddemocracy.org or the fall 1991 edition of *Radical Teacher*) is still relevant, but there are some things one might want to add. Given the evolution of mass media and the investment of many youth in the media, some would argue for the inclusion of some kind of media literacy component.

The most obvious addition might be some way to think seriously about gender. Buying into a version of the prevailing sex role definitions gives young men and women in the inner city something to be proud of in ways that the broader society reinforces. There is probably no clearer illustration of Marx's point (or Gandhi's, Martin Luther King's, or Charlie Cobb's) about the oppressed supporting the systems that oppress them. Young people are so deeply invested in their gender self-definitions that if we can get them to think analytically about that, it opens them up to thinking critically in general.

Like their predecessors, many contemporary programs struggle to find a balanced way to think about individual responsibility in the context of socially structured oppression. One might make a case that contemporary teacher-organizers are often not as sophisticated as Ella Baker or Septima Clark, who could look unblinkingly at the flaws, the baggage, carried by poor people while seeing with equal clarity the social forces bearing down upon them. Certainly, many progressives fear that admitting the idea of the "responsibility" of the marginalized plays into conservative hands. The difficulty becomes how to acknowledge the reality of negative elements in youth culture, let us say, without reducing youngsters to that.

Race remains an issue for many of those concerned with liberatory education, and it could hardly be otherwise. Can White people "teach freedom"? Given the history through which we have come, does not the mere assumption of the authoritative role of teacher by Whites replicate the traditional White-Black hierarchy? Or, are there ways White people can teach with awareness of and respect for African American traditions and sensibilities? Thinking critically about social issues is a path, and once students start down it, it may not matter very much exactly how they got started. One could read the history of Highlander, which played a key part in the development of many young Black activists, that way (and yet, if Highlander had not added a Black woman to its staff in the 1950s, it is not at all clear that the work in the Sea Islands would have gone as well).

Lawrence Goodwyn (1976) argues that the development of collective self-confidence is one of the prerequisites of mass movements. One of the factors making that difficult for contemporary liberatory education efforts is the dead hand of the 1960s. Comparing ourselves and the people around us to imagined icons of the 1960s merely reinforces our sense of historical inadequacy. In fact, it would be hard to make an empirical case that youth in the 1980s and 1990s were dramatically less idealistic than those of the sacred 1960s.

The difference may be that latter generations did not operate under such favorable structural conditions (such as the Cold War and the decline of cotton agriculture) and did not manage to find vehicles for expressing their politics that were as powerful as some of those that developed in the 1960s. That's different from saying the desire wasn't there. In fact, one of the reasons to have young people study the 1960s is to move them beyond romanticizing the era so that they can see themselves as not so different from the people who made history then.

Many in the SNCC understood struggle as inevitably involving the fight to maintain a sense of comradeship and identity with one's colleagues. They once thought of themselves as a band of brothers and sisters, a circle of trust. Many of the SNCC's members give some credit for that to Ella Baker. "The SNCC of which I was a part," says Casey Hayden, "was nurturing, warm, familial, supportive, honest and penetrating, radical and pragmatic. I think of it as womanist. I see Ella in all of that" (Hayden, 2003, p. 101). Joanne Grant's film on Baker, *Fundi*, makes a point of showing her asking participants in a meeting if they had any personal concerns that needed to be addressed before business started.

That element of struggle, maintaining a sense of comradeship, may be particularly difficult for African Americans right now, many of whom are growing up in communities that don't exhibit the level of internal solidarity that once characterized Black communities. In particular, it may be that patterns of interactions among African American youth, especially boys, have in places become unsupportive and mean-spirited, a culture of put-down and insult, masquerading as joking (Payne, 2003; Potts in Chapter 16; see Kelly [2002] for a different interpretation).

In this light, it is striking that many programs explicitly encourage more supportive patterns of interaction. In Children's Defense Fund Freedom Schools, scholars are asked to "recognize" one another. (In fact, when scholars in those schools refer to the "Freedom School way" it seems to mean, more or less, "be positive.") At least three of the other programs described in this volume—the Benjamin Mays Institute (Chapter 16), Brotherhood/Sister Sol (Chapter 11), and Project Daniel (Chapter 13)—have similar traditions. At this historical moment, it may well be that for youth coming out of urban communities, the deliberate teaching of social solidarity becomes particularly important. They need to be encouraged to see what's right in one another.

It is useful to think of two main streams of emancipatory education among Black people. One is the stream consisting of Citizenship schools, Freedom schools, and their successors. The other would be initiatives in the tradition of cultural nationalist or African-centered education, education that "acknowledges Afrikan spirituality as an essential aspect of our uniqueness as a people and makes it an instrument of our liberation" (Council of Independent Black Institutions, www.cibi.org, retrieved November 27, 2007). The distinction is a little artificial in the sense that many people are involved in both, but it is useful to underscore that the African-centered tradition would probably have existed even in the absence of the civil rights movement. For much of the 1980s and 1990s, rites of passage programs—adapted from African coming-of-age training—were probably the most widely available form of education for liberation in Black communities. Paul Hill Jr., who heads the National Rites of Passage Institute, says that over the years he has received many inquiries

> predicated on the assumption that today's teenagers are without moorings or elders capable of transmitting enduring human values and cultural traditions that reflect our uniqueness as descendants of Africans. . . . [I]f wise elders do not initiate adolescents, won't adolescents initiate themselves? (2004, p. 31)

Many of the projects in the Freedom School tradition have proven short-lived. African-centered institutions struggle for resources like everyone else, but some of them have demonstrated considerable staying power. The Council of Independent Black Institutions (CIBI), which insists that its member institutions raise most of their funds within the Black community, is 35 years old. Perhaps because the transmission of values is so central to their vision, no matter what else is going on, cultural nationalists will be working with children. Nor do they have an awkwardness in addressing negative peer culture. From their position, Western culture is itself problematic.

The confluence between the resurgence of interest in social justice education and the dominance of hip-hop as the mode of cultural expression for a generation raises some interesting issues about the future of education for liberation. It is clear that the two will feed off each other. Hip-hop has strong elements of social critique built into it, and even some of its most negative elements—the misogyny, individualism, and materialism—can serve as points of entry into important conversations. Some of the people in this history have thought of struggle as threefold: a battle against structures of inequality, a battle to develop oneself and overcome one's own baggage, and a battle for supportive and principled relationships among comrades. Some hip-hop has certainly demonstrated to speak to the first; we shall have to see how much capacity it has to speak to the latter two.

On the Sea Islands, where Septima Clark began her life's work, when a respected person passed away, after the internment, custom called for children to step across the grave. The best parts of the spirit of the deceased were understood to pass into the children. As a nation, we have done a terrible job of passing our children over the graves of their ancestors and, given their already tenuous relationship to the rest of society, that failure often falls with greatest weight on African American and other children of color. That may be the best way to think of what education for liberation does at its best: It is a way to pass children over the graves of their ancestors, to give them a moral grounding in the past that will help them ask their own questions in the present and seek their own answers.

PART I

PROJECTING IMAGINATION
BEYOND CIRCUMSTANCE

*[The slaves] were able to absorb that one book [the Bible], image by image,
and to find in it answers to their own hopeless-seeming situation. They were
able to project their imaginations beyond their present circumstances. For
example, to the anguished question of the Prophet Isaiah, "Is There No Balm
in Gilead?", our slave ancestors were able to answer, Yes: "There Is a Balm
in Gilead" . . . they were able to imagine solutions to their own deeply
desperate situation. . . . Simply put, I think that we have lost a fundamental
belief in the power of our own human spirits and imaginations to project
adequate images of what is possible for us. We have lost hope, and have
therefore lost control over our own futures. Our slave ancestors never made
this deadly mistake. We need to re-learn the first fundamental lesson they
learned.*

—James Alan McPherson

Chapter 1, excerpted from Steven Hahn's prize-winning *A Nation Under
Our Feet*, makes clear how desperately White supremacists after the Civil
War fought against Black educational aspirations. "There is an eternal
hatred . . . against all men that [are] engaged in teaching schools, and
giving instruction to the humbler class of their fellow men." The excerpt
after that, from Robert C. Morris's *Reading, 'Riting and Reconstruction*
makes it clear that White supremacists had very good reason to fear what
was happening in those humble classrooms.

To Build a New Jerusalem

Steven Hahn

[After the Civil War, the] politically symbolic and practical elements of Klan vigilantism were similarly evident in attacks on black churches and, especially, schoolhouses. Aside from Union League[1] meetings, no institutions or organizational forums proved more vulnerable, and this was in part because churches and schoolhouses often served as the locations of league meetings. But they represented as well the wider aspirations, networks, and solidarities that the Klan moved to destroy. Between February and June 1871 alone, just a few months after the Klan had made its first show of local strength, 26 schools were burned in Monroe County, Mississippi, with many of the teachers forced to seek refuge in the county seat of Aberdeen. "There is an eternal hatred," reported a Tennessee legislative committee investigating the Ku Klux Klan in 1868, "existing against all men that voted the Republican ticket, or who belong to the Loyal League, or [are] engaged in teaching schools, and giving instruction to the humbler class of their fellow men."

Schools, like churches (and there was much overlap between the two), were sites of African American initiative and empowerment, and, unlike most churches, of interracial cooperation and alliance. During the Civil War, Northern religious denominations and charitable organizations began to establish schools for ex-slaves in areas of Union occupation—generally staffed by abolitionist women and men—and once the war ended these efforts spread over the South, principally under the auspices of the American Missionary Association. But they built on a base of "educational activism during slavery," and they tapped an intense thirst for education among those who had been held in bondage. Observers marveled at the enormous enthusiasm and commitment among male and female, young and old, parent and child; and by early 1866 hundreds of day and evening schools, Sabbath schools, "native" schools, and plantation schools were in operation. The Freedmen's Bureau school inspector estimated "the whole number of pupils" in the former slave states at more than 90,000 and believed that "much more is being done."

The task was daunting. The missionary associations, aid societies, and Freedmen's Bureau provided some assistance, but outside of the cities and larger towns and away from the densest plantation areas, the burdens of establishing and running schools fell chiefly to the freed people themselves. They had to pool their meager resources, rent or purchase a tract of land (or prevail upon their employer to provide a parcel for them), build a school-house, and hire a teacher. Those who lived in nonplantation districts had a particularly difficult time "owing to the great scarcity of freedpeople" and the distances that separated them. But even where plantations—and there-fore large concentrations of Black folk—were to be found, and even after Republican Reconstruction governments began funding public schools, pov-erty and the rhythms of household labor threw up enormous obstacles for any educational project. Most remarkable, therefore, were the lengths to which many freedmen and -women would go "to secure the advantages of education" for themselves and especially for their children. They moved to more promising locales, walked miles to attend classes, and sacrificed sleep and sustenance. "They are anxious to learn," a less than sympathetic White North Carolinian conceded, "and will deny themselves of any comfort to send their children to school."

Freedpeople clamored for schooling because they viewed it simulta-neously as a rejection of their enslaved past and as a means of power and self-respect in the postemancipation world. Literacy would permit them to negotiate the new relations of production and exchange, involving as they now did contracts, store accounts, mortgages, and promissory notes. It would allow them to fend off the duplicities of "unprincipaled [sic] employers" and merchandisers and to make use of the judicial system. It would expand their political horizons and better equip them to exercise the new rights of citi-zenship. And it would enable them to read the Bible. Freedpeople could be seen "during the intervals of toil" holding "some fragment of a spelling book in their hands, earnestly studying." One Scottish traveler who visited a night school in Montgomery, Alabama, noticed "a perfectly Black man of about 50 years of age studying a big Bible that lay on the desk before him" and discovered that "he is a labourer on a farm a good way out of town" who comes "every night as punctual as the clock," usually "without his supper that he may be here in time."

Impressive as such individual exertions were, book learning was likely to be a family and collective undertaking, and one in which familiar hierar-chies of authority could be disrupted or inverted. When the "colored citi-zens" of Oak Hill in Granville County, North Carolina, petitioned the local

Freedmen's Bureau agent to see about furnishing a teacher for the "log school house" they expected to put up, they signed as heads of 22 families, at least four of whom were women. Black women seem indeed to have played a particularly active part in advancing the cause of education by helping to form school committees, raise the necessary funds, ready the buildings, and find and board the teachers. They seem, as well, to have seized every available opportunity to gain literacy and then, like many school-age children, to have become teachers in their own rights. . . .

But the schoolhouse was an educational center in an even broader sense. It was not only a place where freedmen, women, and children could learn to read, write, and cipher; it was also a place where they could be taught about the course of Reconstruction, the substance of their rights, the goals of the Republican Party, and the importance of voting. Local leaders, Union army officers, and Freedmen's Bureau agents might address community assemblies there, and teachers usually saw their educational role as extending well beyond book learning. Klans assumed an almost inextricable connection between the schoolhouse and the Union League or Republican Party because much of what went on there appeared to aid the ends of partisan mobilization. . . . Indeed, Klans widely assumed that schoolteaching was a mere cover for more overt political objectives and that schoolteachers were chiefly concerned with emboldening the freedpeople, turning them against White employers, and currying their favor for the Republican Party. "There was a Carpetbagger from Connecticut teaching a Negro school between Greensboro and Newburn," a vigilante in the western Alabama Black belt recalled. "He pretended to be teaching, but he was organizing the Negroes in some kind of League and was drilling them every Saturday." A Black Union League president nearby, complaining that local Whites were "badly opposed to order and peace and well fare of the colored people," told the governor that "several men of the most pernicious character" had accosted their "peaceful teacher." "Cursing him," they vowed to "fix him well . . . the first time they found him in the league, or reading newspaper or in the act of giving instruction to colored people in regard to equality of race, or privilege acquired by from the damned *radical party*." Both of these teachers, White Northerners, escaped with threats; others who stood their ground were generally whipped and driven off. Black teachers—women and men— fared even worse. They could expect to be humiliated and whipped or murdered.

As early as 1867, African Americans composed about one third of the teachers to be found in the fledgling freedmen's schools, and their proportion grew over the course of Reconstruction. This, in good measure, reflected a mix of attainment and intimidation: the increasing literacy of former slaves and the declining willingness of Northern Whites to venture into the South.

But it also reflected the role of local schools as vehicles of Black political power and patronage.

When, therefore, vigilantes burned schoolhouses, assaulted teachers, and harassed appointed or elected school officials, they struck at a newly constituted political hub, and one that could align the balances of local power in several ways.

NOTE

1. *Editor's Note*: Union Leagues, also known as Loyal Leagues, promoted loyalty to the Union and the policies of Abraham Lincoln. In the Reconstruction South, they operated as an adjunct to the Republican Party and often organized armed militias to counter White supremacist violence.

CHAPTER 2

"We Are Rising as a People"
The Content of Instruction in Freedmen's Schools

Robert C. Morris

The school is located in an abandoned Baptist church, shaded by lofty live-oak trees, with long, pendulous moss everywhere hanging from their wide-spreading branches, and surrounded by the gravestones of several generations of White communicants. The walls of the makeshift classrooms are adorned with pictures of Lincoln, Garrison, Phillips, and Whittier. On the only blackboard in the school is written: "Try, try again" and "Knowledge is power."

By 10:00 a.m. all of the 145 pupils are in their seats and busily engaged in reading, spelling, or arithmetic. One class of 12 students reads an exercise from Clark's *First Lessons in English Grammar*:

Columbus discovered America.
Fulton invented steamboats.
Howard alleviated suffering.

The teacher interrupts briefly to explain that General Howard is commissioner of the Freedmen's Bureau. . . .

The teacher of an advanced class is leading her pupils in a prepared oral exercise on the subject of government and citizenship:

What was the wisest country of old times?
Egypt in Africa.
What are the people of the United States called?
American citizens.

Excerpted from Robert C. Morris, 1981, *Reading, 'Riting and Reconstruction: The Education of Freedmen in the South, 1861–1870*. Chicago: University of Chicago Press, pp. 174–181. Reprinted with permission.

What are the rights of an American citizen?
Life, liberty, and the pursuit of happiness.
What are his duties?
To obey the laws, defend the country, and vote for good men.

Pointing to a picture on the wall, the instructor continues:

Who is that?
President Lincoln.
Was he a good man?
Yes, yes!
What good thing did he do?
He set the colored people free.

The class for older children and adults is reading from *The Freedman's Third Reader*, published by the American Tract Society. The story for today is about Toussaint L'Ouverture, the slave who led the successful Haitian revolt against French rule. A student begins reading on page 81:

Toussaint L'Ouverture has been very justly called "one of the most extraordinary men of an age when extraordinary men were numerous." Born a slave in St. Domingo, his first employment was tending cattle on the plantation of his master. As a child he was gentle, thoughtful and of strong religious tendencies. He early learned to read and write, had some knowledge of arithmetic, geometry, and Latin, and was diligent in gathering stores of information which fitted him for a higher sphere.

Toussaint's good conduct and ability gained the love and esteem of his master, and he was soon promoted to offices of trust and honor. . . .

War having broken out in St. Domingo between the French and Spaniards, involving both the free people of color and the slaves, Toussaint joined his brethren in arms, and stepped in a moment from slavery to freedom. Yet, while struggling for the rights of his race, he had no feelings of revenge to gratify, but was the same amiable and charitable person as ever.

When his late master and family were in danger he risked his own life for their escape, sent them to a safe retreat in America, with provision for their support, and afterwards remitted to them not only all he could save from the wreck of their fortune, but also valuable additions from his own property.

As the hour approaches 2:30 p.m., teachers conclude the day's lessons and instruct their students to assemble in the main hall for closing exercises. As always, these exercises begin with a song. Led by a pleasant-toned melodeon, the entire school joins in a chorus of "Howard at Atlanta":

> We are rising as a people, with the changes of our land,
> In the cause of right and justice let us all united stand.
> As we rose amid the conflict, when the battle storm was high,
> With returning peace we're rising, like the eagles to the sky.

This was followed by renditions of Whittier's" Song of the Negro Boatmen" and "John Brown's Body."

Promptly at 3:00 p.m. classes are dismissed, and the children are admonished to return to their jobs in the cotton fields as soon as possible. Classes will resume at 10:00 a.m. on Monday morning.

In the absence of detailed information on any one freedmen's school, this composite picture gives some idea as to the type of educational exercises used by bureau instructors throughout the South. While subject to many of the limitations involved in reconstructing past events, it is by no means fictional. Rather, it is based directly on contemporaneous accounts written by teachers, missionaries, soldiers, agents of the federal government, and other interested observers from both sides of the Mason-Dixon Line.

By modern standards these exercises seem quite tame. During the passionate post–Civil War period, however, they were the subject of heated and often violent controversy. Southern Whites continually complained that freedmen's teachers used their classrooms to belittle the South, to stir racial hatred, and to propagandize on behalf of the Republican Party. As one Virginia editor explained to an instructor from Nantucket, Rhode Island, "The idea prevails that you come among us not merely as an ordinary school teacher, but as a political missionary; that you communicate to the colored people ideas of social equality with the Whites." The editor claimed that he approved of education for freedmen, but regarded such teaching of "politics and sociology" as "mischievous" and likely to "disturb the good feeling between the two races."

The Sumter, South Carolina, *Watchman* in 1866 printed a vivid example of the type of lesson that most alienated the former Confederates. The subject was the hated antislavery militant John Brown:

> Who talks of deeds of high renown?
> I sing the valiant martyr Brown.
> I love the Doctor of the West,
> May his pure soul in quiet rest.

Let Nations weep the martyr's death.
Let children lisp with early breath,
The name of Brown, above all men,
Who e'er have lived in mortal ken.

A more common form of tribute to "Old Ossawatomie" was manifested in the widespread use of the song "John Brown's Body" (also known as "John Brown's Soul"). Indeed, it appears to have been an indispensable part of the school curriculum. Much to the disgust of Southern Whites, Negro students especially enjoyed the version that referred to hanging Jefferson Davis "on a sour apple tree." In Norfolk, Virginia, this line prompted one student to ask her teacher if the recently captured president of the Confederacy had been hanged yet. On being told "no," the student was extremely disappointed.

Many educators continued to use "John Brown's Body" even after it became readily apparent how deeply Southern Whites resented its lyrics. Francis Cardozo seemed almost proud to report that residents of Charleston could scarcely control their rage when they heard his students singing "Rally 'round the Flag," "John Brown's Soul," and "other patriotic songs." The black principal's defiant attitude intensified resentment. One woman, "very finely dressed, and apparently quite lady like," stopped at the door of Cardozo's school while the children were singing and said "Oh, I wish I could put a torch to that building! *The niggers . . .*"

Such allusions to Jefferson Davis were especially evident in the period immediately after the assassination of President Lincoln. In May 1865 Miss L. D. Burnett asked her students in a Norfolk school where Davis was captured. An 8-year-old student answered: "Running away in the woods, with his wife's dress & petticoat on." On another occasion, Miss Burnett asked who was happier—Lincoln, "who was murdered," or Jeff Davis. The answer: "Mr. Lincoln 'cas' he's in Heaven." Finally, the bureau instructor asked if Davis wouldn't be just as happy "if we would let him go to some country & live there unmolested." The answer: "No he'd think of the folks he's killed."

PART II

Building the Army of Democracy

It is my belief that creative leadership is present in any community and only awaits discovery and development.

—Septima Clark

When college students first encounter Septima Clark and Ella Baker, they often ask why they hadn't heard of them before. There are many parts to that answer—the still common tendency among scholars to overlook women, the ambivalence these women felt about putting themselves in the spotlight, the willingness of some of their male colleagues to push them aside when they could—but no doubt a part of the answer has to do with the particular form of politics they espoused. Developing people is just undramatic. Nurturing supportive relationships pales in interest besides giving a good, hard-hitting speech or organizing a confrontational demonstration. It is not just that we undervalue women but that we undervalue those forms of politics—and often don't even think of them as politics—most likely to be associated with them. Thus, radicals keep producing political forms, which, although formally oppositional, reflect some of the same masculinist, hierarchical values that define the society they are opposing, and which, therefore, at the extremes, devolve into ego-driven politics of masculinist theater, devoid of much human feeling and, thus, incapable of sustaining itself.

In Chapter 3, David Levine analyzes the reasons for the early successes of the Citizenship Schools, and Deanna Gillespie continues the story in Chapter 4, examining the spread of the program into the Savannah, Georgia, region, which had, in the years after World War II acquired a well-deserved reputation for activism. The Savannah story is usually rendered in terms of dynamic male leaders, but Gillespie shows that women and their networks were crucial to the spread and effectiveness of the Citizenship Schools. Ella Baker became a role model for many younger activists in the 1960s; Charles Payne outlines her thinking and demonstrates that her basic working style seems to have been in place during the Depression.

CHAPTER 3

The Birth of the Citizenship Schools
Entwining the Struggles
for Literacy and Freedom

David Levine

In a 1981 interview, civil rights leader Andrew Young commented, "If you look at the black elected officials and the people who are political leaders across the South now, it's full of people who had their first involvement in civil rights in the Citizenship Training Program."[1]

Informally known as Citizenship Schools, this adult education program began in 1957 under the sponsorship of Tennessee's Highlander Folk School, which handed it over to the Southern Christian Leadership Conference in 1961. By the time the project ended in 1970, approximately 2,500 African Americans had taught these basic literacy and political education classes for tens of thousands of their neighbors. The program never had a high profile, but civil rights leaders and scholars assert that it helped to bring many people into the movement, to cultivate grassroots leaders, and to increase Black participation in voting and other civic activities (Branch, 1988; Morris, 1984; Payne, 1995).

Focusing on the formative years of the program as a Highlander project in the Charleston area, this essay explores how an educational endeavor can nourish a movement for social justice by transforming its participants. Citizenship School teachers and students improved their literacy skills and civic knowledge, expanded their problem-solving abilities, and challenged the unjust social order of the segregated South. The success of the schools was due to three crucial ingredients: a sustained focus on overcoming illiteracy to strengthen Black electoral power, an interactive pedagogy that built upon the experience and culture of the students, and an explicitly political approach

Original version published in the *History of Education Quarterly*, *Vol. 44*, No. 3, Fall 2004, pp. 388–414. Reprinted with permission from Blackwell Publishing.

to education that assertively linked the acquisition of knowledge with collective efforts to overcome racism.

BEGINNINGS

In the waning months of 1956, Myles Horton of Tennessee's Highlander Folk School and Septima Clark, a South Carolina teacher, asked Clark's cousin Bernice Robinson to teach an adult literacy class on Johns Island, a rural area a few miles outside of Charleston. She reacted to this request with unqualified dismay. Although she had a high school diploma, she couldn't imagine how her experience as a clerical worker, seamstress, and beautician qualified her to teach: "I never been no teacher and I'm not going to be a teacher. I'll help in *any* way . . . but I ain't no teacher."[2] Horton and Clark relentlessly insisted that Robinson was the best, in fact the only, person for the job, and that the project would die unless she took this volunteer position. This moral brinkmanship worked. On the evening of January 7, 1957, Robinson stood in a makeshift classroom facing 14 adult students.

The setting of this classroom offered a dramatic contrast to the urban amenities Robinson enjoyed as a Charleston resident. Johns Island, along with Edisto, Wadmalaw, and James islands, lie close to each other and Charleston, separated from the mainland by narrow rivers. They are flat and swampy, divided between tidal marshes and dense forests that teem with sea and animal life. Most of the approximately 10,000 Black residents of the islands cobbled together livelihoods as fishermen, farmers, farm or factory workers, craftspeople, or domestic servants. The dramatic beauty of the islands contrasted with the grim reality of racial oppression. In 1957, Black residents of the islands had to contend with total exclusion from governmental power, nearly total exclusion from the right to vote, and the segregation of public institutions. Many adults did not have more than a second- or third-grade education (Clark, 1990; U.S. Bureau of the Census, 1963).

The classroom itself was located at the back of the Progressive Club, a converted three-room building that a local civic group had bought to house a co-op store and this literacy program. Robinson arrived for that first class with a few borrowed elementary textbooks, a South Carolina voter registration form, and a copy of the United Nations charter to tack on the wall. Anxiously surveying 14 expectant pairs of eyes, she contemplated how to start:

> I guess I was as nervous, I was *more* nervous than the people, because they didn't know what they were coming for. They were just coming to learn or to see what they could learn, that sort of thing. And, they came in that night and I told

them that they ask[ed] me to teach this class. But, I'm not going to be the teacher, we gonna learn together. You gonna teach me some things and maybe there are a few things I might be able to teach you, but I don't consider myself a teacher. I just feel that I'm here to learn with you, you know, learn things together. I think that sort of settled the folks down.[3]

Robinson quickly realized that this group of adults would find the third- and fourth-grade primers she had brought along irrelevant and demeaning. She asked them what they wanted to learn and constructed a curriculum defined by their needs and interests. Some wanted to learn to read the newspaper, some the Bible, others to fill out mail-order catalogues and money orders, and to pass the voter registration test. Some hoped to read and write their own letters, so they could communicate with relatives and not depend on a White to read their incoming correspondence to them. The men who worked at the Charleston docks wanted to learn enough math to keep track of how much cargo they handled and how many hours they worked. Through creative improvisation and warm respect for her students, Robinson soon constructed a strikingly successful classroom experience directly responsive to the learning interests and needs of these mature students.[4]

This promising beginning was built on years of painstaking pedagogical experimentation and political networking devised at Highlander. By the time Myles Horton and his colleagues from Highlander connected with Black activists in the Charleston area, they had already fashioned a distinctive approach to adult education. From its birth in 1932 through the 1940s, the school functioned as a key training center for White rank-and-file union activists in the South, building a close relationship with the CIO. Most of the staff espoused both a nondoctrinaire socialism and a commitment to radical educational experimentation. Myles Horton was the leading figure among the talented Highlander staff (Adams and Horton, 1975; Horton, 1990).

From its early days, Highlander made probing attempts to break the color line that crippled working-class solidarity in the South. By the mid-1940s, it was one of the very few places where Southern Black and White union members could meet to share common problems. In the 1950s, alienated from the labor movement by the conservative impact of McCarthyism, Highlander turned increasing attention toward the nascent civil rights movement (Levine, 1999, pp. 80–83; Highlander Reports, 1954). The crucial connection that led to the creation of the Citizenship Schools was provided by Septima Clark and Esau Jenkins, key figures in Charleston's Black community. Clark was a native Charlestonian and elementary school teacher who had taught on Johns Island from 1916 to 1918, and then again from 1926 to 1929. Animated by strong drives for both self-improvement and Christian service, Clark's personal style was modest and soft-spoken. But she also possessed quiet courage and determination to confront injustice, qualities that drew her to Highlander (Clark and Blythe, 1962; Clark, 1990). After attending a 1954 workshop at the folk school, she looked for ways to connect the school to Black people in the Charleston area. She made sure to involve Esau Jenkins, a former student, who became a businessman and community leader on Johns Island. In addition to forming the Progressive Club, Jenkins was also president of the Citizens Club, another Johns Island organization established to promote attempts to register to vote and civic involvement. By the mid-1950s, the club had around 200 members. Those who worked with Jenkins politically admired his warmth, his persistent determination, and his capacity to convince people to take practical steps toward their own emancipation (Woodruff, 1984, p. 2).[5]

It soon became clear to Highlander staff, particularly Horton, that the Charleston area could be an ideal place to try to create a civic empowerment project based in a Black community. To facilitate this effort, they hired Clark as a part-time staff member in February of 1955. Between 1955 and the start of the first Citizenship School class in January of 1957, Highlander staff and Black activists on the Sea Islands and in Charleston sought to deepen their relationship and explore various avenues toward community-based political engagement. Much of this process was informal and low-key, especially during the first year. Myles Horton made several trips to Johns Island, trying to get a feel for its people and their needs by fishing with them, helping out with farm work, and playing with their children. In February and March of 1955, the school sponsored a Charleston conference for Black leaders, and in May 1955, an all-day community meeting on Johns Island featured panel discussions on why Blacks should organize and why only 30% of Black South Carolinians were eligible to vote.

During the summer of 1955, Clark and Jenkins brought several Johns Island's residents to Highlander for residential workshops. During his first Highlander visit, Esau Jenkins had pledged to run for school trustee, aiming to prove to Sea Island Blacks that an African American could run for office and not get killed (Woodruff, 1984, p. 2). He finished third and received 192 out of 200 black votes. This showing spurred a revitalized Citizens Club to set up a committee to promote voter registration. Jenkins and his colleagues were able to register 100 Blacks in 1955, equaling the total number who had registered during the prior decade. A White magistrate with a record of treating Blacks unfairly was facing a tough election. Perceiving the growth in Black registration on Johns Island, he approached Jenkins for support, which Jenkins promised in exchange for a promise of better conduct from the judge. With Black support, the judge was reelected and his treatment of African Americans in the courtroom underwent a marked improvement (Kennedy, n.d.).

Despite some encouraging victories, Esau Jenkins became increasingly aware of the extent to which illiteracy was preventing Blacks from voting. The historic neglect of Black education on the four Sea Islands near Charleston meant that when the Citizenship Schools began in the late 1950s, a high proportion of the adult Black population needed and were eager to obtain literacy instruction. Based on her experience teaching on Johns Island, Septima Clark believed that almost all of its adult Black residents were illiterate. Clark also found that Black tenants often pledged the work of their entire families to their employers. This meant that fifth-grade youngsters did not start school until December or later, after the cotton crop was picked, and could only attend until early spring, when they left to help prepare the next crop (Clark and Blythe, 1962, p. 39).

One day, as Jenkins drove his bus between Johns Island and the mainland, Alice Wine (one of his riders) asked him to teach her how to read and write so she could obtain the ballot. He passed out portions of the state constitution and voting laws among his unregistered passengers and soon was conducting impromptu classes on the bus. Wine was able to memorize part of the state constitution and pass the registration test, but Jenkins did not feel qualified to give her basic literacy instruction. This prompted him to ask Highlander for aid in setting up some kind of adult education (Carawan and Carawan, 1994, pp. 198–209).

By 1956, Jenkins and Clark were actively looking for a place to hold an adult education class. Eventually, Highlander agreed to lend the Progressive Club $1,500 to buy an old school from a White man who had recently purchased it from the county for $1,000. The club set up a cooperative store in the front of the building, and, according to Clark, decided to have the class take place in the two back, windowless rooms where it would be hidden from island Whites (Clark, 1990, p. 47).

As the schools got off the ground, two crucial and complementary ingredients to their success were the capacity of Highlander to allow strong women to play crucial roles and to challenge organizers to reflect upon and change their political practice. From the start of the first days of school in 1932, Myles Horton and his male colleagues were able to work effectively with strong women such as Zilla Hawes and Zilphia Horton (Glen, 1996, pp. 29–31, 138–139, 188–189). Although there is little evidence that the folk school focused on the oppression of women, Highlander encouraged an attitude of respect that encompassed both women and people of humble backgrounds. As Septima Clark grew as an organizer through her work with Highlander, she was also able to enrich the practice of the school by constantly challenging those around her to deepen the program's capacity to develop the underprivileged. When she and Horton first began planning how to spread the Citizenship Schools beyond the Sea Islands, he wanted the focus to be on large-scale registration of voters rather than deep literacy training. It took a number of shouting matches for her to convince him that intensive literacy instruction should remain at the core of the program.[6]

During her tenure at Highlander, Clark was alert to how gender and education could interfere with the painstaking work of engaging with poor people:

> It was funny to me, but most of the educated men seemed to have that trouble relating. They didn't have the patience at first to work in small towns or listen to the poor people who came in. Myles Horton had trouble sitting and listening to the people from places like Thomasville, Georgia, tell about the happenings there. It was hard for him to sit and listen to them say, "Now this happened the night that that sow had its calf on such-and-such a moon." He wanted them to come right to the point, and they wouldn't do it [laughing]. I found that true with most of the men.[7]

Even though Esau Jenkins became increasingly aware of the need to develop leaders, he had traditional notions about the role of women. Clark recalled with pleasure one of the rare instances when his perspective was challenged:

> All the women would be doing would be serving the tables. And one Sunday a woman said, "Mr. Esau, yes, we want such-and-such a thing," talking about typing classes for the children. And he said, "Just sit down there and say nothing." And she said, "Yes, we want typing classes, and we want a typing teacher, too!" And I put that down as a benchmark . . . [that] this woman [could] stand up there and say something [to Jenkins].[8]

Through persistent efforts, Clark and Horton convinced Jenkins to modify his leadership style. When they first began working with him, he often did most of the talking at community meetings and did not perceive the importance of developing leaders. Through discussions on how to move the work forward, and through his participation in the Highlander residential experience, they helped Jenkins alter his approach. In April of 1955, he wrote Horton, "My ideas of community leadership have changed in many ways. I have found that giving others something to do in helping make better citizens in the community is very important. My old way of doing was slow." Jenkins appointed one person from each of 15 church congregations on Johns Island to remind people of Citizens Club meetings. With Clark's encouragement, he also began to expand his conception of who could be an appropriate leader. Clark (a teetotaler herself) recalled, "There were some bootleggers there [on Johns Island] that made moonshine whiskey . . . that he felt shouldn't be invited to the meeting. I said, 'We've got to work with everyone on this island.' Then he got the idea too that everybody needs to help . . ." (Tjerandsen, 1980, p. 155).[9]

CITIZENSHIP SCHOOLS IN ACTION

Robinson began her classes without the benefit of any preconceived model. She worked out a classroom routine that began with prayer led by a rotating leader. This was followed by a review of homework—about 30 minutes of reading with spelling instruction centered on the difficult words that the students encountered. Math followed, and finally a discussion of voter registration and civics. The group also viewed films and participated in song sessions led by Guy Carawan, a young White folksinger from Highlander.

Robinson traced money orders onto pieces of cardboard so that all the students could practice filling them out. She brought in newspaper supermarket ads for math lessons and drew vocabulary words from voter registration tests. She had the eight students who were totally illiterate trace their signatures over pieces of cardboard. They also told her stories about their activities that were then read aloud by the students with some reading skills.[10]

For adults whose last school experiences were dim childhood memories, entering a classroom must have been a somewhat alien experience. In his autobiography, Myles Horton recalled:

> At the beginning there was a problem over pencils. Many of the people in the class were in their sixties, and most of them were used to holding a plow or a hoe, or throwing a fishing net. When they'd first hold a pencil, nine times out of ten they'd break it. The physical adjustment wasn't easy. You could hear those pencils snapping all over the room. We decided right there that no teacher should ever show any concern about pencils, because that would be intimidating, but simply hand students another one and say there are plenty more. Because they had so many obstacles to overcome, we tried to make unimportant things like that as insignificant as possible. (Horton, 1990, p. 3)

From every indication, Robinson was a natural teacher with a keen understanding of how essential it is to turn a classroom into a trusting community. A number of her students brought in teenage daughters they didn't want to leave alone at home, whom she taught to knit and crochet. A few of the girls snickered at the adults stumbling as they read, so Robinson brought in public speaking materials and assigned them oral presentations. As they stammered in front of the class, "we would just laugh at 'em, kidding them and say, 'See how it feels now when you're not doing something right, you don't want nobody to laugh at you so let's not laugh at others.'"[11]

Given the commute from Charleston, the biweekly two-hour sessions, and her preparation work on other nights, Robinson was putting a tremendous amount of time into the class. But the rewards of the work provided more than enough compensation:

> I became *so involved* with those people, that nothing else really mattered. Just to see a 65-year-old woman, who finally recognized her name in a bunch of names on the board, meant something to me. . . . I could never explain or express how I felt when I put all those names on the board and I said to her, 'Now, can you find your name up there on the board?' '*Yes ma'am*, I surely can.' She took the ruler out of my hand. 'That's my name there, Annie, and that's my other name down there, Vastine.' I had goose pimples all over me. That woman could not read or write when she came. She could recognize her name in that short space of time [since she had started attending].[12]

Toward the end of the class, some of the students tried to register to vote. Robinson would find them waiting for her when she arrived to teach, waving certificates of registration at her and saying, "I got it! I got it!" By the end of the class, attendance had risen to 37 and all of the original 14 students had registered (Glen, 1996, p. 163).[13]

It was clear from the very first class meeting in January of 1957 that Robinson was indeed the right person for the job. Her inventiveness, sympathetic attitude, and willingness to have students help define the learning agenda proved highly successful with the first group of students. She reported, "I have never before in my life seen such anxious people. They really want to learn and are so proud of the little gains they have made so far. When I get to the club each night, half of them are already there and have their homework ready for me to see." Horton quickly grasped that an unusually powerful experience was unfolding in this plain, windowless classroom. During one visit, he observed a crowd of 30 to 40 in the co-op store separated by a partition from the classroom, intently listening in on the lesson (Horton, 1989, pp. 224–225).

By 1958, word of the Johns Island pilot class, which Robinson and her students began calling a "Citizenship School," had generated considerable interest among Blacks on the Sea Islands and in Charleston. Clark and Robinson sought out new teachers. Although there are no formal rosters of the Citizenship School teachers during the first few years, the gendered association of women with education shaped the demographics of the program. Most teachers mentioned in accounts of the early program were women. More formal records kept during the SCLC phase of the program indicate that about two thirds of teachers were female.[14] Esau Jenkin's daughter, Ethel Grimball, started a class on Wadmalaw Island; and Allene Brewer, a social worker and pastor's wife, began one on Edisto Island. Her students took up an "each man get a man" initiative to increase voter registration, and Brewer periodically brought people into Charleston to register. Mary Davis organized a class mostly comprised of domestic workers that met in her beautician's shop in North Charleston and was taught by Bernice Robinson. Her students were soon supplementing their literacy studies with a campaign to win more paved streets for their neighborhood. In 1959, classes began on Daufauskie and St. Helena's islands. Some of the early Citizenship School teachers appear to have designed fairly ambitious curriculums. Ethel Grimball used a variety of reading, writing, and math texts designed for adults to individualize instruction, and had her students study paragraphs in the state constitution and practice filling out voter registration applications. Allene Brewer's course of study included reading, writing, math, sewing, history, and the review of citizenship responsibilities. Highlander records indicate that in the winter of 1958–1959, 106 students, ranging in age from 15 to 76, attended classes in North Charleston and on Wadmalaw, Edisto, and Johns islands. The steady growth in Citizenship Schools prompted Highlander to hire Robinson on a half-time basis in 1959 to supervise the schools (Tjerandsen, 1980, pp. 167–170).

The limited number of taped interviews and letters that document the early days of these schools convey enthusiasm and gratitude for the program. Minnie R. Washington, of Edisto Island, commented, "The adult school means so much to me I cannot express my appreciation by words. The only thing I am so sorry the school terms was so short. I would like to thank our teacher Mrs. Brewer for helping us out so wonderful in sewing, arithmetic" (Oldendorf, 1998, pp. 13–14). At an Edisto Island meeting, a resident commented to a Highlander staff person on the effect of the schools on students and the political climate in the community:

> Adults who give such fine cooperation and are willing to improve themselves, to share with others, are great potential leaders in their community. Many [who did not attend the classes] were afraid to come to the school. Some were ashamed to admit what they did not know. Some were afraid of losing their jobs. But little by little they are catching on and expressing regret that they did not come but will come next time. (Tjerandsen, 1980, p. 168)

One student who attended an early Citizenship School taught on Wad-malaw Island was Anderson Mack Sr. Mack, a lifetime resident of Wadmalaw Island, illustrates how the Citizenship School experience could change some-one's life. In an interview, he recalled that he did not start attending school until the age of 12, only receiving a second-grade education. By the time he reached adulthood, "I couldn't sign my own name. I was zero. . . . You go to the restroom, you don't even know the men's restroom from the lady's rest-room." When he was 25, he began attending a Citizenship School class of about 20 older farmers and road workers taught by Ethel Grimball. He re-members learning reading, writing, grammar, and basic math. Grimball guided his hand on the blackboard as he learned cursive writing. He believes her class had "great effect on my life." At the time he started, he was doing road maintenance work for Charleston County Public Works. The skills and self-confidence he gained through the Citizenship School class helped him succeed as a supervisor at his job, and he became a respected community leader. He helped start the first child-care center on the islands, near the Bethlehem Church on Johns Island. With advice from Esau Jenkins, he also helped start a kindergarten on Wadmalaw Island. He then worked with oth-ers to create a community center for the island, an endeavor that involved purchasing a 7-acre site, starting a program, which first operated out of a mobile home, and mobilizing volunteer labor to build a permanent struc-ture. In 1998, the Wadmalaw Community Center still sponsored youth and senior citizen programs and a land use committee. Mack's tradition of civic service continued through his son, Anderson Mack Jr., who now runs the housing rehabilitation program of the Sea Island Rural Missions community agency.[15]

Even before the birth of the Citizenship Schools, the first stirrings of the civil rights movement had evoked repressive responses in South Carolina, including Charleston County. In June of 1956, the Charleston schools in-formed Clark that her teaching contract would not be renewed. Although no reason was given for her dismissal, the state legislature had passed a law in 1955 prohibiting state employees from belonging to the NAACP, and Clark refused to hide her membership in that group. Esau Jenkin's children James, Marie, and Ethel [Grimball] were all prevented from getting public school teaching jobs in the area because of their father's activism.[16] Ironically, in Clark's case, this bit of repression allowed her to become more deeply in-volved in the struggle. At Horton's invitation she became director of work-shops at Highlander, moving to the center in June of 1956.

Some registrars began to switch the sections of the state constitution the applicants were required to read and turn away people who were trying to register after failing the test once. After Jenkins's strong showing in the Johns Island school trustee elections, the positions were made appointive. As the

Black population of Charleston approached 50% in the mid-1950s and the percentage of Blacks voting increased, the city council was reduced from 24 members elected from wards to 12 elected at large (Fraser, 1989, p. 408).

LEARNING FOR LIBERATION

Horton, Jenkins, Clark, and Robinson—the major architects of the program—believed that the most effective teachers would be the peers of the students, rather than credentialed educators who might consider themselves superior to their pupils. The basic qualifications to become a Citizenship School teacher were some high school education, the ability to write legibly, and a commitment to serve the community. According to Clark, they were looking for "degree quality people who did not necessarily have a degree."[17]

Clark and Robinson, who played dominant roles in shaping the curriculum and teaching methods in this early period, consistently emphasized the need to focus on skills and topics of intense interest to students, and to allow student voices to emerge within the educational process. They expressed notions of the learning process that, if not identical, shared a high commitment to student-centered education. Clark suggested that the successful teacher balanced and united the interests and aspirations of students with their own beliefs of what knowledge, actions, and values should be promoted by the learning experience: "I found out that you don't tell people what to do. You let them tell you what they want done and then you have to have in your mind certain things that you feel they need to do. And so you get their thoughts and wind your thoughts around. . . . But if you have a cut-and-dry program for them, you'll lose out every time."[18] For Robinson, the program worked because it employed a "basic tenet" of the Highlander philosophy, "That the direction and substance of a program must emerge *from* the people and not [be] *brought* to them however well intentioned. This is what is called the 'percolator effect' rather than the 'drip' technique. If a program is to work the people must have the power of making decisions about what they want to do."[19] Underlying this pedagogy was a fundamental belief in the dignity, life knowledge, intellectual competence, and capacity for growth possessed by these adult learners, even when they were illiterate or struggling on the edge of literacy.

BUILDING ON CULTURAL STRENGTHS

Other adult education programs were unable to equal the success of the Citizenship Schools. Starting in 1931 (and working with the help of prominent

South Carolina adult educator Wil Lou Gray), a Miss Gregory had tutored
Edisto Island Blacks with very limited results. Even well-respected literacy
programs were less effective than Citizenship Schools. Clark estimated that
the levels of literacy achieved by the Adult Education Association program
in 140 hours and the Laubach program in 98 hours were achieved by Citizenship School students in about 80 hours. In Horton's opinion, the Citizenship Schools offered no particular innovation in methods over other programs,
but were more successful because of their radical affirmation of students'
dignity, their challenge to obtain first-class citizenship, and their use of community people as teachers (Clark, 1990, pp. 60–70; Horton, 1990, pp. 96–
122).

    This belief in the strengths of Black Sea Islanders was not fanciful. Blacks
on the cluster of islands near Charleston suffered from a neglect and poverty
that should not be romanticized. But they also possessed strong traditions of
mutual aid, creative expression through crafts and storytelling, practical
survival skills, and the social cohesion provided by strong family ties. After
the abolition of slavery, extended family groups often settled together in clus-
ters of three to eight houses along a path or road, in close proximity to shared
farmland and/or a garden. Childrearing responsibilities were shared by grandparents, aunts and uncles, and cousins. If birth parents had to leave the island to make a living or had precarious financial resources, it was not unusual
for relatives to take primary responsibility for rearing a child. Family land
ownership was informally handed down, and provided an important source
of identity even for those who had left the islands. Although these deep family connections have been weakened by migration, they continue to play a
strong role in the lives of island residents (Jones-Jackson, 1987, pp. 22–24;
Agbasgebe, 1987, pp. 57–58).

    Even though each island had several churches dating back to the 19th
century, the difficulty of transportation prompted many neighborhoods to
build "praise houses," small, wooden structures for community worship that
were within easy walking distance. One such praise house, Moving Star Hall
on Johns Island, exemplified the centrality of grassroots religious initiatives.
The hall, a clapboard structure warmed and illuminated by a pot-bellied stove,
was built by the Moving Star Society around 1914. In 1959, the folksinger
Guy Carawan accompanied Esau Jenkins to a Christmas watch meeting at
the hall. Worshippers gathered from 11:00 p.m. until dawn, moving informally through a series of *a capella* religious songs, personal testimony, and
varied tellings of the nativity story. The hallmark of Moving Star services
was participation. Carawan was deeply impressed by the ability of congre-
gation members to pray, preach, or lead a song; to interweave their singing;
and to blend separate rhythms created by voices, hands, and feet. As Jenkins

explained, such gatherings helped sustain the community: "The songs that you are listening to are coming from people who know what hardship is. Those songs are the thing that gives us courage, when it seems as if we don't have any friends. We realize that when we were turned loose, we didn't have any property, we didn't have any education, we didn't have any friends. Those songs . . . [make] them think about God Almighty, who has helped them all the way."[20]

Through the incorporation of song and prayer, discussion of common problems, and a curriculum that drew upon daily experience, the Citizenship School classes melded the acquisition of new skills and forms of struggle with traditions of cooperation and solidarity that were embedded in the lives of students. By building on the life experience of her students, Robinson fashioned procedures that prefigured the "whole language" methods that began to emerge in K–12 education during the 1960s and 1970s: "I started off with things that were familiar with them. They were working in the fields and I'd have them tell me stories about what they did out in the fields and what they had in their homes. I'd write these stories out and work with them on the words. I'd say now, 'This is your story. We're going to learn how to read your story.'"[21] When Horton came down to visit Robinson's class early on, the students serenaded him with a rendition of "Jacob's Ladder" refurbished with civil rights lyrics, "Every voter, makes us stronger."[22] We do not have enough evidence to verify if other teachers built as strongly as Robinson on the life experiences of students. It is clear, however, that the shared background and learning agendas uniting the students and teachers made it likely that pupils had a strong sense of being culturally at home when they attended these classes. We do know that from the very beginning indigenous and civil rights music often played an important part in Citizenship School classes and other meetings. The singing was frequently led by Guy Carawan and his wife, Candie, who together played an important role in recording local music and sponsoring Sea Island folk festivals (Carawan, n.d.).[23]

This foundation of respect for the impoverished Black communities of the Sea Islands marked a fundamental departure from the perspective of White school officials that Black students were capable of little learning. It gave Citizenship School teachers the conviction that their students could achieve great things, if properly inspired by high expectations and the lofty goal of acquiring "first-class citizenship." Just as importantly, it suggested that the culture and traditions of mutual aid and solidarity that sustained poor, rural African Americans were resources that could be tapped to build the local struggle for equality and enrich the civil rights movement across the South (Tjerandsen, 1980, pp. 188–189).

MELDING EDUCATION AND POLITICAL ACTION

A substantial proportion of Citizenship School students in the Charleston area were able to pass the voter registration test, and the political momentum that the classes helped generate inspired others to register and vote. In 1959, Robinson launched a voter registration campaign in Charleston for which she organized a "coaching staff" of women (one each from 12 wards) who taught residents how to read, and in particular, how to read ballots. They were able to register almost 700 new voters. In 1960, Blacks on Edisto Island outvoted Whites for the first time, and Wadmalaw Island Black citizens fell just a few votes shy of matching the White vote. In 1964, the Black vote gave Wadmalaw the distinction of being the only part of Charleston County won by Lyndon Johnson. Septima Clark estimated that between 1957 and 1962 the number of Blacks registered to vote on Johns Island rose from 200 to 800 (Tjerandsen, 1980, pp. 188–189).

Soon after the start of the schools, Jenkins realized that even after they had gained rudiments of literacy and the right to vote, poor Blacks still did not have the knowledge they needed to effectively exercise political power. He began to popularize what he called "second step citizenship education."

> I decided since we had got quite a few people registered through the adult citizenship schools that we wouldn't let the Highlander spirit die. So I started what we call a second step political education because the people in the school—they'd register and they'd vote because we told them to vote. But they didn't have the political education and the understanding of voting—what it means. So we decided to teach them then what the ballot means.[24]

This entailed teaching how government functioned on the local, state, and federal levels and how to use newspapers to follow current events. It also meant helping new voters learn to reject those who tried to get their votes through bribery or specious claims of friendship, demand that politicians explain and justify their platforms, and focus their support to gain the maximum electoral impact. In May 1958 a meeting on Edisto Island convened to form a group that came to be called the "Self-Development of People." Jenkins explained, "Suppose we get 400 or 500 Negroes registered on this island and no organization. . . . With no organization to guide you your vote will be scattered thin or sold out to some politician who decides to be good overnight and only for one night."[25]

This second step phase generated substantial activism on the islands. On Edisto, students who had participated in the "each man get a man" registration campaign met on a monthly basis after the school ended to study candidates and issues, and Edisto's "Self-Development of People" organization mobilized the Black vote and initiated community improvement projects. The Board of Concerned Members of Wadmalaw Island, which grew directly out of the first Citizenship School on that island, was eventually able to win the election of a Black woman to the precinct executive committee and provide critical support to a White state legislator who helped residents gain mail delivery to individual boxes, school bus routes that included side roads, and three day-care centers. In March of 1963, the Progressive Club proudly opened its new Johns Island community center, which included a small gym and facilities to host conferences, and sponsored a boy scout troop and a young citizens group (Carawan and Carawan, 1994, pp. 174–195).

REASONS FOR THE SCHOOL'S SUCCESS

I would pose three hypotheses to explain why the schools started in the Sea Islands and not elsewhere. Although the Sea Islands were rapidly losing their historic isolation during the 1950s, their Black population was still, in many ways, insulated from the direct, intimate, and daily control of a White elite that felt immediately threatened by Black enfranchisement. Sea Island Blacks risked White ire when they registered, but it was less likely to be a life-threatening venture compared, for instance, with the experience of Blacks in Mississippi (Payne, 1995, pp. 7–47). In addition, the kind of communal institutions I have described were not unique, but did have more breathing room in which to thrive compared to other Southern Black communities. Finally, Clark, Horton, Jenkins, and Robinson acted to implement the immensely powerful combination of the Highlander pedagogy and spirit and cultural resources embedded within Black Sea Island life.

When the SCLC took over the Citizenship Schools in 1961, the small staff assigned to the program was able to expand the impact of the endeavor to encompass the entire South. Their work was arduous, but adult students around the South were drawn to the program by goals similar to those cherished by the first participants of Johns Island: opportunities to enjoy the varied personal uses of literacy and to participate in the civil rights movement. Organizers throughout the South who believed that the movement should be built from the bottom up found the program an ideal means to implement their values and strategic orientation. During the heat of many civil rights battles, symbiotic relationships grew between Student Nonviolent Coordinating Committee (SNCC) and Congress on Racial Economy (CORE) field staff and the core workers within the Citizenship Education Program (Payne, 1995, pp. 166, 169, 294).

Other factors bolstered the schools. The passage of the 1965 Voting Rights Act was in part fueled by the support by the Kennedy and Johnson administration for Black voter registration. This commitment emerged as early as 1961, when Kennedy administration officials became deeply involved in setting up the Southern Regional Council's Voter Education Program (VEP). The VEP provided crucial economic support to voter registration drives that, in turn, provided much of the motivation to set up Citizenship Schools (Branch, 1988, pp. 479, 515, 636, 677, 716).

The Citizenship Schools bear striking similarities to other adult education projects with liberatory agendas. For example, during the early 1960s, Paulo Freire and his colleagues developed "literacy circles" with Brazilian peasants that eventually inspired adult educators around the world (Curtis, 1990). Although hardly identical, there are striking similarities between his pedagogical ideas and the North American Citizenship Schools: respect for the culture and intelligence of the despised and exploited poor, the conviction that teacher and students should act as partners who learn from each other, and the conviction that learning is an essential ingredient in revolutionary change.

It is safe to assume that there was substantial variation in how effectively these ideals were put into practice during the early phase of the Citizenship School program. Bernice Robinson's drive, inventiveness, and empathy would have been hard to match, and many of the teachers were less well educated than she was. The decentralized nature of the program allowed wide latitude in the diligence and methods of each teacher (Levine, 1998, pp. 202–236).

But whatever the instructional variations, the program flourished through an ethos that emphasized how much, rather than how little, poor people are capable of. There is little doubt that the Citizenship Schools opened the doors of learning for both students and teachers, and played a core role in energizing the civil rights movement. The civic improvement activities encouraged by the schools, truly subversive when initiated by poor Blacks in the South of the 1960s, are considered routine today. Perhaps what remains subversive is the concept of an educational program that is simultaneously practical in its goals and unabashedly convinced that "ordinary people" possess the power to transform themselves as they work to transform the society in which they live.

NOTES

1. Andrew Young, interview by Elliot Wigginton, 1981, Highlander Library, Highlander Research and Education Center, New Market, Tennessee, 3.
2. Bernice Robinson, interview by Sue Thrasher and Elliott Wigginton, November 9, 1980, Highlander Library, HREC.

3. Bernice Robinson, interview with Thrasher and Wigginton.

4. Bernice Robinson, Interview with Thrasher and Wigginton.

5. Herbert U. Fielding, interview with author, January 28, 1998, Charleston, South Carolina; Bill Jenkins, interview with author, July 1997, Charleston, South Carolina.

6. Septima Clark, interview with Sue Thrasher, June 20, 1981, Highlander Library, HREC; Septima Clark, interview with Jaqueline Hall, July 25, 1976, Southern Oral History Project Collection, Wilson Library, University of North Carolina, Chapel Hill, North Carolina.

7. Septima Clark, interview with Sue Thrasher, June 20, 1981, Highlander Library, HREC.

8. Septima Clark, interview with Jaqueline Hall, July 25, 1976, Southern Oral History Project Collection, Wilson Library, University of North Carolina, Chapel Hill, North Carolina.

9. Highlander Research and Education Center Collection, State Historical Society of Wisconsin, Madison, Wisconsin, Tape 46.

10. Bernice Robinson, interview with Thrasher and Wigginton.

11. Bernice Robinson, interview with Thrasher and Wigginton.

12. Bernice Robinson, interview with Thrasher and Wigginton.

13. Bernice Robinson, interview with Thrasher and Wigginton.

14. Citizenship Education Program. In the Southern Christian Leadership Conference Collection. The Martin Luther King, Jr. Center for Nonviolent Change, Atlanta, Georgia.

15. Anderson Mack Sr., interview by author, January 26, 1998, Wadmalaw Island, South Carolina.

16. Myles Horton to Leonard Reiser, 1955, Tape 168, HREC Collection, SHSW; Bill Jenkins, interview with author, July 1997, Charleston, South Carolina.

17. Septima Clark, interview with Jaqueline Hall.

18. Septima Clark, interview by Peter Wood, February 3, 1981, Charleston, South Carolina, Highlander Library, HREC.

19. Bernice Robinson, "Reaching Out: 'Empowerment of the Estranged, the Powerless,'" Box 4, Bernice Robinson Collection, The Avery Research Center for African-American History and Culture, Charleston, South Carolina.

20. Esau Jenkins, "Esau Jenkins: Talks," tape transcript, Box 16 Folder 10, HREC Collection, SHSW

21. Bernice Robinson, interview by Sandra Brenneman Oldendorf, 1986, Charleston, South Carolina.

22. Bernice Robinson, interview by Oldendorf.

23. Guy and Candie Carawan, interview by Sue Thrasher, 1982, Highlander Library, HREC.

24. Esau Jenkins, undated interview, Highlander Library, HREC.

25. "Edisto Island: Organizing," Reports 1958–1965, Box 154 Folder 19, HREC Collection, SHSW.

CHAPTER 4

"They Walk, Talk, and Act Like New People"

Citizenship Education in Southeastern Georgia, 1960–1965

Deanna M. Gillespie

In January 1963, Savannah resident Dorothy Boles opened an adult literacy class at the Independent Christian Lodge in her neighborhood. In this class, students learned lessons that held the promise of full citizenship, turning education into a political tool. At the end of 3 months, Boles reported on her students' progress. She wrote, "They wanted to show [their] new courage and gratitude by writing the Mayor of Savannah in regard to the streets not being sufficiently paved in Carver Village. They are now waiting for an answer." Boles added, "There is nothing else to report except that since this school started, they walk, talk, and act like new people with determination and more courage to face the future."[1]

In the years preceding the Civil Rights Act of 1964 and the Voting Rights Act of 1965, Citizenship Education Program (CEP) teachers worked to reverse the effects of decades of racial discrimination and legal segregation. In their classes, they created space where they and their students performed first-class citizenship, sowing the seeds for collective action and political empowerment. This "awakening," as CEP teacher Cassie Pierce named it, was perhaps the most important result of their efforts.[2]

CEP was a unique adult education program designed to increase Black voter registration through lessons in literacy. The program started in 1957 as a local effort on Johns Island, South Carolina. Over the next 3 years, the Highlander Folk School devoted substantial staff resources to open Citizenship Schools across the Sea Islands. By 1960, Highlander director Myles Horton sought a new administrative home for the growing program. In the spring of 1961, the Southern Christian Leadership Conference (SCLC) assumed responsibility for CEP (Horton, 1989; Morris, 1984, pp. 154–155; Tjerandsen, 1980, pp. 1–8).

Existing CEP scholarship emphasizes these early years, focusing on key personalities and institutions (See, for example, Tjerandsen, 1980; Horton, 1989; Oldendorf, 1990; Levine, 1999, 2004). While these studies offer important insight about this period, they raise additional questions. For example, what happened after SCLC assumed responsibility for the program? How did local communities incorporate CEP into ongoing civil rights activities? How did the program expand Black women's grassroots efforts across the southeast? This paper explores these questions, focusing on CEP implementation in and around Savannah between 1960 and 1965.

Shifting focus not only extends the CEP narrative, it also complicates interpretations of civil rights action in southeastern Georgia. Existing studies richly describe demonstrations in urban Savannah, characterizing the dynamic local movement as the product of internal tensions between strong-willed and charismatic male leaders (Bolster, 1972; Tuck, 1995, 2001). However, situating CEP in the center of the narrative highlights African American women's leadership in a regional movement that stretched beyond Savannah to mobilize Black communities in surrounding rural counties.

CEP teachers' attendance records and narrative reports reveal that they believed that their work centered on three important objectives: improving literacy skills, increasing voter registration, and improving community conditions. They did not dwell on the internal tension within the Savannah movement. Instead, they used literacy education as a vehicle for grassroots community mobilization and leadership development.

African American women had long supported Savannah's local civil rights leaders and organizations. In the 1940s, they spearheaded efforts to build a local orphanage and joined an NAACP-organized effort create a voting bloc for the 1944 state election.[3] As civil rights action gained momentum in the late 1950s, African American women's networks and organizational skills provided critical support for renewed protests. According to NAACP chapter president W. W. Law,

> [Black women formed] a committee of . . . housewives, by and large. And when we would hold the mass meeting . . . and determined what we had to do the next week, we would give those instructions to Miss [Virginia] Mack. She would communicate with all of the women who [had phone] directories. One woman would call . . . the people in the "A" section and "B"—and that's how the word would get around the city. Blacks would know not to go into the stores or whatever else we were doing.[4]

Across southeastern Georgia, CEP built on and extended these efforts. In contrast to these ongoing efforts, CEP drew direct connections to Black women's historical traditions in education. In this program, they were more than participants, supporters, and followers; they were teachers.

When CEP was introduced in southeastern Georgia in early 1960, it fit into an emerging strategy to increase voter registration. That spring, as the Savannah NAACP chapter planned large-scale demonstrations, Hosea Williams, the branch's outspoken political action committee chairman, assertively promoted a plan to expand voter registration activities (Bolster, 1972, p. 233). He called for a new organization that could serve as an alternative for Black professionals who supported the NAACP's goals but faced economic reprisal if they officially joined the organization. The chapter board agreed and created the Chatham County Crusade for Voters, appointing Williams as director (Bolster, 1972, p. 233; Tuck, 1995, pp. 547–595; 2001, pp. 128–129).

As he assumed leadership of the Crusade, Williams met with Bernice Robinson. During the meeting, Robinson described her experiences teaching the first Citizenship Schools on Johns Island, and explained Highlander's efforts to extend the program beyond the South Carolina coast. Williams listened with interest as she outlined how the Sea Islands Citizenship Schools had achieved two of his primary objectives: increasing voter registration and mobilizing communities.[5] He readily agreed to work with Highlander to train teachers and set up classes in Savannah. Between September and December 1960, the Crusade and Highlander collaborated to open 30 local schools. During these 3 months, 9,000 African Americans registered to vote in Chatham County, due in part to the Citizenship School program. Based on this success, Highlander staff assisted the Crusade in securing grant funds to expand its efforts (Tjerandsen, 1980, pp. 178–179).

Bolstered by his success in Savannah, Williams traveled to surrounding rural areas, engaging local activists from the 18 counties in Georgia's First U.S. Congressional District. By January 1961, three representatives from each county formed the governing board of the renamed Southeastern Georgia Crusade for Voters. Each county group set out to organize local affiliates that could initiate voter education activities across the region. Citizenship Schools formed the cornerstone of these efforts, as representatives regularly identified teachers to attend Highlander training sessions.[6] In 6 months, 630 students had enrolled in Citizenship Schools, resulting in 110 new registered voters in 13 coastal counties.[7]

Across the region, African American women responded to Williams's invitation to teach local classes. Citizenship Schools directly connected Black women's civil rights activism to gendered traditions of education as a political strategy. Since the late 19th century, teaching remained one of the few professions open to African American women. According to historian Stephanie

Shaw, "regardless of the type of school, and particularly in the South, teachers did not anticipate the luxury of merely teaching. Nor did they define their work that way" (Shaw, 1996, p. 176). Many of them fully understood the radical potential of an educated African American electorate in the Jim Crow South. Across the region, they actively expanded their activities beyond the classroom, engaging entire communities in their efforts to "lift the race" (Fairclough, 2001, pp. 42–67). Drawing on this tradition, local Citizenship School teachers established a clear and recognizable identity.

While Citizenship Schools preserved Black women's leadership in education, the program structure broadened these traditions to engage a new group of activists. Consistent with Highlander's emphasis on community leadership development, Citizenship School teachers were recognized leaders who did not necessarily have formal training or education credentials. Unlike other adult education programs, Citizenship Schools intentionally avoided a hierarchical relationship between teachers and the adult students in the classroom. According to Septima Clark, "we wanted to find a person who was not a licensed teacher, one who would not be considered highfalutin, who would not act condescending to adults" (Clark, 1990, p. 48).

This criterion for teachers ensured that local classes preserved the program's origins in practical education and the Highlander approach to social change. Horton argued that given the opportunity, oppressed people could develop their own solutions to social problems. Local teachers had a responsibility to teach the fundamentals of literacy, but they also needed to create an environment that encouraged participatory democracy. In contrast to the racial uplift ideology of the early 20th century, Citizenship School teachers were not "lifters," but instead provided the tools and encouragement for students to "lift" themselves.

Throughout 1961, Williams and local leaders identified and recruited potential teachers across the First Congressional District. During this same period, Horton stepped up negotiations with SCLC staff members to transfer the expanding program. In the summer of 1961, SCLC leaders agreed and assumed responsibility for the renamed Citizenship Education Program (CEP). The SCLC board hired Andrew Young to direct the program. Young, a Congregationalist minister, brought organizational and fundraising experience. Clark followed the program to SCLC, serving as its director of teaching. Her presence and expertise provided continuity between Highlander and CEP's new home. Bernice Robinson offered additional continuity, leading teacher training workshops and supervising local classes through support from Highlander. Dorothy Cotton, an SCLC staff member already based in Atlanta, was named director of education.

For Hosea Williams in southeastern Georgia, the administrative transfer altered both institutional and financial support for his efforts. He depended on Highlander for teacher training as well as scholarships to pay the costs associated with the training. As Young, Cotton, and Clark prepared to extend the program across the southeast, the funds available to support ongoing efforts in southeastern Georgia dwindled. Williams opened discussions with Dorothy Cotton at SCLC, inquiring about available support for teachers attending Highlander training. In her response to Williams, she explained, "SCLC . . . affiliates will select persons from their areas to attend the [teacher training] schools at Highlander. . . . SCLC will be able to relieve the affiliates of some of the cost as soon as certain grants are available to us." She closed the letter with an invitation to affiliate, "if you desire."[8] After 10 months of negotiation, the Crusade officially affiliated with SCLC in December 1961, making CEP in southeastern Georgia an "SCLC program."[9] Local teachers now received training and stipend payments from SCLC, strengthening their connection with the organization.

Six months earlier, SCLC had moved teacher training workshops from Highlander to the Dorchester Center, located approximately 40 miles south of Savannah. Like Highlander's earlier workshops, the 5-day training sessions offered the opportunity for local leaders and SCLC staff members to get acquainted in a relaxed, retreat-like setting. Throughout the week, teachers attended a series of workshops to become familiar with CEP materials and teaching methods.

Staff members led discussions on the functions of government, the Constitution, and African American history, using these sessions to teach civics and history lessons. According to Young, "these were adults who knew a lot about life; it was merely certain knowledge about citizenship they needed, basically because such knowledge had been denied them" (Young, 1996, p. 147). SCLC staff members also used the workshops to demonstrate the group learning model that teachers would use in their local schools. Cotton later reflected, "We'd tell people to pay attention not just to what we're talking about but how we do it."[10] In these sessions, community leaders first performed their emerging identities, gaining the confidence needed to conduct local classes.[11]

Following training, teachers returned to their home communities to recruit students and begin classes. In Savannah, association with SCLC lent credibility to local teachers' efforts and enhanced the Crusade's reputation. However, in rural communities, this association, particularly with Martin Luther King Jr., proved to be a double-edged sword. According to Daisy Redding in Twin City, "I found out people idolize Dr. Martin Luther King Jr., [but] they are afraid. Afraid of what the white people might say and do."[12] In Alamo, Dollie Williams's students expressed concern about "Dr. Martin Luther King and his gang." Williams explained, "Dr. King was not an enemy to them, that he was helping in this nonviolent fight for their freedom."[13]

According to rural teachers, potential students' responses reflected the very real fear of economic reprisal as well as disagreement within African American communities about leadership and tactics.

In and around Savannah, many teachers adapted SCLC's recruiting guidelines to fit their local situations. Teachers canvassed their neighborhoods and posted advertisements announcing upcoming CEP classes. For teachers in Savannah, the Crusade provided important resources for publicizing classes and recruiting students. CEP teacher, Adline Bradshaw enlisted assistance from a young man in the Crusade office. She reported, "He printed several [leaflets] . . . that read, 'Stop! Look! And Listen! Adult Citizenship School at West Savannah Community Center, Mrs. Adline Bradshaw, teacher.' I [took] these and left one at every door in my neighborhood."[14]

Other teachers used more direct approaches to recruit students. Savannah teacher Cassie Pierce reported that her "class was organize[d] by soliciting door to door and friends [telling] one [another] about it."[15] In rural communities, where teachers had limited resources for advertising and publicity, face-to-face contact and personal connections served as primary methods to recruit students. In Collins, Pearlie Ealey made appeals to her neighbors, "entering the homes of those who are total[ly] illiterate . . . and begging them to let me help them help themselves and others."[16]

Recruitment brought teachers face-to-face with the effects of decades of discrimination and segregation. In contrast to direct action protests, Citizenship Schools required potential students to admit publicly that they could not read. According to Adline Bradshaw, "I didn't get very much cooperation from our [church] members because [they] thought it was embarrassing to let people know that they couldn't read and write, so for that reason, they wouldn't attend classes."[17] Similarly, Cassie Pierce reported, "the problem [seems to be] getting the most illiterate to school. They seem ashamed or [afraid]."[18] For adults who had struggled to develop strategies to overcome illiteracy, enrollment in Citizenship Schools required a personal admission of perceived failure as well as a commitment to political action, both presenting risks for potential students.

Savannah CEP teachers could refer to local traditions of organized resistance in recruitment efforts. In some cases, teachers worked with students who had been disenfranchised by literacy tests and poll taxes enacted in 1948. For example, Ida Smalls-Mack reported:

Some of my students . . . told me that during the time they were first registered, they were not required to be able to read and write; but after [Herman] Talmadge became Governor of Georgia, those persons whose names were on the book were required to re-register and if they did so, their names remained on the book.[19]

In this context, CEP offered a mechanism to capitalize on this public memory to mobilize for change.

In contrast, rural teachers did not have this same public memory and extensive organizational structure to build upon. Teachers directly confronted long-standing traditions of paternalism and intimidation, as well as recent memories of Klan violence. Rural students recognized that attending CEP classes represented a highly charged public act that could easily disrupt racialized social and economic relationships. According to Pearlie Ealey, "the adults [in Collins] were somewhat afraid to participate in civic affairs because they were afraid they would lose friendship with the Whites."[20] Similarly, Susie Greene in Wadley reported that community residents "were afraid to attend . . . because of their jobs." In her discussions with these residents, Greene clarified CEP's purpose, "assuring them that we were not trying to desegregate the schools in the citizenship school."[21] Beginning with this narrow definition, Greene attracted students and reduced negative attention from the White community.

Once teachers recruited between 8 and 15 students, they began classes. They operated schools for 3 consecutive months, holding meetings twice a week for 2 hours each night. In many cases, teachers creatively addressed problems to ensure that students continued through the program. For example, in rural communities, agricultural work often interfered with class attendance.[22] However, Susie Greene reported, "the people here are busy picking cotton. I am working with them individually."[23] Agricultural workers were not the only groups unable to attend class regularly. Daisy Jones faced similar difficulties in her Savannah class. Like Greene, Jones also offered individual instruction in students' homes "because the inconvenience of their work hours would not permit them attend [the] regular session."[24] Recognizing that many rural students did not have reliable transportation, Dollie Williams enlisted her husband to "take [her] to school and . . . also pick up all the students. . . . After class, he would take them back home."[25]

In class, teachers used Highlander's group-centered educational model to guide students through CEP participant workbooks. SCLC staff members retained much of Highlander's original structure, but revised the workbooks to include additional information about nonviolence, African American history, and SCLC. Consistent with the organization's foundations in Christianity, the revised workbooks opened with a lesson on "The Bible and the Ballot." In this lesson, SCLC staff members described CEP as missionary work. Teachers and students were called upon to "release the captives of this segregated society, and bring liberty to those who are oppressed. We must preach the good news of equality and brotherhood to the poor. . . . This was Jesus's work, and now it is ours."[26] This lesson set the tone for local classes, adding sacred significance to citizenship education.

CEP teachers incorporated this emphasis into their classes. They relied on local churches for critical support, including space, materials, and access to congregations. In addition, visibly connecting CEP to churches, rather than more secular civil rights organizations, gave the program credibility and respectability. In this context, local teachers were not viewed as civil rights agitators, but instead were respectable churchgoing women, performing God's work for the collective good. This identity served an important function. Connecting CEP to Black women's leadership in churches allowed SCLC to recruit through existing networks. For local teachers, CEP offered a vehicle for extending their church-based community activities. Cassie Pierce of Savannah articulated this connection, writing, "I thank God that time presented itself to be of service [in] my little way to the people. This is Christianity."[27]

Linking CEP with local churches also helped teachers incorporate rituals that followed a recognizable and familiar structure. For example, Florence Jenkins in Savannah reported that her class "had devotion . . . sang a song from our Freedom Song Sheets, prayed, and read the Scripture from the 133rd Psalms."[28] These rituals reinforced the sacred significance of citizenship and offered opportunities to actively engage students in learning. According to Dollie Williams in Savannah, "Some of them had special things they wanted to learn like read the Bible, add, subtract, [and] some wanted to learn to raise hymns and be able to be in different departments of the church work." She explained, "I would follow my class program but I would fit in a few minutes on the Bible."[29] Similarly, Cassie Pierce in Savannah reported, "In our devotionals, there are some that are inspired to [do] the reading of the scriptures. Their desires are great. They . . . want to read it well someday. I have them in intervals to learn Bible verses."[30]

In addition to "The Bible and the Ballot," CEP workbooks included basic literacy lessons designed to teach concepts in citizenship. In one lesson, students improved their vocabularies and reading skills by learning how individual letters formed words related to voting and government functions. For example, students learned that the letter "a" started words such as *attorney*, *amendments*, and *alderman*. Brief selections about African American history and lessons in nonviolence served as reading comprehension exercises. In addition, students learned writing and math skills within the context of their daily activities, filling out money orders and working math problems related to farming or voter registration.[31]

This practical approach to learning reflected Myles Horton's participatory democracy model. According to Horton, empowerment for social change occurred through two related processes. First, "you had to start where [the people] were and deal with their problems. . . . What you do is try to get people to have more confidence in themselves and their peers, and to understand that it's up to them, there's nobody else [who] can do it."[32] This personal and group empowerment allowed participants to recognize each other as resources and catalysts for change.

Once individuals began to rely on each other, Horton explained, "Given genuine decision-making powers, people will not only learn rapidly to make socially useful decisions, but they will also assume responsibility for carrying out decisions based on their collective judgment" (Horton, 1990, p. 134). For Horton, a truly democratic society was grounded in innovation and responsibility, where individual citizens reached consensus on needed changes and worked to achieve results for the collective good. CEP classes offered the space for previously marginalized groups to experience this democratic process in which they were equal participants and assumed responsibility for social change (Levine, 1999, pp. 41–53; Morris, 1984, pp. 141–149; Tjerandsen, 1980, pp. 200–204).

To meet students where they were, CEP teachers adapted everyday activities to teach basic literacy and encourage community involvement. According to Lou Anna Riggs in Midville, "We discuss and thrash out any individual problems that occur. For instance, a school bus driver wanted to know how many miles he drives per school term, driving 36.6 miles one way per day. This problem was solved and fully discussed. The entire class benefited."[33] Teachers also encouraged students to discuss current events in class. According to Savannah teacher Cassie Pierce, "Our discussions [on] government and current happenings . . . created interest and made the class interesting and enjoyable by all. We'd sometimes get so deep in the subject matter, we'd stay overtime."[34] These additional activities allowed teachers to exercise a level of autonomy within a program with increasingly rigid reporting requirements and curriculum.

In CEP classes, teachers measured progress in individual terms, reporting students' achievements and milestones. In Collins, Pearlie Ealey reported on several students' progress. According to Ealey, "One lady who felt inferior to others because of being somewhat illiterate . . . has learned to read and write and has recently been appointed Chairman of the Deaconess Board of her church. An unwed mother became aroused about not [finishing] high school and is now taking courses through the mail in order to qualify for her high school diploma."[35] Similarly, Mary Troupe reported individual progress in her CEP classes in Alamo. According to Troupe, "One gentleman . . . [attended] one month [and] said, 'I've learn[ed] to read and write better. I can even read the newspaper, and sign my [own] papers without anyone's help, for that I am thankful.'"[36] These individual accomplishments sowed the seeds for collective action across southeastern Georgia.

Like racial uplift discourse at the turn of the century, empowerment through literacy was simultaneously conservative and radical. Although the program's rhetoric reinforced existing policies and practices, literacy and social responsibility subverted racial constructions in important ways. As students and teachers performed first-class citizenship, they presented a compelling challenge to political and educational barriers. In CEP classes, Southern Black adults clearly demonstrated their commitment to both learning and political engagement. Local teachers understood the radical potential of their classes and often reported their accomplishments in terms of increased voter registration and community organization.

Students who successfully registered to vote returned to CEP classes to share their stories, turning an individual act into public ritual. For example, Adline Bradshaw reported, "I . . . have a man in my class, about 65 [years old]. . . . I told him he could read well enough to go and register. He went to the courthouse and read the paragraph that they gave him to read without missing a word and wrote two lines. We were so proud of him when he returned to class the next night. The whole class shook hands with him."[37]

In Savannah and rural counties, individual success stories served as inspiration for other students. In Twin City, Joe Walker reported on his successful trip to the courthouse. According to his teacher, Daisy Redding, "After [he read his] report and [told] how easy it was for him to become a first-class citizen, more members of the class went out to register and bring in their reports."[38] Similarly, in Alamo, Mamie Hall reported, "I carried two very nervous students up to register and they made it just fine. The people in the office were very nice. They asked me to bring all I could."[39] Through these narratives, CEP students learned what to expect from their fellow classmates, alleviating fear and anxiety.

By early 1964, these individual actions translated into significant increases in voter registration across southeastern Georgia. In a report to SCLC, Hosea Williams reflected on the previous year's activities. According to Williams,

> Exactly 110 Citizenship School teachers and 14 Supervisors have been trained . . . for the Southeastern Georgia Crusade for Voters. During the past 12 months, 27 effective Adult Citizenship Schools have been operated, training a total of 540 students. . . . Our 27 Adult Citizenship Schools played a very important part in registering 13,000 new voters throughout the First District.[40]

In addition to quantifiable increases in voter registration, Williams also reported that the schools had sparked individual changes that planted the seeds for collective action. In his report, he asserted, "We have been able to organize our people because the program has enlightened them to the advantages of . . . voters over non-voters, good citizenship over citizenship, literacy over illiteracy, community participation over complacency, and human dignity over worldly possessions."[41]

In both rural communities and urban Savannah, CEP teachers reported that their students initiated community improvement projects. In Midville, Lou Anna Riggs's students "signed a petition to get better roads in this area. This project is underway now."[42] In Wadley, Susie Greene's students formed "a committee on drop-outs and absentees, one on petitions for street lights, sewage, and drainage and getting a by-pass cut in the Negro section and streets paved. 107 people signed."[43] Through these projects, students performed their new identities, demonstrating first-class citizenship through action.

Especially in rural counties, CEP graduates turned their energies to support a variety of community organizations. In Collins, Pearlie Ealey reported that former students "have become registered voters, participants in P.T.A., voter registration organizers, registration workers, church members, church supporters, blood donors, and other community, county, and district organization participants."[44] As students joined these organizations, they reinforced the program founders' belief that CEP classes could nurture leaders for social change. Demonstrating that "first-class citizenship" extended beyond the courthouse, former students enacted participatory democracy and social responsibility in community organizations, broadening CEP's influence beyond the local classroom.

From 1960 to 1965, CEP teachers and their students influenced civil rights action in important ways. Throughout the early 1960s, direct action protests and CEP classes worked in tandem in urban Savannah. Increasingly confrontational demonstrations, including night marches, drew large numbers of young people to Williams and the Crusade. In contrast, CEP classes and their teachers represented a "less militant" alternative (Morris, 1984, p. 239). Importantly, the program insured that African American women remained a vital part of the Crusade, diversifying Williams's image beyond confrontational direct action. Through CEP, the Crusade expanded activities in Savannah's Black neighborhoods, nurturing potential leaders for community action.

Outside of the relative protection of Savannah's African American community, direct action protests were not a viable organizing strategy. In rural areas, local Black leaders encouraged their neighbors to register to vote and organized to support Black schools.[45] In this context, CEP classes expanded civil rights activism opportunities, particularly for Black women. Unlike protest activities led by Black male leaders, Black women who taught citizenship classes appeared to be less threatening to existing White power structures. In 1964, Williams claimed, "the Citizenship Program meets less resistance on the part of the White community than any program attempted."[46]

In January 1964, on the eve of a massive voter registration drive, Martin Luther King Jr. addressed an audience in Savannah, Georgia, and declared,

"Savannah . . . is the most integrated city south of the Mason-Dixon line" (Raines, 1977, p. 443). His statement celebrated the African American community's 18-month long economic boycott and acknowledged Savannah's place as the first Southern city to desegregate all public facilities. This achievement represented the culmination of several factors, including effective local leadership, broad-based commitment to change, and coordinated direct action and voter registration activities. Although CEP never gained the public recognition of protests in Albany and Birmingham, the program provided an alternative strategy for organizing in rural areas, a strategy grounded in Black women's community activism.

NOTES

1. Dorothy Boles, Narrative from the W. Gwinnett Citizenship School, undated, Box 160, Folder 1, Southern Christian Leadership Conference Collection, Citizenship Education Program Papers, Martin Luther King Jr. Center for Nonviolent Social Change, Atlanta, Georgia (hereafter abbreviated: SCLC-CEP).

2. Cassie Pierce, Citizenship Narrative, March 16, 1963, Box 160, Folder 17, SCLC-CEP.

3. W. W. Law, interview by Clifford Kuhn and Tim Crimmins, November 15, 1990, transcript, Box E-2, Folder 1, Georgia Government Documentation Project, Special Collections, Georgia State University Library, Atlanta, GA.

4. W. W. Law, interview by Kuhn and Crimmins.

5. Bernice V. Robinson, "Report on Field Trips for May-June-July," August 1960, Box 38, Folder 2, Highlander Folk School Collection, Wisconsin State Historical Society, Madison, WI (hereafter abbreviated: WSHS-HFS).

6. Hosea L. Williams, "History and Philosophy of the Southeastern Georgia Crusade for Voters," undated, Box 139, Folder 22, SCLC-CEP.

7. Highlander Folk School, "Memorandum on Citizenship Program," Box 136, Folder 28, SCLC-CEP.

8. Letter from Dorothy Cotton to Hosea Williams, February 6, 1961, Box 160, Folder 26, SCLC-CEP.

9. Letter from Hosea Williams to Dorothy Cotton, December 14, 1961, Box 160, Folder 26, SCLC-CEP.

10. Harry Boyte, "The Dorchester Center: An Interview with Dorothy Cotton, 1991", p. 3, Center for Democracy and Citizenship website, http://www.publicwork .org/pdf/interviews (accessed March 15, 2004).

11. For more detailed description of SCLC's teacher training workshops, see Levine, 1999, pp. 182–197.

12. Daisy P. Redding, "My Experience While Working With Citizenship Classes," March 16, 1963, Box 160, Folder 50, SCLC-CEP.

13. Dollie M. Williams, "Research Paper," March 12, 1963, Box 158, Folder 6, SCLC-CEP.

14. Adline Bradshaw, "A Narrative of My Citizenship School," undated, Box 160, Folder 2, SCLC-CEP.

15. Cassie Pierce, "Citizenship Narrative," March 16, 1963, Box 160, Folder 17, SCLC-CEP.

16. Pearlie Ealey, "The Effect of the School in the Community," November 1962, Box 158, Folder 51, SCLC-CEP.

17. Adline Bradshaw, "A Narrative of My Citizenship School."

18. Cassie Pierce, "A Narrative on Citizenship School," February 26, 1963, Box 160, Folder 16, SCLC-CEP.

19. Ida Smalls-Mack, "Narrative II," March 15, 1963, Box 160, Folder 14, SCLC-CEP.

20. Pearlie Ealey, "Questionnaire for Workshop on Training Leaders for Citizenship Schools," undated, Box 158, Folder 49, SCLC-CEP.

21. Susie Greene, "Questionnaire for Workshop on Training Leaders for Citizenship Schools," undated, Box 160, Folder 56, SCLC-CEP.

22. Mary Lois Byrd, "Attendance Report," February, 1964, Box 158, Folder 43, SCLC-CEP; Daisy P. Redding, "Attendance Report," August, 1963, Box 160, Folder 51, SCLC-CEP.

23. Letter from Susie Greene to Dorothy Cotton, September 10, 1962, Box 160, Folder 56, SCLC-CEP.

24. Daisy Jones, "The Effect of the School in the Community," January, 1963, Box 160, Folder 11, SCLC-CEP.

25. Dollie M. Williams, "Research Paper."

26. Southern Christian Leadership Conference, "Citizenship Workbook," undated, Box 153, Folder 23, SCLC-CEP.

27. Cassie Pierce, "My Narrative on Citizenship School," February 26, 1963, Box 160, Folder 16, SCLC-CEP.

28. Florence Jenkins, "The Effect of the School in the Community," June 14, 1963, Box 160, Folder 9, SCLC-CEP.

29. Dollie Williams, "Research Paper."

30. Cassie Pierce, "My Narrative on Citizenship School."

31. Southern Christian Leadership Conference, "Citizenship Workbook." See also Levine, 1999, pp. 241–244.

32. Bill Moyers, "Bill Moyer's Journal: An Interview with Myles Horton, The Adventures of a Radical Hillbilly, Parts I and 2," *Appalachian Journal* 9 (Summer 1983), 248–285, quote on p. 260.

33. Lou Anna Riggs, "Narrative," undated, Box 159, Folder 39, SCLC-CEP.

34. Cassie Pierce, "Citizenship School," March 16, 1963, Box 160, Folder 17, SCLC-CEP.

35. Pearlie Ealey, "The Effect of the School in the Community," 1963, Box 158, Folder 51, SCLC-CEP.

36. Mary Troupe, "The Value of the Adult Citizenship School," undated, Box 158, Folder 4, SCLC-CEP. See Levine, "Citizenship Schools," pp. 247–253.

37. Adline Bradshaw, "A Narrative of My Citizenship School."

38. Daisy P. Redding, "My Experience While Working with the Citizenship Classes."

39. Mamie Hall, "Pleasant Hill Citizenship School," June 14, 1963, Box 158, Folder 2, SCLC-CEP.

40. Hosea Williams, "Memorandum on Adult Citizenship Program," 1964, Box 160, Folder 33, SCLC-CEP.

41. Hosea Williams, "Memorandum on Adult Citizenship Program."

42. Lou Anna Riggs, "Narrative."

43. Susie Greene, "Better Conditions in a Community as a Result of Citizenship Training," undated, Box 160, Folder 55, SCLC-CEP.

44. Pearlie Ealey, "Collins and Reidsville Citizenship Struggle," Box 158, Folder 51, SCLC-CEP. See Levine, "Citizenship Schools," p. 240.

45. Booker T. Hagan and Charles L. Bailey, interview by author, December 15, 2005, Claxton, Georgia.

46. Memorandum from Hosea Williams to Andrew Young, 1964, Box 160, Folder 33, SCLC-CEP.

CHAPTER 5

"Give Light and the People Will Find a Way"

Ella Baker and Teaching as Politics

Charles M. Payne

But one of the guiding principles has to be that we cannot lead a struggle that involves masses of people without identifying with the people and without getting people to understand what their potentials are, what their strengths are.

—Ella Baker

The essence of [Fidel Castro's] own thinking could lie in the certainty that in undertaking mass work it is fundamental to be concerned about individuals.

—Gabriel Garcia Marquez

Ella Baker spent her life trying to make people understand their own potential and their own capacity to act on the issues that mattered to them. Among those most familiar with African American struggles from the Depression through the modern civil rights era, her name is iconic. Among those who worked with her, she commands the special respect reserved for people who have brought us to new levels of self-awareness. Only recently has scholarship brought her story to broader audiences (Grant, 1998; Ransby, 2003; see also Grant, 1981; Cantarow, O'Malley, & Strom, 1980).

Ella Baker remains a compelling figure because of her confidence in the capacities of ordinary citizens; because of her persistence, her rejection of dogmas and ideological fixity, and her rejection of hierarchies of race, class, education, nationality, and gender; because of her willingness to sublimate her ego to her politics; because of her limitless confidence in young people;

Portions of this essay appeared previously in Charles Payne, *I've Got the Light of Freedom* (Berkeley: University of California Press, 1995) and in *Southern Cultures*.

because of her commitment to working for causes, not organizations; and because of her insistence on principled and supportive human relationships—in short, because of the clarity of her commitment to democracy as both means and end. For over half a century, wherever the struggle was, she was on its cutting edge—the NAACP in the 1940s, the Southern Christian Leadership Conference in the 1950s, and the Student Nonviolent Coordinating Committee in the 1960s, in addition to working with dozens of less well-known organizations. Wherever she was, her voice tended to be distinctive. Barbara Ransby, one of her biographers, calls her both a radical democrat and a radical humanist, and says her feminist sensibilities were sufficiently strong to discomfit many a traditional leader.

It may be fair to say of Ella Baker that she understood teaching to be the most fundamental political act. She often insisted that the problems we confront are so complex that we need all forms of political challenge, from electoral politics to top-down, charismatic politics. Voting, lobbying, petitioning, agitation, community organizing, mass disruptions and civil disobedience are all well and good. Nevertheless, over the longer haul, concessions from the power structure are ephemeral. If ordinary people aren't capable of standing up for their own interests, whatever concessions are won today can be withdrawn tomorrow.

Ella Baker's historical importance rests significantly on the impact she had on the young people who reshaped the country in the 1960s. It was Baker who responded to the energy of the sit-ins by calling the meeting out of which the Student Nonviolent Coordinating Committee grew; it was she who helped develop its distinctive democratic and antihierarchical ethos, its emphasis on developing local leadership. SNCC, to a degree that is still not widely appreciated, went on to reshape the very idea of activism not only in the Black struggle, but in the other struggles that define that decade. Casey Hayden, for example, who helped shape the thinking of one wing of the early feminist movement in the 1960s, attributes her own empowerment largely to Baker. "So in this way, the women's movement traces back to Ella Baker" (Hayden, 2003). One SNCC member, Bob Moses, bestowed upon Baker the Swahili title of *Fundi*, which translates as "the person who passes the best collective knowledge from one generation to the next." If Martin Luther King was the paradigmatic spokesperson of the Southern movement, we can think of Miss Baker—and it is movement tradition to refer to her as *Miss* Baker—as its paradigmatic teacher.

If we wish to understand the developmental trajectory of education among African Americans, it is important to note that one of its most important progenitors had pretty much worked out her approach to it as early as the Great Depression. (One might say the same of Septima Clark [Brown, 1986].) If we look at the work she did in the 1930s and 1940s, we can see the framework of ideas that would inform SNCC Freedom Schools in the 1960s and Black Panther Liberation Schools in the 1970s.

Born in 1903, Baker's youth was spent in Virginia and rural North Carolina. She described her background as offering strong examples of racial pride and outright defiance of White supremacy as well as strong egalitarian traditions and a powerful sense of community. She often traced a line between her own activism and her mother's active involvement in the well-being of others as a rural missionary: "I was young when I became active in things and I became active in things largely because my mother was very active in the field of religion" (Ransby, 2003, p. 13).

After her graduation from Shaw University in North Carolina, she moved to Harlem where she seems to have tried to expose herself to every political current in the city, from Harlem to Greenwich Village. In 1931, she was able to spend a semester at the Brookwood Labor College. Brookwood is a part of a largely lost history of worker education. Located near New York City, Brookwood offered courses in the history, practice, and theory of labor struggle, playing the kind of generative role that the Highlander Center played in the South. Many important organizers of the Congress of Industrial Organizations were trained at Brookwood, and one of its faculty helped found the Fellowship of Reconciliation, which nurtured the nonviolent wing of the civil rights movement. The teaching there was eclectically radical, trying to get students to think for themselves rather than accept any received wisdom (Howlett, 1993). Barbara Ransby says this was Baker's first encounter with "open, democratic" pedagogy and she "saw enormous transformative potential" in it (Ransby, 2003, p. 74).

What she learned at Brookwood and from her other experiences with New York activists may have reinforced and formalized some of what she had absorbed from the egalitarian values of the community she grew up in. In any case, the kind of work she subsequently did with youth was certainly consistent with what she would have been exposed to at Brookwood. From 1934 to 1936, she worked with the Harlem Library, where part of her work involved developing educational programming for young people. A letter of recommendation from her supervisor suggests that the young Ella worked very much like the mature Ella:

> Her work was particularly good in organizing and acting as adviser to Young People's Forum. The group appealed to was from 16 to 26 years of age, one not ordinarily touched by our educational activities. Miss Baker successfully formed an active organization, which she brought into touch with other youth groups in the neighborhood and city. The public meetings included forums on social, economic, and cultural topics, literary and musical programs, debates and contests.

> Prominent speakers were brought into these meetings, but it was Miss
> Baker's plan always to place emphasis on increased participation by
> the members themselves. . . . Although Miss Baker left us for a better
> position, many of these people still show an active interest in the
> library's community program.[1]

The focus on exposing young people to a variety of viewpoints; on broadening their social experiences and networks; on active, participatory learning;
on learning through dialogue and debate and interaction; and on working
in such a way that the work continues after the initial organizer is gone
would all sound familiar to the young people who worked with her 30 years
later.

Working with young people would, of course, become one of the hall-
marks of her career. During her junior year in college, she gave a prize-
winning speech in which she claimed, "The salvation of the world is in its
youth. . . . Hence it is of paramount importance that the trend of youth's
thoughts be guided."[2] In her case, that was probably more than the usual
rhetoric. Later in her life, she repeatedly noted that youth, given their freedom from both old ideas and adult responsibilities, could play a special role
in what she liked to call social action. During the Depression one of the
projects that best reflected her emphasis on youth was her work with the
Young Negro Cooperative League.

To the modern ear, there may be nothing particularly radical about the
idea of economic cooperatives and consumer education, but the cooperative
movement of the 1930s was rooted in the upheavals of that moment and in
some of its manifestations could be as radical as any ideas current at the time.
It could be a practical form of Marxism. One leader in the movement said:

> The state of disorganization into which the world has fallen is the
> result of an unworkable method of social organization, sponsored and
> led by the White masters of our economic and political system. Crises,
> with their inevitable suffering and injustices, and wars, with their
> unavoidable brutality and demoralization, are an integral part of the
> profit system which holds the world in its grip.[3]

It could be seen as a practical Garveyism as well, a response to racial self-
doubt. Another leader in the movement thought:

> The Negro has long considered himself an inferior being. He has
> doubted his ability to run a business successfully. Through consumers'
> cooperation, the Negro will . . . gain self-confidence and . . . self-
> esteem and self-reliance.[4]

Ella Baker was among those drawn to the cooperative movement not just as a response to hard times but as a path to a more humane society. In 1930, she was one of the founders of the Young Negro's Cooperative League. That's *Young Negroes* as opposed to *Old Negroes*, the latter connoting to YNCL's founders a lack of militance, a bourgeois orientation, absorption in old-fashioned religious hokum. Membership was ordinarily restricted to those under 35 years of age to keep the old fogies and old ideas out. It was a very exact parallel to the *Negro* against *Black* debate of the 1960s. The League insisted that women be included on an equal basis with men and that ordinary members have a real voice in decision making. Ella Baker became its national director, and the League grew to 22 local councils by 1932. Along with stimulating local buying clubs and cooperatives, the League placed great emphasis on the ongoing education of its members. According to Barbara Ransby, the founders "insisted 'we must be trained before trying to lead people' and that therefore in the first year 'each council [will be] engaged in extensive educational work'" (Ransby, 2003, p. 84). For Baker, this meant genuine education, not merely giving predigested information to consumers. About this time, she wrote a prospectus about consumer education in which she pointed out:

> The main object is to aid the consumer to a more intelligent understanding of the social and political economy of which he is a part. The approach is to be more informational and suggestive than dogmatic and conclusive, yet the aim is not education simply for its own sake, but education that leads to self-directed action (Grant, 1998, p. 38).

In 1936, she was hired by the Works Progress Administration to work in consumer and worker education. We can be sure that the government officials who included worker education in the WPA were not trying to foment radicalism at public expense. Still, it was only natural that union activists, radicals, and socialists would drift toward anything that purported to be teaching workers.[5]

Thus, her time with the WPA deepened her already considerable exposure to radical and progressive modes of thought. In 1941, she began her 5-year stint with the national office of the NAACP. She had been angling for the job of national youth secretary (which might have gotten interesting). As it turned out, she was initially an assistant field secretary, a job that meant organizing and supporting branches all over the South in particular and eventually the national director of branches, a position that gave her a chance to experiment in a new way with some of her ideas about mass education.

Like many of the leaders with whom she had worked in the Deep South, and like many young people at the time, she was increasingly impatient with the NAACP's conservatism, its lack of internal democracy, its middle-class orientation at the national level, and its centralization; too many decisions were being made in New York instead of by the people closest to the problems. A memo written by assistant secretary Roy Wilkins in 1945 so perfectly captures some of her concerns that one suspects they collaborated on it:

> We certainly lack a program of action for our branches. We certainly lack field workers. It is almost fantastic that we have more than 800 units and 500,000 members and two or three people in the field. We need more regional offices. We need some alert, well-trained, militant young people on our staff. We need closer coordination between the things we are trying to do on a national level and the activities on the local level. We need instruction and understanding on national legislative programs.[6]

When she was still working in the field, Baker "observed that local NAACP programs were often ineffective because branch leaders did not know what to do."[7] Almost as soon as she became director of branches, she initiated, despite the skepticism of some of her superiors, a series of regional trainings for people who had leadership responsibilities at the local level, under the theme, "Give Light and the People Will Find a Way." Before she left the association in 1946, she was able to conduct 10 of them for nearly 1,100 local officers.

Similar in structure and intent to Highlander workshops, the conferences (one of which was attended by Rosa Parks) were both skill-enhancing and consciousness-raising. Before they came, delegates were asked what issues they wanted addressed. What they asked for ranged from basic issues of organizational development (getting committees to function, holding on to members, mounting publicity campaigns) to more substantive requests for information on what to do about police brutality or employment discrimination or about reintegrating veterans into the community. The conferences then presented other local leaders who had successfully addressed those issues or national officers with pertinent expertise. At the same time that they tried to help local leaders find more effective ways to attack local problems, the conferences also tried to help them see how local issues were expressions of broader social problems. The leadership conferences were an immediate hit. The Texas delegates who praised their conference for "a wonderful fellowship and [the] contacts . . . and the many and varied benefits resulting from the exchange of experiences and expert information" spoke for many others.[8]

Baker pointed out in a 1946 memo that it had proven difficult to speak to the needs of large chapters and smaller ones in the same meetings. It was difficult to cover enough ground in the day and a half typically allotted.

Characteristically, she also pointed out that the regional meetings all "attempted to become legislative bodies; and this reveals the increased demand for influencing national program and policy."[9] Still, she saw them as meeting a definite need. As a national officer of the most prominent civil rights organization of the time, Miss Baker tried to do what she so often urged on others. She always maintained that leaders should be centrally concerned with replicating themselves, with giving others the experiences that will allow them to lead in their own right.

Before World War II, then, certain Black activists had encountered progressive ideas about teaching and about human potential and how it could be nurtured, wrapped that around their understanding of the African American experience—what Miss Baker called "that rich spiritual inheritance which 240 years of servitude could not kill"[10] and developed their own version of the pedagogy of the oppressed, 40 years before Paulo Freire's book of that title. Their work and their thinking then became a part of the inheritance of the postwar freedom struggle, enriching and amplifying it. We might ask, what is their legacy for our times? What might it mean to look at contemporary issues through the eyes of the great organizer-teachers, like Ella Baker? There are many ways to approach that, but only three points will be mentioned here.

The foundation of the thinking of a Septima Clark or an Ella Baker is their profound confidence in the capacity of ordinary people to grow and develop. If we can just give light, we can leave the rest to the people. That confidence by itself vaults them ahead of most contemporary American thinking about social inequality. The forces of hegemony successfully keep critics on the defensive by framing the issue in terms of the character of the poor. Do they really want to succeed? Couldn't they do more to help themselves? Organizer-teachers don't have to expend much energy in that unwinnable battle. To the degree that they are focused on what people can become and the developmental steps they need to get there, they can look unflinchingly at what people actually are at the moment. Their deepest commitment isn't just to what people are, but to what they can become. In fact, they cannot do their jobs if they romanticize overmuch. They can acknowledge that the poor contribute to their own problems without reducing them to that. Organizer-teachers can believe simultaneously in individual agency and a structural critique of society.

Secondly, a prominent feature of contemporary discourse among progressives is the iconization of the 1960s, to the denigration of subsequent generations. What happened to all the activism? Why don't we have people in the streets now the way we did then? These cross-generational comparisons tend toward the simplistic. There was *more* activism then; the character of that activism is seldom interrogated. One suspects that Ella Baker would want to know something about this. Did the activism represent some part of a developmental process? Did the participants really own it, or were they just led to the barricades? While she agreed with what someone like Stokely Carmichael (later Kwame Ture) said about Black Power, it worried her that not everyone who talked about it had thought it through the way he had:

> But this began to be taken up, you see, by youngsters who had not gone through any experiences or any steps of thinking and it did become a slogan, much more of a slogan, and the rhetoric was far in advance of the organization for achieving that which you say you're trying to achieve.[11]

Finally, organizer-teachers are not likely to be overly encouraged by short-term victories or discouraged by defeats. Certainly, this was the case for Miss Baker:

> Every time I see a young person who has come through the system to a stage where he could profit from the system and identify with it, but who identifies more with the struggle of Black people who have not had his chance, every time I find such a person I take new hope. I feel new life as a result. (Baker, 1973, p. 352)

> It isn't impossible that what those who came along with me went through, might stimulate others to continue to fight for a society that does not have those kinds of problems. Somewhere down the line the numbers increase, the tribe increases. So how do you keep on? I can't help it. I don't claim to have any corner on an answer, but I believe that the struggle is eternal. Somebody else carries on. (Cantarow, O'Malley, & Strom, 1980, p. 93)

NOTES

1. Ernestine Rose to NAACP, June 11, 1942. Papers of the NAACP, Library of Congress (hereafter NAACP), Group II, box A572.

2. "The Challenge of the Age and The Negro Youth," n.d., box 1, folder 2. Ella Baker Papers (hereafter EBP), Schomburg Center for Research in Black Culture.

3. Letter from J. P. Warbasse to the First National Conference, 1931, EBP, box 2, folder 1.

4. Oscar Cooley to Mr. George Schuyler, March 31, 1932, EBP, box 2, folder 1.

5. Joanne Grant interview with Ella Baker, n.d., box 2, folder 11, EBP.

6. Memorandum to Mr. White from Mr. Wilkins, October 10, 1945, EBP, box 3, folder 10.

7. Ella J. Baker, "A Digest of the Regional Leadership Training and In-Service Training Program Conducted by the Branch Department during 1944–1946," July 10, 1946, EBP, box 4, folder 7.

8. "Minutes of the Texas NAACP Board meeting, n.d., NAACP series IIC, folder 375.

9. Ella J. Baker, "A Digest of the Regional Leadership Ttraining and In-Service Training Program Conducted by the Branch Department During 1944–1946," July 10, 1946, EBP, box 4, folder 7.

10. "The Challenge of the Age and the Youth of the Land," EBP, n.d., box 1, folder 2.

11. Interview with Ella Baker, 1968, p. 67, Moorland Spingarn Oral History Collection, Howard University.

PART III

THE 1960S: FROM FREEDOM TO LIBERATION

What will [your students] be like? They will all be different—but they will have in common the scars of the system. Some will be cynical. Some will be distrustful. All of them will have a serious lack of preparation both with regard to academic subjects and contemporary issues—but all of them will have knowledge far beyond their years. This knowledge is the knowledge of how to survive in a society that is out to destroy you . . . and the knowledge of the extent of evil in the world. . . . You will help them to see there is hope and inspire them to go after it.

—Jane Stembridge, SNCC, *Notes on Teaching in Mississippi*

We've noted before that the style of pedagogy associated with Freedom Schools has deep roots. In Chapter 8, Daniel Perlstein emphasizes the connections between the open-ended pedagogy that characterized the schools and the long tradition, perhaps more closely associated with Dewey than with any other person, of progressive education. He is particularly concerned with the interesting question of the way in which overall racial ideology influenced choice of pedagogy, arguing that more progressive teaching styles were predicated upon a relatively optimistic sense of America's racial future. SNCC was anything but a singular experience, so it is not surprising that some SNCC members would have a different take. For Fannie Theresa Rushing, for example, a member of SNCC and founder/teacher in the Chicago Residential Freedom School, radicalization of the movement did not mean retreat to more conservative pedagogies. Rushing also emphasizes the issue of whose liberation we are talking about. Are we talking about liberating individuals or communities? How does the answer affect what and how we teach?

One can imagine that Ella Baker or Septima Clark would have been tickled by the Oakland Panther school described in Chapter 10 by Charles

Jones and Jonathan Gayles. They would have enjoyed the vigorous sense of democratic practice, the emphasis on putting young people in roles ordinarily considered beyond them—running a radio station, adjudicating disputes, and making teachers out of people who had no credentials but their own intensity.

CHAPTER 6

Prospectus for a Summer Freedom School Program

Charles E. Cobb, Jr.

(December 1963). It is, I think, just about universally recognized that Mississippi education, for Black or White, is grossly inadequate in comparison with education around the country. Negro education in Mississippi is the most inadequate and inferior in the state. Mississippi's impoverished educational system is also burdened with virtually a complete absence of academic freedom, and students are forced to live in an environment that is geared to squashing intellectual curiosity and different thinking. University of Mississippi Professor James Silver, in a recent speech, talked of "social paralysis . . . where nonconformity is forbidden, where the White man is not free, where he does not dare express a deviating opinion without looking over his shoulder." This "social paralysis" is not limited to the White community, however. There are Negro students who have been thrown out of classes for asking questions about the freedom rides, or voting. Negro teachers have been fired for saying the wrong thing. The state of Mississippi destroys "smart niggers" and its classrooms remain intellectual wastelands.

In our work, we have several concerns oriented around Mississippi Negro students:

1. The need to get into the schools around the state and organize the students, with the possibility of a statewide coordinated student movement developing.
2. A student force to work with us in our efforts around the state.
3. The responsibility to fill an intellectual and creative vacuum in the lives of young Negro Mississippians, and to get them to articulate their own desires, demands and questions. More students need to stand up in classrooms around the state, and ask their teachers a real question.

Originally published as Cobb, Charles. 1991. Prospectus for a Summer Freedom School Program. *Radical Teacher*, *40*:36. Reprinted with permission of author.

I would like to propose summer Freedom Schools during the months of July and August, for 10th- and 11th-grade high school students, in order to:

1. Supplement what they aren't learning in high schools around the state.
2. Give them a broad intellectual and academic experience during the summer to bring back to fellow students in classrooms; and
3. Form the basis of statewide student action, such as school boycotts, based on their increased awareness.

I emphasize 10th- and 11th-grade students, because of the need to be assured of having a working force that remains in the state high schools putting to use what has been learned.

The curriculum of this school would fall into several groupings:

1. Supplementary education, such as basic grammar, reading, math, typing, history, etc. Some of the already-developed programmed educational materials might be used experimentally.
2. Cultural programs such as art and music appreciation, dance (both folk and modern), music (both folk and classical), drama, possibly creative writing workshops, for it is important that the art of effective communications through the written word be developed in Mississippi students.
3. Political and social studies, relating their studies to their society. This should be a prominent part of the curriculum.
4. Literature.
5. Film programs.

Special projects, such as a student newspaper, voicing student opinion or the laying of plans for a statewide student conference, could play a vital role in the program. Special attention should be given to the development of a close student-teacher relationship. Four or five students to one teacher might be good, as it offers a chance of dialogue. The overall theme of the school would be the students as a force for social change in their own state.

If we are concerned with breaking the power structure, then we have to be concerned with building up our own institutions to replace the old, unjust, decadent ones that make up the existing power structure. Education in Mississippi is an institution that can be validly replaced, as much of the educational institutions in the state are not recognized around the country anyway.

CHAPTER 7

Organizing Freedom Schools

Charles E. Cobb, Jr.

I'm thinking of freedom songs, almost obscure now, or viewed as quaint musical icons of a different era; but 3 decades ago, their vital lyrics provided much sustenance to the Southern civil rights movement: *Ain't gonna let nobody turn me 'roun*, we sang. *We'll never turn' back*, and *Keep your eyes on the Prize.*

All the songs affirm. They express what we are going to do. They assume that "freedom" is affirmative, that freedom starts with deciding what you want to achieve and is reached by finding the ways and means of organizing toward that goal or goals. You'll find no reasoning that the struggle for human and civil rights is in any way determined by what cannot be done. Only, as the old song goes . . . that *freedom is a constant struggle.* Always, a constant faith in human ability and possibilities.

We tend to analyze the movement in terms of strategy and tactics, especially because it is true that the effectiveness of those strategies and tactics did indeed break down the barriers preventing Blacks from exercising voting rights and brought an end to at least the legal justifications for racial segregation in public schools and public accommodations. But such a narrow approach misses the point, or perhaps more exactly, is only a half-right portrayal of what was unfolding in the Deep South during the 1960s.

As powerful and rigid as the structures of White supremacy were, they were more easily defeated than the manner in which thought—and with thought, behavior—imprisoned the communities in which we worked.

Yes, we wanted an end to segregation, discrimination, and White supremacy. However, at the core of our efforts was the belief that Black people had to make decisions about and take charge of the things controlling their lives; the effective movement was grounded in grassroots local leadership. We were organizers in Mississippi, not leaders, even if at moments we led. The distinction was important to us, and a practical necessity.

Most of us organizing soon learned that our main challenge was getting Black people to challenge themselves. Stated another way, people would have to redefine themselves. That was the foundation on which White supremacy could be effectively challenged. As SNCC organizer Larry Guyot, a native Mississippian, put it once: "To battle institutions we must change ourselves first."

While the ever-present threat of economic reprisal and personal assault was of genuine concern to any Black person considering an attempt at voter registration, the words an organizer heard most often in a sharecropper's home were: "Register? That's White folks business, boy." And it reflected something more than fear. In Issaquena County, a narrow, almost all-Black strip of cotton plantation land along the Mississippi River, Henry Sias, well into his sixties when I met him in 1963, cautioned me in two ways during a long conversation. Be careful was the first. "These White folks know you're here." Then later, and more tellingly: "We could do [register, vote, take county offices], but to tell you the truth, we don't know what we could do. Won't think on it. That's what I mean when I say we down far."

The most important struggles in Mississippi were within the Black community: whether to allow a movement worker to speak in church or use the church for mass meetings and voter registration workshops; whether to trust that worker with your life, your family's life, or your family's economic survival. Every step in the fight against racism and discrimination was preceded by a deeper and more profound struggle that involved confronting oneself.

The Freedom Rides to Jackson notwithstanding, SNCC and CORE organizers were working in Mississippi because a handful of Mississippians had already confronted themselves in this way and had decided to risk everything for change. They were the virtually underground NAACP chapters, sometimes at odds with the national organization, working invisibly at voter registration; the Amzie Moores who had to guard the filling station he owned with rifles simply because it was a Black-owned gas station in the White-ruled Delta; the Herbert Lees pressing for school desegregation, and he paid for it with his life. There were others, young and old.

They trained us in how to listen to people and talk to people. And to measure risk. What they thought in urging us to work in Mississippi was that if we listened and learned we could help the communities they led see a way toward change.

The arguments for and against the 1964 Mississippi summer project framed the issue of change in terms of race, nonviolence, and the need for national pressure on the state. But at its most basic, the debate was over whether hundreds of White college students would take over the movement and, with what was presumed to be their superior resources, education, and connections, stifle local Black leadership, some of it just developing. Or, did the inarguable and immediate facts of terrible violence, economic reprisal, and the low level of national concern outweigh this? After all, violence *was* on the increase. Federal authorities still insisted that their hands were tied in responding to it. Media, for the most part, did not get to the out-of-the-way rural counties where SNCC and CORE organizers worked. And insofar as success could be measured by attempts at voter registration, few in the prevailing climate of terror were attempting it.

In a sense, the debate was never resolved, although by default, plans for the summer project went ahead; the students were on their way. If SNCC/ COFO didn't bring them down, the National Council of Churches said it was going to. Organizers, no matter where they stood in the complex debate about the summer project, finally said if they're coming down, we'll organize them. It was in this ambivalent context that the idea of "freedom schools" emerged.

One of the things you learn as an organizer is to constantly be on the lookout for issues and openings that encourage people to challenge their ideas and habits. The person who may not see the value of attempting voter registration, or who may see the value but may not be willing to run the risk, might eagerly embrace the idea of a farm workers' union. Many more people attended church "mass meetings" than braved the danger of going to the voter registrar's office at the county seat.

In Mississippi, as was the case throughout the South, on education there was broad Black consensus: Black schools were inferior to White schools; and along with this, the almost contradictory belief that education was one of the main avenues to greater opportunity and a better life.

The oppressive narrowness of Southern Black public schools still seems almost unbelievable today, despite the grim problems confronting contemporary public education. In the Mississippi Delta, the fall school term was delayed while cotton was picked. New brick school buildings built to give the illusion of "separate but equal" contained virtually bookless libraries and science labs with no equipment.

But more than the inadequacies of the physical plant, the idea of ideas, thought, and creativity among Black people was ruthlessly suppressed. As we wrote in the original freedom school proposal: "Here an idea of your own is a subversion that must be squelched; for each bit of intellectual initiative represents the threat of a probe into the why of denial. Learning here means only learning to stay in your place. Your place is to be satisfied—a 'good nigger.'" It is true that many teachers struggled heroically against these conditions, giving inspiration and imparting knowledge in spite of the state. However, the schools as institutions remained part of the apparatus of repression. Indeed, the police were likely to be called if an organizer showed up on school grounds.

Few parents would accept a direct challenge to the existence of even these public schools. For although Black schools were more like sandbars than islands of hope, they were something in a land of nothing, something that offered some chance of a better life.

What if, it occurred to some of us, we could extend the worlds of possibilities opening up to us through activism, in a broader, more institutional way in the communities where we organized? What if we showed what was possible in education? We had already been approaching this through "literacy workshops" within the context of organizing for voter registration. And SNCC itself had created a "nonviolent high school" during the 1961 protests in McComb, Mississippi. A few of us had even begun to experiment with programmed learning materials in Selma, Alabama, as well as the Mississippi Delta. But we hadn't really tackled education as an approach to community organizing in and of itself.

Significantly, the model for how to do this emerged from a specific political organization that also grew out of grassroots organizing: the Mississippi Freedom Democratic Party.

The Department of Justice had long claimed that apathy was one of the important reasons for the low number of Blacks registered to vote. We argued that in Mississippi and throughout the Black-belt South, to ask Blacks to enter a hostile White county seat was to guarantee that few Blacks would attempt to register.

A "freedom registration" and "freedom vote" was one result of our effort to prove the point. Blacks were registered at home with simple forms. Candidates were selected to run for state offices. Thousands of Blacks both registered and voted within this "mock" but meaningful framework. And, thus, the MFDP was born.

Freedom schools were a variation of this idea. We could "parallel" the state structure "to fill an intellectual and creative vacuum in the lives of young Negro Mississippians."

Although the actual planning of the freedom school project was delegated (among those key early planners were Myles Horton of the Highlander Center; SCLC's Septima Clark, a former schoolteacher; New York teacher and United Federation of Teachers activist Norma Becker; Noel Day, who wrote a citizenship curriculum in question and answer format; and Staughton Lynd, who wrote "A Guide to Negro History" and later became statewide director of the freedom schools), the idea of the bringing schools into existence became integrated with the daily work of field organizers in the months leading up to the summer project. For those of us still trudging plantation roads, it offered an additional route by which the paralysis freezing Black Mississippians in a place where they were acted upon instead of acting could be challenged.

Traditional and widely embraced notions of education were transformed by placing programs—whether remedial reading or African American history—in the arena of social change. As with the voter registration drive and all other organizing in the state, the essence of the schools was that Black people could begin to rethink in their own terms the ways and means of shaping and controlling their own destiny. Fannie Lou Hamer put it to me this way, "We can start learning to learn."

About 2,000 students attended classes in some 40 schools. If the number seems small, it was twice what we had estimated attendance would be. There were remedial classes as well as courses in literature, the humanities, creative writing, foreign languages, art, drama, typing, and Afro-American history and culture. Discussion of civil rights and social changes was continuous. It should be pointed out that many students were attending public schools in the summer, for cotton was picked in the fall.

As a practical matter, the schools effectively struck a balance between the reluctance of organizers to use inexperienced, White student volunteers in the dangerous rural areas of the state and the need to deal with the reality that they were coming and would have to be used in some manner that was concretely beneficial during the summer.

That the program in some respects seemed to accept traditional liberal concepts and approaches to education, which in many ways did not then—and does not now—grapple with deeper flaws in education and society, does not negate the important benefit of the schools' contribution to expanding the idea in Black Mississippi that Black people could shape and control at least some of the things that affected their lives. Perhaps the fact that the schools existed at all was their greatest success. As Staughton Lynd noted in a report to COFO that summer, the schools helped "to loosen the hard knot of fear and to organize the Negro community."

The freedom schools hardly broke down hundreds of years of oppression, but near the end of the summer, when freedom school students from around the state convened, they reflected a substantial growth of political awareness. Their resolutions asked for slum clearance, low-cost federal housing, jobs programs, and even sanctions against South Africa, among a long list of proposed reforms.

After the summer, some freedom schools continued. But never would the number of schools or the number of students attending them equal those of that first summer. For a variety of reasons, the movement was changing. In part, it was a victim of its success. We had in one sense accomplished what we set out to do: A public accommodation law had been passed; a voting rights law seemed certain. Mississippi was now prominently on the political map. New organizations, such as the Mississippi Child Development Group, with deeper financial pockets were establishing themselves.

Many of us were unsure of what to do next. Grassroots organizing—the lifeblood of the movement—diminished. Many organizers scattered. Some were shattered and never recovered. Others took advantage of the opportunities they had helped create. Increasingly, Black elected officials filled the vacuum. And at the first dinner of the Congressional Black Caucus, one congressman proclaimed, "We are the new civil rights movement." That, of course, was not and is not true. The "new" civil rights movement, like the "old," is still made up of the people organizing in many Black communities today, often as invisible as the movement was 30 years ago.

CHAPTER 8

Freedom, Liberation, Accommodation: Politics and Pedagogy in SNCC and the Black Panther Party

Daniel Perlstein

A "degenerating sense of 'nobodiness'," Martin Luther King Jr. declared (1985, p. 435), constitutes the Black child's unique and most fundamental burden. The struggle to assert Black humanity in the face of racism's brutalizing power echoes across the history of African American education. Far more than today's calls to eliminate the racial achievement gap in standardized test scores, campaigns to overcome "nobodiness" have demanded a profound rethinking of educational approaches and visions. Rarely has this struggle been pursued with as much dynamism or animated as much educational thought and activism as during the civil rights and Black liberation movement years of the 1960s and 1970s.

The sit-ins at the outset of the 1960s heralded the pedagogical flowering of the civil rights movement. In addition to protesting racial injustice, however, these activists sought to live their beliefs. A commitment to fostering both personal and social transformation infused the new activism with pedagogical concerns, and over the next decade, activists envisioned new, liberatory forms of education.

Between the early 1960s and the mid-1970s, activists developed, abandoned, re-created, and again abandoned open-ended, progressive approaches to the study of social and political life. The educational programs they developed drew on, extended, and challenged the long-standing progressive

A version of this chapter was originally published as Perlstein, Daniel, Minds Stayed on Freedom: Politics, Pedagogy, and the African American Freedom Struggle, *American Educational Research Journal* 39:249–277. Copyright (2002) by the American Educational Research Association. Reproduced with permission of the publisher.

tradition in American education. This chapter focuses on the political ideas and ideals that shaped the movement's evolving pedagogical impulse.

The educational efforts of the Student Nonviolent Coordinating Committee (SNCC) and the Black Panther Party epitomize the relationship of activists' political analysis to their pedagogical ideas. Both groups created celebrated alternative schools as part of a larger commitment to the fundamental transformation of Black consciousness and life.

SNCC AND PROGRESSIVE PEDAGOGY

The sit-ins derived their power from the ability of protesters to reconstitute the meaning of their own humanity, while they also demanded the abolition of unjust laws. In their own words, Student Nonviolent Coordinating Committee activists viewed the freedom struggle as "the closest thing in the United States to Paul Goodman's 'anti-college' where students learn because they want to learn, learn in order to do and to discover who they are" (Fifth Annual Spring Conference, 1981, p. 1).

As activists expanded their protests into a mass movement, they engaged poor Southern Blacks in the same project of self-discovery and social transformation to which they had committed themselves. No less than the activists themselves, SNCC's Charles Sherrod explained, the masses of Southern Blacks were "searching for a meaning in life" (Carson, 1981, pp. 57–58). The "freedom" that the movement sought, as SNCC's Charlie Cobb argued, "is affirmative; [it] starts with deciding what you want to achieve and is reached by finding the ways and means of organizing toward that goal" (1999, p. 134).

Although SNCC activists "wanted to end segregation, discrimination, and White supremacy," Cobb explained,

> the core of our efforts was the belief that Black people had to make decisions about and take charge of the things controlling their lives. . . . Most of us organizing soon learned that our main challenge was getting Black people to challenge themselves. Stated another way, people would have to redefine themselves" (1999, p. 134).

This commitment to a politics of self-discovery, self-expression, and self-determination imbued SNCC's work with pedagogical concerns.

The movement, in the words of activist Jimmy Garrett, was "for the Black people, a search for acknowledgment of presence and a desire for recognition" (1969, p. 8). Activism was sustained by a belief that nonviolence would transform the consciousness of Whites and lead the nation to live up to its professed ideals. "Through nonviolence," SNCC proclaimed in its 1960 statement of purpose, "mutual regard cancels enmity. Justice for all overthrows injustice. The redemptive community supersedes systems of gross social immorality. . . . Integration of human endeavor represents the crucial first step toward such a society" (Rothschild, 1982, pp. 7–8). Far from being a mere tactic for social change, activists' rhetoric of non-violence articulated both the desire for full participation in a reformed America and a belief that America was open to transformation through Blacks' self-actualizing activity.

Mississippi became the focal point of SNCC's work, and in the Freedom Summer of 1964, the organization spearheaded the creation of a network of freedom schools there, staffed primarily by Northern White college students. Activists argued that Mississippi's schools were the worst in the United States. The "complete absence of academic freedom squash[ed] intellectual curiosity" and produced "social paralysis." Because of segregation, SNCC charged, "Negroes and Whites aren't allowed to know each other." How, activists demanded, "can a people who are separated from their fellow men live the truth?" (Perlstein, 1990, p. 303).

At the same time as SNCC activists believed that Black consciousness was distorted by Jim Crow schooling, they were convinced that Blacks could draw from their experience an understanding of the nature and promise of American society. "The value of the Freedom School," volunteer teachers learned, "will derive from what the teachers are able to elicit from the students in terms of comprehension and expression of their experiences" (Freedom School Curriculum, 1991, p. 7).

Organizers' faith in students' ability to make sense of their world—their faith that American society was not irretrievably alien to students—inspired them to embrace a student-centered curriculum. The Freedom Schools, Charlie Cobb argued, would "fill an intellectual and creative vacuum in the lives of young Negro Mississippians, and to get them to articulate their own desires, demands and questions" (1981, p. 1).

The commitment to giving students the opportunity to construct meaning from their experiences drew on the belief that African American students could collectively reshape their world. To "train people to be active agents in bringing about social change," teachers were instructed to begin by having students describe the schools that they attended. The Freedom School curriculum included a dozen sample questions such as, "What is the school made of, wood or brick?" Students were then asked to compare Black schools with White ones. Similarly detailed questions focused on housing conditions, employment, and medical care. Later, students explored social differences among Whites and why poor Whites identified with the power structure. SNCC activists explained to Freedom School volunteers,

> We have attempted to design a developmental curriculum that begins on the level of the students' everyday lives and those things in their environment that they have already experienced or can readily perceive, and builds up to a more realistic perception of American society, themselves, the conditions of their oppression, and alternatives offered by the Freedom Movement. It is not our purpose to impose a particular set of conclusions. Our purpose is to encourage the asking of questions, and the hope that society can be improved. (Freedom School Curriculum, 1991, p. 9)

For activists, then, the act of questioning was not just a step in a process of intellectual growth but also a repudiation of subordination and an assertion of democratic fellowship.

The politics and pedagogy of the Freedom Schools were embodied in a widely celebrated lesson taught by SNCC activist Stokely Carmichael. Carmichael began the class by writing four pairs of sentences on a blackboard. "I digs wine" was matched with "I enjoy drinking cocktails"; "The peoples wants freedom" with "The people want freedom"; and so on. "What do you think about these sentences?" Carmichael asked.

"'Peoples,'" Zelma answered, "isn't right."

"Does it mean anything?" Carmichael persisted.

"Peoples," Milton acknowledged, "means everybody." Conventionally incorrect usage, students affirmed in answer to Carmichael's continued questioning, was widely spoken and understood in their community.

At the end of the hour-long lesson, it was left to a student rather than to the teacher to draw the conclusion that rules about what constitutes correct English are used to reproduce an unjust social order. "If the majority speaks" nonstandard English but it has lower status than proper English, a student named Alma explained, "then a minority must rule society" (Stembridge, n.d., pp. 1–2).

For Carmichael, teaching consisted entirely of asking a series of questions. SNCC activist Jane Stembridge observed that Carmichael "trusted" students' understanding of political and social life and their ability to articulate that understanding. He "spoke to where they were" and relied on "the movement of the discussion" to deepen analysis (n.d., p. 3). Activists publicized Carmichael's lesson because it epitomized SNCC's political analysis and ideals.

Freedom Summer, historian Vincent Harding suggests, represented the movement's view that "human beings are meant to be developmental beings; that we find our best identity and purpose when we are developing ourselves and helping to develop our surroundings" (Harding, 1998, p. 137). The hope that Blacks could participate fully in American democratic life was a precondition for activists' pedagogy, as for their politics. The freedom schools, according to SNCC's Charlie Cobb, reflected "traditional liberal concepts and approaches to education." Although the schools did not "grapple with the deeper flaws in education and society," they contributed "to expanding the idea in Black Mississippi that Black people could shape and control at least some of the things that affected their lives" (1999, p. 137).

POLITICAL SHIFTS AND PEDAGOGICAL CHANGES

In the years that followed the Mississippi Freedom Summer, the trust—in America and in students' understanding—that infused SNCC's activism and Stokely Carmichael's teaching began to dissipate. The eclipse of integrationism was heralded by the electrifying demand for "Black Power," which Carmichael popularized in 1966. Although SNCC launched the politics of Black Power in the rural South, the slogan also resonated among Blacks confined in Northern ghettos, for whom the goals and strategies of the nonviolent, integrationist Southern civil rights movement held limited appeal. SNCC activists' growing conviction that America was hopelessly racist and that efforts to reshape Black humanity could not rely on the decency of Whites mirrored the wider trajectory of the civil rights movement. This ideological shift precluded pedagogies growing out of students' American experience and led to increasingly didactic approaches to teaching.

Declining faith in integration was in part ironic testimony to the movement's success in raising Black consciousness. "Young Black people," activist Jimmy Garrett observed, "began to see that the inequalities placed upon them by American society were not individual inequities taking place at odd moments, but rather a group activity against a group of people regardless of their education or economic status. They began to see that there were continuous activities by the White community to shut them out of the major society" (1969, p. 8).

The movement's successes were not, however, the only source of activists' disenchantment. SNCC's dependence on White volunteers to focus national attention on Mississippi testified to the enduring power of American racism. According to activist Dave Dennis, organizers had come "to Mississippi looking for the dissimilarities" between the South and the American mainstream. They saw federal intervention as the solution to the Southern race problem. During and after the summer, however, the refusal of the federal government and the Democratic Party to fully support equal rights, together with interracial tensions among activists in Mississippi, increasingly convinced organizers that "the only difference is that the political oppression and control in Mississippi is much more conspicuous, much more overt" (Perlstein, 1990, p. 322).

As activists confronted racism on a national scale, they were forced to conclude that Southern segregation laws were only the most visible form of

American racism. The movement's successes in dismantling Jim Crow offered little guidance in challenging the deeply rooted system of racial and economic oppression manifest in Northern ghettos. There, government agencies, business groups, and labor unions combined to promote the growing comfort of White citizens and the growing alienation of Blacks. Meanwhile, the Northern school integration movement foundered in the face of opposition from White parents, real estate interests, and educators. Racism in schools, the legal system, housing, and employment continued to oppress Blacks despite the right to vote and the absence of segregation laws (Perlstein, 2004, pp. 62, 136).

The belief that America itself was hopelessly racist precluded political mobilization through a language of shared American values. Gradually, as the notion that one could live the truth while living in America receded, so too did the belief that the open-ended questioning of students' experiences could foster their understanding of themselves and of possible avenues for social change. A focus on self-discovery and self-expression among the voiceless was replaced by a desire to articulate a critique of society to the oppressed. Ironically, then, more radical critiques of American society led to seemingly more traditional banking approaches to teaching.

The years following the Freedom Summer saw SNCC retreat, step by step, from the pedagogy it had developed for Mississippi. In the summer of 1965, SNCC created a Residential Freedom School in Chicago for Black youth from around the United States. To the dismay of activists, the Southern civil rights movement offered few lessons that applied to life in the ghetto. "We went into the southside talking about 'freedom,' which to the Southern kid meant the vote, education, eating where you wanted to, etc.," noted activist Judy Richardson. "But 'freedom' to the southside kids meant getting out of the ghetto and they couldn't really see how this fit into what the Southern kids were talking about." Amid the oppressive, seemingly intractable conditions of ghetto life, the pedagogy that had succeeded in Mississippi generated few insights. In even the best lessons, teaching became abstract and removed from activism and experience. Meanwhile, declining faith in the possibility of creating a truly integrated society led organizers to bar Whites from teaching Negro history, a role they had played in 1964 (Richardson, 1981a; Richardson, 1981b, pp. 3, 6, 12, 13).

SNCC's 1966 Atlanta Project continued the movement away from the integrationist ideal. Atlanta leader Bill Ware noted that Freedom Summer had "presupposed that Mississippi schools were so far below the national norm that Freedom Schools were needed to help bring Mississippi Negroes up to some kind of national norm." Rather, Ware claimed,

> our experience in this country has taught us something about this country: it lies. . . . The country has taught [Black people] that they are intrinsically infe-

rior. . . . The lies that little Black children learn about themselves leave a crippling scar, . . . which results in their feeling that they are worthless and that they cannot approve of themselves. (Ware, 1981)

Whereas 1964's Freedom School organizers enlisted White volunteer teachers from across the United States, the Atlanta group recruited from Atlanta's Black colleges; whereas in 1964 organizers delegated curriculum development to a wide range of Black and White activists, the 1966 group opted not to entrust such work to outsiders. Abandoning national ambitions, the Atlanta effort represented an increasingly isolated form of activism.

Among Black activists, declining trust in White activists was matched by a declining interest in the study of American society and a declining sense that pedagogy should flow from students' experiences. When Washington, DC, SNCC activists planned a 1968 "liberation school," three of the four courses covered African history and culture (Reports on Washington, DC, Liberation School, 1981). The transmission of information had become more important than students' exploration of their own experiences.

Veteran activist Jimmy Garrett embodied SNCC's evolving politics and pedagogy. Through the mid-1960s, Garrett had ardently embraced SNCC's integrationist vision as a vehicle for the empowerment of African Americans. A freedom school, he argued in a 1965 proposal to bring SNCC's educational program to Los Angeles, was "an area, atmosphere, situation—any place where young people, whether Black or White, rich or poor, come to deal with real questions as they relate to their lives," a place that lets "young people challenge not only the authority which stifles them, but also . . . challenge themselves" (1981, p. 1). Then, in 1965, came the Watts "riot," a 6-day rebellion in which thousands of Blacks participated and to which authorities responded with massive military force. Although Garrett continued to believe in the democratic ideal of people's articulating and enacting their desires, his faith in the possibility of winning Black rights in the United States and his commitment to integration began to wane.

In 1966, Garrett left SNCC's Los Angeles office and headed to San Francisco State College. There, he led efforts to create the first Black Students Union (BSU) in the United States. Under Garrett's leadership, the BSU brought militant demands for Black Power and community involvement to Northern campuses. Garrett and the San Francisco State BSU, together with a group of students at nearby Merritt College that included Black Panthers Huey Newton and Bobby Seale, spearheaded the struggle to establish the first Black Studies programs at American universities. Although Garrett drew on the Mississippi Freedom School curriculum in imagining Black studies, the new program abandoned SNCC's trust in students making sense of their own experience (Waugh, 1969, p. 6; Hine, 1992, p. 12; Major, 1971, p. 82; Smith,

Axen, & Pentony, 1970, p. 131; Garrett, 1998–1999, p. 161). Rather, argued SNCC veteran Mike Thelwell, the goal of Black Studies was "the rehabilitation of . . . a culture and a heritage they have been taught to despise" (1969, pp. 704, 712). Instead of campaigning for integration, Garrett now argued for Blacks to "build their own institutions" (Orrick, 1969, pp. 78, 80, 124).

The BSU quickly became the preeminent voice of Black students, and when the group initiated San Francisco State's Third World Liberation Front, the college became one of the principal centers of campus activism in the United States. Still, as Garrett became skeptical about the possibility of integration into the American mainstream, he became skeptical also about the power of grassroots organizing. Convinced that "an organized minority controls the world," Garrett, like many activists in the late 1960s, became increasingly persuaded that an organized minority could catalyze the radical transformation of American society (Orrick, 1969, pp. 81, 100).

Garrett's growing skepticism about integrating Blacks into American society shaped his educational efforts. BSU programs, he declared, sought to "build Black consciousness" by teaching Black elementary, secondary, and college students "their history and values as a People." No longer did Garrett see Black and White students as united by common yearnings. "Black people are not Western," he argued in 1969. "They are Westernized. In much the same way as one might get simonized. We are painted over with Whiteness." Criticizing the assimilationist politics of the *Brown* decision and the civil rights movement ideals that it embodied, Garrett argued that Black children failed in school "because the information that Black children receive is alien to them, dealing almost completely with White culture. . . . There is little in any curriculum that starts with Black people as a specifically cultured people" (Orrick, 1969, pp. 80, 87; Garrett, 1969, p. 8).

In the late 1960s, activists maintained the commitment to self-determination for Blacks that had always shaped SNCC's work, but they no longer believed that the creation of an integrated American society would allow them to achieve their goal. As activists concluded that Black oppression was a permanent feature of American society, they became convinced that Black students could not draw from their American experience an understanding of their real needs, desires, or identity. A progressive pedagogy that trusted students to discover the truth gave way to one in which students were informed about politics and culture. Whatever one labels the alternative to progressive pedagogy—teacher-centered, traditional, and direct instruction are popular terms—its essential characteristic is that a predetermined body of information or skills that students lack is delivered to them. Such an approach won increasing support among Black activists.

BLACK POWER, REVOLUTION, AND DIRECT INSTRUCTION

San Francisco State's BSU worked closely with the Black Panther Party. James Garrett's grim drama of racial conflict, *And We Own the Night*, was first performed at a 1967 Panther rally. Fellow SNCC veteran Stokely Carmichael was among the featured speakers at the play's premiere. Like Garrett, Carmichael had renounced the optimistic integrationism and open-ended pedagogy of SNCC's early years (Garrett, 1968, p. 69; Black Theater, 1968, p. 173; *S.F. Chronicle*, 1967, p. 2).

Carmichael argued that unlike poor Whites, who were merely exploited in America, Blacks were "a colonized people" (Hoffman, 1968, pp. 8, 18). Whereas Carmichael's 1964 lesson on African American vernacular had legitimized claims for full citizenship in a fully democratized America, in 1968 he used Black English to justify a separatist politics:

> We are an African people, we have always maintained our own value system. . . . Take the English language. There are cats who come here from Italy, from Germany, from Poland, from France—in two generations they speak English perfectly. We have never spoken English perfectly. . . . Never did, never will, anyhow they try to run it down out throat, we ain't gonna have it. (1971a, pp. 113–114)

Carmichael's new understanding transformed his educational project. No longer did he trust students to draw from their experience a sufficient political understanding. "The honky," Carmichael maintained, "has channeled our love for one another into love for his country—his country." Meanwhile, the victims of colonization "have been so dehumanized, we're like a dog that the master can throw out of the house, that the master can spit on, and whenever he calls, the dog comes running back" (1971a, pp. 113, 120–121).

Carmichael worked to transmit to students a Black humanity that was not dependent on the dominant White American culture. "The first stage" of the liberation struggle, he argued,

> is waking up our people . . . to the impending danger. So we yell, Gun! Shoot! Burn! Kill! Destroy! They're committing genocide! until the masses of our people are awake. Once they are awake, it is the job of the revolutionary intelligentsia to give them the correct political ideology. (1971b, pp. 185, 190)

Carmichael and Garrett, together with countless other Black activists, found a model of revolutionary activism in the Black Panther Party. Founded in 1966, the Panthers first gained fame through public displays of weaponry and militant confrontations with the police. Advocating a synthesis of Marxism and nationalism, the Panthers proclaimed the need to replace rather than reform American institutions. They were, SNCC activist Julian Bond told ABC news correspondent Edward P. Morgan in 1970, the "standard of militance, of just forcefulness, the sort of standard we haven't had in the past" (1995, p. xix). "More than any other group of the 1960s," echoes historian Clayborne Carson, "the Black Panther Party inspired discontented urban African Americans to liberate themselves" (1995, p. ix). No less than with SNCC, pedagogical concerns infused Panther activism.

A commitment to transmitting their revolutionary analysis led the Panthers to use a banking language in their educational proposals. The group's 1966 program demanded "education for our people that exposes the true nature of this decadent American society" (Newton, 1996, p. 121). The main purpose of "the vanguard party," Panther founder Huey P. Newton explained, was to "awaken . . . the sleeping masses" and "bombard" them "with the correct approach to the struggle" (1972, pp. 15–16). "Exploited and oppressed people," argued Panther leader Eldridge Cleaver, needed to be "educating ourselves and our children on the nature of the struggle and . . . transferring to them the means for waging the struggle" (Williamson, 2000, pp. 6, 9–10, 13).

George Murray, a San Francisco State instructor and Panther minister of education, led efforts in the summer of 1968 to develop the Panthers' political education program for members, modeled on Mao's 1929 campaign to educate Red Army troops (Heath, 1976, p. 149). Political education classes became a central Party activity, recalled Panther Chief of Staff David Hilliard, through which Party leaders and theoreticians could "disseminate" their ideas to the cadre (Hilliard and Cole, 2001, pp. 143, 161).

In addition to classes for the cadre, the Panthers promoted political education in the community through lectures about Panther ideology. "Imagine people living in a cave," Huey Newton explained:

> They've been there all their lives. At the end of the cave shines a light. Now one person among them knows the light is the sun. The rest are afraid of the light. They've lived in darkness and think that the light is some kind of evil. Now let's say the person who knows about the light tells them it's not evil and tries to lead them out of the cave. They'll fight and probably overpower and maybe even kill him. Because all they know is darkness, and so quite logically they would be fearful of the light. So instead he has to gradually lead them toward the light. Well, it's the same with knowledge. Gradually you have to lead people toward an understanding of what's happening. (Hilliard and Cole, 2001, p. 121)

Like progressive education, the transmission of political theory required consideration of the intellectual steps through which students could move from what they knew to a fuller understanding. Still, the Panthers did not believe they could rely on Blacks living in darkness to discover the path to liberation. It was up to their teachers to light the way.

No less than SNCC's earlier commitment to eliciting students' own questions, the Panthers' commitment to teacher-centered inculcation transformed Black consciousness. "I had been taught only to revere White people," former Panther Regina Jennings would recall. "Panther teachers . . . taught us from an Afrocentric perspective, whereby the needs and interests of African people determined our perception of the world. The void I used to fill with drugs was now filled instead with a pure and noble love for my people" (1998, pp. 259–260).

As the Panthers expanded their educational program, they began to teach children as well as adults. Here, too, their goal was to transmit Party ideology to Blacks living in an environment so oppressive that it precluded their discovering the truth. Among the most prominent of the Panther educational programs was a network of "liberation schools" through which the Panthers taught children "about the class struggle in terms of Black history" (*Black Panther*, 1969b, p. 14). First established in 1969, the Panther liberation schools were perhaps the closest counterpart in the late 1960s to SNCC's 1964 freedom schools. Both had an ephemeral existence, but both epitomized the political and pedagogical values of the most dynamic African American activism of their day. Together, the two programs therefore illuminate the evolving relationship of politics and pedagogy.

Whereas SNCC had once embraced a pedagogy of open-ended inquiry, the Panthers applauded explicit, direct instruction in revolutionary analysis. "Black people and other poor and oppressed people must begin to seek an education, a true education that will show them how those in power wage outright war against us," the Party argued. "Our eyes must be opened to the social brutality." To open Black eyes, the Panthers' schools would "expose those people that are in power and who are waging a war against us" (Davis, 1969, p. 14). At the high school level, Panther leader Bobby Seale elaborated:

> we will probably teach more about revolutionary principles. At the grammar school level we will . . . teach little Black kids about how to identify not only a White pig, but also a Black pig. . . . We're going to be talking about downing the class system, cultural nationalists and capitalists, both Black and White, who are the same: exploitative. (Peck, 2000, p. 5)

The first liberation school opened in Berkeley, California, on June 25, 1969. There, elementary and middle-school students were taught to "march to songs that tell of the pigs running amuck and Panthers fighting for the people." Employing a curriculum "designed to . . . guide [youth] in their search for revolutionary truths and principles," the Panthers taught the children "that they are not fighting a race struggle, but, in fact, a class struggle . . . because people of all colors are being exploited by the same pigs all over the world." The children learned to work for the "destruction of the ruling class that oppresses and exploits, . . . the avaricious businessman, . . . and the racist pigs that are running rampant in our communities" (Douglas, 1969, p. 2).

At the Panthers' San Francisco Liberation School, "everything the children do is political. . . . The children sing revolutionary songs and play revolutionary games." The entire curriculum contributed to students receiving a clear and explicit ideology. Teachers avoided lessons "about a jive president that was said to have freed the slaves, when it's as clear as water that we're still not free" (*Black Panther*, 1969c, p. 14). Instead, students learned the origins and history of the Black Panther Party and could "explain racism, capitalism, fascism, cultural nationalism, and socialism. They can also explain the Black Panther Party Platform and Program and the ways to survive" (*Black Panther*, 1969a, p. 13).

In Chicago, a Panther free breakfast program offered an occasion to talk to children about community concerns. Akua Njeri and her fellow activists "explained to the children that we are not the people out there committing a crime. . . . The police are the ones who are committing the crime because they just snatch us up at whim, particularly African men, and beat us up. . . . We let the young brothers and sisters know what the real deal was" (Njeri, 1991, p. 15).

Black children went to school "and learned nothing," Njeri argued, "not because they're stupid, not because they're ignorant. . . . We would say, 'You came from a rich culture. You came from a place where you were kings and queens. You are brilliant children. But this government is fearful of you realizing who you are. This government has placed you in an educational situation that constantly tells you you're stupid and you can't learn and stifles you at every turn'" (1991, pp. 15–16). In the Panthers' eyes, the public schools of Northern cities were no different from Jim Crow schools in the segregated South. Activists' use of direct instruction was needed to counter the brutalizing impact of American schools and society.

In 1971, the Panthers built on the liberation school pedagogy with the establishment of an elementary school for the children of Party members. In addition to providing academic classes, Oakland's Intercommunal Youth Institute (IYI) offered instruction in the ideology of the Party, together with field work "distributing the *Black Panther* newspaper, talking to other youths in the community, attending court sessions for political prisoners and visiting prisons." The children also learned to march in the Panthers' military uniforms. An IYI student reported to *Black Panther* readers that, unlike public school students, "at this school we don't have to salute the flag." Instead, "over here they teach us about what the pigs are doing to us" and about "philosophy, ideology, dialectical materialism, and stuff like that" (*Black Panther*, 1971a, 1971b).

COMMUNITY ORGANIZING
AND PROGRESSIVE PEDAGOGY

Gendered concerns about the brutalizing impact of racism on Black men played a central role in the Panthers' politics and pedagogy. America, Huey Newton charged, treats the Black man as "a thing, a beast, a nonentity." Refusing to "acknowledge him as a man," society reduced him to "a constant state of rage, of shame, of doubt" (1972, pp. 80–81). Armed self-defense and teacher-centered approaches to education challenged America's dehumanization of Black men.

Within a few years of the Party's founding, however, the Panthers' politics and approach to education began to shift. Abandoning revolutionary aspirations, activists gradually returned to community organizing and rediscovered progressive teaching methods. The Panthers' "militaristic style," notes historian Tracye Matthews, diminished as women, many from relatively privileged backgrounds, played an increasingly prominent role in Party activity (1998, pp. 277–278). (The rise of women in the Party owed a good deal to the brutal government campaign to jail or kill the male leadership.)

In the face of the government assault, the Party, as David Hilliard has put it, became "a split organization," its militant displays of Black manhood degrading into macho thuggery while its community service programs encouraged grassroots organizing, the "two halves operating in completely separate spheres" (Hilliard & Cole, 2001, p. 363). The opposing tendencies in Panther activism—a declining capacity to articulate revolutionary demands and a growing capacity to foster grassroots activism—reshaped the Panthers' educational ideas. As grassroots organizing gained strength, the commitment to progressive pedagogy returned to activists' educational work. "All you have to do is guide [children] in the right direction," explained Panther teacher Val Douglas. "The curriculum is based on true experiences of revolutionaries and everyday people they can relate to. . . . The most important thing is to get the children to work with each other" (Douglas, 1969, p. 2).

Increasingly, the Intercommunal Youth Institute fostered student-centered learning, along with the inculcation of Panther ideology. In language echoing Deweyan pragmatism and the Mississippi freedom schools, the Panthers justified the teaching of "the basic skills—reading, writing, math, science"—by arguing that such study enabled students to "begin to define the phenomena around us and make all phenomena act in a desired manner" (*Black Panther*, 1971a).

Progressive approaches shaped social relations in the school. Activists contrasted the IYI, where students were "regarded as people whose ideas and opinions are respected," with public schools, where children who questioned the dominant ideology were "labeled troublemakers." At IYI, the Panthers encouraged students to "openly criticize all areas" of school activity and allowed them to "make most of the decisions in reference to activities that take place. . . . The purpose for this is to give each one the opportunity to make decisions, to do things for themselves, and to put things into practice" (*Black Panther*, 1971a).

For a few years, historian Craig Peck notes, the IYI mixed "vestiges of prior Panther ideological training" with "progressive educational modes." At the same time that students learned liquid and dry measures by baking brownies, they learned English by writing to political prisoners. The Panthers' mix of progressive and transmissive pedagogies mirrored the ambiguity of their politics. As they swayed between revolution and reform, the Panthers were undecided as to whether the Black community had the capacity to articulate its own demands or whether it had to depend on a vanguard to reveal the truth about its situation: "We know that because the People, and only the People, are the makers of world history, we alone have the ability to struggle and provide the things we need to make us free. And we must . . . pass this on to all those who will survive" (Peck, 2000, p. 19; *Black Panther*, 1974f, p. 9; 1971a, p. 1).

Whatever the merits of the IYI curriculum, the Panthers' political evolution precluded their maintaining the institute's delicate educational balance. As Craig Peck argues, the very opening of the IYI reflected a profound shift away from revolutionary aspirations toward reformist electoral politics (2000, p. 11). By 1973, the Panthers acquired a new, larger home for the Oakland school and assigned to it a central role in the Party's new focus on local electoral campaigns (*Black Panther*, 1976b, p. 4). In its decade-long existence, the institution's mission changed from the training of future Panthers to the establishment of a "progressive" school that could model a "humane and rewarding educational program" for poor urban youth (*Black Panther*, 1974c, p. 4; 1974h, p. 4).

IYI pedagogy shifted increasingly away from the inculcation of revolutionary political theory toward open-ended lessons reminiscent of the earlier Freedom Schools. "The goal of the Intercommunal Youth Institute," the Party now explained, was to "teach Black children basic skills necessary to survive in a technological society and to teach children to think in an analytical fashion in order to develop creative solutions to the problems we are faced with" (*Black Panther*, 1973a, p. 4). IYI students, *The Black Panther* now told readers, received "the greater portion of their education through direct experience." The school used field trips, including ones to the zoo, an apple orchard, Mount Diablo, and the trial of the San Quentin Six, to "teach the children about the world by exposing them to numerous learning experiences" (*Black Panther*, 1974a, p. 5). Claimed IYI director Brenda Bay, "the world is [the students'] classroom." Through "individualized instruction," the school offered children "equipment to analyze and interpret their experiences." (*Black Panther*, 1973c, p. 4). "We're not here to teach our children *what* to think," Panther leader Bobby Seale announced at a 1973 school ceremony. "We're here to teach our children *how* to think!" (*Black Panther*, 1973b, p. 3).

In 1974, the IYI was renamed the Oakland Community School (OCS), further distancing it from its revolutionary Panther roots. Activists increasingly embraced the progressive ideal of free personalities freely experiencing their world. "We consider [children] people who have personalities of their own and experiences of their own," the Panthers maintained. "The difference between them and us is the lack of experience on their part" (*Black Panther*, 1974e; 1974h).

OCS offered poor Oakland youth "individual attention in reading, mathematics, writing, and really, an understanding of themselves and the world," new school director Ericka Huggins told educator Herb Kohl in a 1974 KPFA radio interview. Whereas, she argued, the public school "does not allow for the individual mind or personality," OCS was "very concerned about children relating to their environment and to this world as it really is." In order for them to do so, the school relied on

> practical experience as a basis of our learning experience. That is, if we want to know what makes trees grow, then we won't go to a book about trees or have a science demonstration and just talk about trees. We might have the children go outside to see a tree or trees of various sizes or trees in various stages of development. We would see what makes them grow and what keeps them from growing and thereby try to understand what would be the best way to help a tree grow. (*Black Panther*, 1974b, p. 4)

Students built their vocabularies through "words we use around town" and "at home": *library, physician, china, chair.* They learned mathematics by going to the store and getting change. In words echoing classic American progressivism, OCS educators argued that through the use of concrete objects to teach arithmetic, "thought and action become one" (*Black Panther*, 1974e, p. 4; 1974h, p. 4).

To enable students to "draw their own conclusions," the OCS educator served "primarily as a demonstrator and a reference" (*Black Panther*, 1974h, p. 4). Teachers, the school's *Instructor Handbook* stressed, "do not give opinions in passing on information; instead, facts are shared and information discussed. . . . Conclusions are reached by the children themselves" (Williamson, 2000, pp. 11–12). "In contrast to public school instruction, which consists mainly of memorization and drilling," *The Black Panther* now maintained, the OCS "encourages the children to express themselves freely, to explore, and to question the assumptions of what they are learning, as children are naturally inclined to do." Moreover, "the children progress at their own rate, and it is not uncommon for a 7-year-old student to learn math with 10-year-olds and reading with 5-year-olds" (Hoffman, 1975, p. 23).

The contrast with public schools extended to student discipline. In "traditional public schools," the Panthers charged, "'discipline' means a set of rules, punishments, and rewards that are imposed by teachers and authority figures." By contrast, "the Institute emphasizes internal discipline" (Hoffman, 1975, p. 23).

Like the Panthers' earlier liberation schools, the OCS reflected activists' egalitarian project of transforming the education and lives of poor Black youth. However, the political analysis underlying the school's pedagogy had shifted. The Panthers' flagship school now sought the expansion of liberal education practices and the integration of mainstream American life rather than the abolition of an oppressive social order.

THE ABANDONMENT OF ACTIVISM
AND THE ECLIPSE OF PROGRESSIVISM

The Panthers' local organizing led to some influence in Oakland politics, but those limited successes could not compensate for the atrophied aspirations they embodied. Activists' embrace of mainstream progressivism therefore proved to be as tenuous as their earlier effort to construct a revolutionary curriculum. By 1974, the Panthers criticized not only the repressiveness of public schooling but also its failure "to adequately teach English or grammar." At OCS, in contrast, students "recite[d] consonant blends" and studied word endings, diacritical marks, and alphabetization (*Black Panther*, 1974e, p. 4). By 1976, Panther leader Elaine Brown repudiated the OCS's ideological roots. "This is not a Black Panther school, per se," she told *Jet* magazine. "It's not a 'freedom school' or a 'liberation school' in the sense that we teach the children rhetoric." *Jet* supplemented Brown's views with descriptions of younger students learning "basic English—not 'Black English' or 'Ghetto English'"—and of older students reading such mainstream works as *Animal Farm* and *Jonathan Livingston Seagull* (Lucas, 1976).

By the end of the 1970s, Craig Peck notes, OCS "instructor handbooks reveal[ed] a minimal attention to Black and ethnic studies and, importantly, contain[ed] no references to the Black Panthers." Moreover, rote education in basic skills continued to supplant progressive methods of instruction. Whereas IYI language arts classes had once focused on the works of Black authors, teachers were now directed to stress "phonics, . . . handwriting, . . . and language mechanics." "In this country," the handbook argued, "language barriers have systematically been used to oppress Black and other poor people in the country. . . . The ability to speak and read Standard English is essential" (Peck, 2000, p. 28). Although perhaps true, earlier Panthers would have observed that this claim confused the means through which oppression is reproduced with the forces that reproduce it. Gone were hopes of even modest social change, and with those hopes went much of OCS's progressivism.

A social science unit on California's government suggests how much the Panthers' hopes for political transformation had narrowed. The unit-plan objectives called for students to state who "the current governor of California is and what his job entails." Whereas in an earlier era the Panthers would have articulated the state's role in policing the oppressed, the OCS instructor now evaluated students' ability to state, "The governor's job is to carry out the laws of the state and make life better for people living in the state" (Peck, 2000, p. 25).

The conventionalism of the OCS curriculum reflected the Panthers' diminished sense of the capacity of Blacks to determine their individual or collective destinies. Instead of "trying to build a model school" or "provide a real education to Black kids," Panther chief Elaine Brown lamented,

> Right now, I think, we're mostly saving a bunch of lives. I mean, we've got a 6-year-old girl whose entire right leg is marred by third-degree burns. She said her 'uncle' had dropped a pan of hot grease onto her leg—her whole leg? There's a 9-year-old boy who's been shooting heroin into his mother's veins before school every morning. Three kids from one family came to us with no shoes. . . . One of my own student's back was imprinted with permanent welts from being beaten so much. . . . [Keeping them away from] the snake pits of their neighborhoods . . . and keeping anybody from doing any more damage than has already been done . . . seems to clear the way to teach them . . . skills. (Brown, 1992, pp. 392–394)

OCS never fully abandoned its critique of racial and economic oppression or its progressive practices. "I love freedom, power, and community" one elementary student wrote on a drawing displayed on an OCS bulletin board (*Black Panther*, 1974f, p. 4). Similarly, the 1975 OCS Christmas pageant featured skits of "the upper-middle-class and wealthy wallowing in their greed" and "Rudolf the Black Nose Liberator" (*Black Panther*, 1975e, p. 4). Educators employed peer tutoring, individualized instruction, and other progressive techniques. Moreover, the school served a community-building function in Oakland, no matter what its pedagogy. Still, as the radical hopes of the late 1960s faded, the school abandoned the idea that students could either make meaning of their world or be instructed so as to understand their oppression.

A LIGHT UNTO THE NATION:
BLACK ACTIVISM AND PROMISE
OF DEMOCRATIC EDUCATION

Calls for schools to build on children's interests, promote active problem solving, and connect learning to life are staples of American education. Contemporary constructivism is but the most recent incarnation of a discourse that has echoed through American educational thought since the days of the common school movement and that achieved its best known expression in the Progressive Era a century ago (Mann, 1844, pp. 100–107; Dewey, 1990, pp. 36, 56).

The enduring appeal of this pedagogy owes much to the way that it resonates with widely held American political values. "The basic thesis of democracy," as W.E.B. DuBois put it, "[is] that the best and only ultimate authority on an individual's hurt and desire is that individual himself" and that "life, as any man has lived it, is part of that great reservoir of knowledge without which no government can do justice" (1973, p. 119). Shared by constructivist and progressive theorists, the ideal of self-actualizing learners defining their environment mirrors the liberal democratic political synthesis of individual autonomy and collective self-determination.

If, however, progressive pedagogy resonates with liberal democratic ideals, it also presumes an environment that nurtures democratic aspirations. Critics have struggled to reconcile the democratic claims of progressivism with reservations about its appropriateness for poor and minority students. The liberal ideal of encouraging "children to become autonomous . . . in the classroom setting without having arbitrary, outside standards forced upon them," as Lisa Delpit has argued, may well serve the interests of privileged students. However, children who have not already internalized "the culture of power" are often left to drift with little chance of academic success or social mobility (1988, p. 285).

Delpit follows in a long line of African American educators and intellectuals who have charged that in imagining meaning making as the relatively painless and unconstrained exploration of a relatively benign environment, progressive educators mistakenly generalize from White experience. Active inquiry into social life, as Horace Mann Bond argued in 1935, presupposes "an elastic, democratic social order in which there are no artificial barriers set against the social mobility of the individual. In such a society classes are assumed to be highly fluid, and there can be no such thing as caste" (p. 167). "The Black child," veteran educator and civil rights activist Septima Clark echoed, "is different from other children because he has problems that are the product of a social order not of his making or his forebears" (Brown-Nagin, 1999, p. 89). "Those streets, those houses, those dangers, those agonies" that surround the Black child, writer James Baldwin reminded teachers, are "the result of a criminal conspiracy to destroy him." Unlike White children, Baldwin argued, African American youth are faced with a paradox: "Precisely at the point when you begin to develop a conscience, you must find yourself at war with your society" (1996, p. 226).

An acute awareness of the contradiction between progressive pedagogical ideals and American political realities shaped Black visions of liberatory education. At times, Black intellectuals and activists have been persuaded that liberal democratic elements in American life were overcoming the brutalizing impact of racial exclusion and oppression. At those moments, Black scholars and educators have gambled that the promise of progressive pedagogy outweighed the special difficulties that confronted Black children in a racist environment organized to dehumanize them. At other moments, whether of heightened commitment to radical social transformation or heightened pessimism about democratic change, support for open-ended progressive pedagogies of experience and discovery has diminished.

Emerging from one of the most dynamic moments of democratic thought and activism in American history, the SNCC Freedom Schools and Black Panther liberation schools illuminate crucial questions confronting educators and constitute a vital chapter in the history of emancipatory education.

Elements of activists' educational program were absorbed at least partially by the public school system. A number of public schools inspired by Freedom Schools have demonstrated that progressive approaches to education can structure classrooms in which disenfranchised students are encouraged to do serious work. The expanded, multicultural history and literature curricula commonly found in schools today are directly traceable to movement lessons about the role of Blacks in the forming of American society. The movement also encouraged the development of cooperative learning and other progressive techniques as tools in promoting equality in schooling (Moses and Cobb, 2001; Banks, 1992; Cohen and Lotan, 1997).

And yet, the greatest significance of the Freedom and Liberation schools does not lie in the practices pioneered in them that were taken up by American schools. The ideas, ideals, and activities of the African American struggle for social justice signal that meaningful change in education is not reducible to any new policy, program, or technique. The movement and its schools serve as a reminder that no curriculum project can fundamentally transform learning if it is not part of a process of transforming social relations as well. Black activists' support for progressive approaches to the education of Black children required the utopian hope—reflected in and sustained by the African American freedom struggle—that the United States would fulfill its democratic promise so that Blacks, too, would be in a position, individually and collectively, to define and shape their situation. When that hope became implausible, pedagogical aspirations shifted along with political ones.

The evolution of movement schooling demonstrates that no single pedagogical approach inherently serves the cause of social justice. SNCC's most significant achievement mirrored progressive ideals. The Black Panthers' most significant achievement in transforming the consciousness of African America—that is, their most significant achievement as an educational agency—occurred in the years when their work was little informed by progressive techniques. Despite their crucial differences, both the SNCC schools and the Panther schools offered students an alternative to the ideologies of racial supremacy and economic oppression that surrounded them. Both exposed students to the culture of power, but also initiated a critique of it. Both conveyed a transcendent sense of possibility. Both modeled for students the possibility of collective learning and action that challenged the pervasive individualism of American life. What distinguishes the movement schools from most of public education is not primarily the techniques they employed. Rather, at issue was whether curriculum and pedagogy would perpetuate racism and other forms of domination or would foster change. Any educational program for disenfranchised students that neglects the centrality of social change omits an essential element of the educational process.

CHAPTER 9

Minds Still Stayed on Freedom?

Reflections on Politics, Consensus, and Pedagogy in the African American Freedom Struggle

Fannie Theresa Rushing

This essay is a reflection inspired by Daniel Perlstein's "Freedom, Liberation and Accomodation," not a refutation of it. As someone who has spent a significant part of her life teaching either in alternative high schools or in colleges and universities, I recognize that the major questions of the paper about how to provide education for freedom, independence, and liberation are as valid today as they were in the past. My perspective is that of someone who was a member of the Student Nonviolent Coordinating Committee for 5 years and who was among the founders of the first and only SNCC Residential Freedom School, which operated in Chicago and Cordele, Georgia.

From that perspective, it is difficult to think of SNCC as having consensus on goals and objectives, much less pedagogy. Our great diversity of opinion was and is our strength. At a given moment, you could have found SNCC members who were completely devoted to open-ended pedagogies, others who thought that was exactly the wrong path, and others still who didn't particularly care about the question.

Dr. Perlstein's core concern is his examination of "the evolution of political and educational ideas in the African American civil rights movement of the 1960s and 1970s, when activists developed, abandoned, recreated, and again abandoned open-ended progressive pedagogical approaches to the study of social and political life." Although I agree with him that both SNCC and the Panthers made considerable contributions to pedagogy in the United States, I cannot agree that both were a part of the civil rights movement. By the 1970s, the civil rights movement of the 1960s was over. A new and understudied movement had taken its place, the Black Liberation Movement. Even though some of the principal actors were the same, for at least a time, and both were parts of the overall struggle of Blacks in this country to make it a democracy, they were different in important ways. I would think that changes in the nature of the movement were at the center of changes in pedagogy more than just analyses of race relations.

Relatively early on for many people in SNCC, racial oppression was increasingly understood as but one dimension of a much more comprehensive system. If the fight against the system was to be successful, the tactics of combat had to change. By the time of the Black Liberation Movement, with its even more international focus, the multidimensional aspect of the struggle was more clearly articulated. This did mean that the content of instruction had to change, but not necessarily the process. Many of us became radical, in part, through constructing and participating in nonstructured open-ended forums where everything was questioned. We never doubted that the process could work the same way for our students.

As a result of struggling to make change, many SNCC activists could see clearly how the United States maintained exploitative, unequal economic relations and political control within the facade of a liberal democratic state. Many of us wanted to continue a process begun in the 18th century, that of making revolutionary participatory democracy in the United States. This commitment to participatory democracy was reflected in organizational structure (such as it was), day-to-day functioning, and programming like the Freedom Schools.

The U.S. system can tolerate protest so long as it is individual. The objectives of the traditional school are to promote individual self-reliance, autonomy, and achievement. The objectives of the Freedom School and the pedagogy of Paulo Freire were to be transformative social change agents. They were not predicated, as the article seems to indicate, on individual self-validation. Looking within one's self for the ability to eradicate oppression is only the first step, not an end in itself. The basic idea initially, it seems to me, was to be able to identify the issues of local oppression and relate that to the county/state/national oppression, and for each person to understand her/his ability to—in connection with others—change oppressive conditions. Freire's idea was "each one–teach one." Again, the emphasis was not on individuation but on social change for the benefit of the larger group. Similarly, one of the objectives of the Freedom School was the improvement of life chances not just for the individual, but for the group.

In retrospect, it becomes even clearer that even as we created Freedom Schools, we were being taught in them. The Residential Freedom School grew out of Chicago Area Friends of SNCC, a support organization for the Southern movement. I came to work for SNCC to support the Southern movement, yet it was impossible just to raise money and resources for the South, when Blacks in Chicago were so severely repressed. As a result, the CAFSNCC office had a long history of struggling with SNCC's national office over the need and right to involve ourselves in direct action in Chicago. There was often deep resentment on the part of Southern staff because the Chicago office did not raise as much money as New York or sometimes did not even raise money because of the press of direct action activities in Chicago. Raising money for the South versus raising hell in the North was a creative tension for us.

One of the most glaring issues confronting Chicago was the question of schools. Benjamin Willis, superintendent from 1953 to 1966, was widely regarded as a racist by Black Chicago. In order to prevent further "White Flight," Mayor Richard J. Daley, in alliance with the State Street Council (downtown business people) and their handpicked employee, Benjamin Willis, were committed to maintaining the neighborhood schools, which in a residentially segregated city meant *de facto* segregation and a corollary lack of resources for schools in Black and poor neighborhoods. This was made even more obvious by the creation of classrooms in mobile trailers—famously called "Willis Wagons"—in Black areas to prevent Black students from transferring to less-crowded White schools.

After 1964, as the movement debated future directions, in Chicago the answer was clear: one movement—North and South. The Residential Freedom School was conceived as an illustration of that new direction and a proving ground for it. The idea was to bring together young, high-school-age students from the South and North to live and study together in a classroom without walls and to explore their collective realities for two months in the summer. One month was to be spent in the North, where the Northern students explained their reality, and the next month was to be spent in the South, where the Southern students explained theirs. SNCC project directors in the South were to do the recruiting and screening of students from the South. In the North, any office that had young people they wanted to send could do so. In Chicago, CAFSNCC had just opened a Freedom Center on 43rd Street in the heart of Bronzeville. As a result, we were best equipped to supply students for the program. We were offering three meals and two snacks a day, plus supervision and field trips; in an impoverished neighborhood, that alone was enough to make it easy to find students. As for staff, anyone interested in the project could come and work. That turned out to be four full-time field staff: John Love, Sharon Jackson, Judy Richardson, and myself.

In Chicago in 1965, our commitment was to open-ended, questioning critiquing; we were not at all didactic. Nor is it my experience that young African Americans in urban areas of the North could not relate to open-ended pedagogy or to the oppression of Southern Blacks. Stokely Carmichael came and gave his "I digs wine" talk as a way to validate the students' language and their ability to understand the world with knowledge that was their own.

There was precious little structure to our work. In the way of curriculum, I did write some notes on African history. However, in the end, rather than lecturing from the notes, pictures on African history and important leaders were placed throughout the church, Monumental Baptist, where the school was housed. I remember finally caving to the insistence on the part of Lucy Montgomery, one of our most consistent supporters, that we at least plan menus for the 50–60 youngsters and staff who were expected to be in the Residential Freedom School. Soon, even that was abandoned, as I realized that the church volunteers had far more experience than any of us in feeding large groups. And besides, unexpected emergencies kept cropping up and wreaking havoc with our plans. Most importantly, the discussion going on among the students was so invigorating that no one wanted to take time from that to do planning.

A major ongoing bone of contention between us and the students was the theoretical question of violence versus nonviolence. The kids had to negotiate daily the reality of urban violence. Instead of the Klan, there was urban gang life, and our Freedom School was in the midst of one of the city's largest ongoing turf battles. In the struggle for soldiers, it was not clear which army would win, the movement or the gang.

Eventually, the violence penetrated the school. After being ignored by the gangs for some weeks, the leadership of one gang arrived at the school and literally held us hostage in the common room for an afternoon and a night. This was their territory. They controlled these streets and they were not prepared to accept a Freedom School or anything that did not acknowledge their leadership. What were the goals of the school? What kind of bullshit were we telling people?

They had a particular axe to grind. The girlfriend of the gang's war councillor had become quite attached to me, and I to her. I had been counseling her on a daily basis that she did not have to be abused by anyone, including her boyfriend. He had come that day to show her and me that he could verbally and physically abuse her when and where he chose. When John Love attempted to intervene on her behalf, two other gang members stepped forward and grabbed him on either side. One held a gun to John's head, daring us all to move. The gang members trashed the room and asked each of us what we were going to do about it. Were we going to be nonviolent? We knew that our students, always skeptical about nonviolence, were watching to see how committed we were to tactical nonviolence when our principles were put to the test.

A kind of stand-off went on for hours, with them threatening and posturing, while we, scared as we were, kept trying to explain what we were doing and kept arguing that we had to find ways to get beyond the violence and fight in other ways for a new day. It was early in the morning before they left, presumably having made their point about who was in charge. I suspect, too, that they had acquired at least a grudging respect for John Love, who never showed any fear throughout the whole ordeal. I also suspect that the evening marked them as much as it did us.

Fortunately, this was the last day of the Northern Freedom School. We were scheduled to leave the next day for the South. We were all traumatized, but we had to pull ourselves together for the sake of the project. We processed it all the way to Cordele, Georgia, only to arrive there on the day after a young Black man had supposedly made advances to a White woman and been jailed. The Klan had threatened to take him from the jail that night. The place where we were to hold the Freedom School was nervous about our arrival and a mass meeting was planned that night to figure out how to proceed. The Klan surrounded the church during the meeting, but we were still able to convince the community to accept us. Terror in the North—terror in the South!

All of this had to be processed with our students—street violence, domestic violence, the Klan, the fear of the Black community, the vulnerability of young Black men. There was another incident, as we were on our way to support a voter registration march, when one of the students from the North, mindful of our urging that everyone take control of their own lives, took that to mean he should drink from the White water fountain at a gas station, nearly bringing the wrath of the White community down on us. We didn't have anything one would ordinarily call a curriculum, but we had their lives to use as a text.

So, at least in my experience, it was not that the open-ended pedagogy of the Freedom School did not function in the North; it did so far better than planned. It was that we as activist/educators had not been schooled enough to understand the environment we wanted to work in. My critique of corporate capitalism, racism, and globalization is much harsher than it was in the 1960s; yet, it has never led me to "banking approaches" to teaching. I still see the importance of and use the Freedom School model for teaching at the university level. My objectives are the same—to give students the understanding of their ability to identify the roots of oppression locally, relate it to the wider world, and in conjunction with others, transform oppressive relationships into liberating ones. In an epoch where diversity is being subordinated to the homogeneity of transnational capital, if our minds are still "stayed on freedom" we must eschew homogeneity, individualism, and teaching methods that deny the right and abilities of students to identify society's problems in favor of a pedagogy of group relationships, goals, and solidarity. Only then can they be real social change agents instead of purveyors of individual achievement, reaffirming a hollow and fallacious meritocracy.

CHAPTER 10

"The World Is a Child's Classroom"

An Analysis of the Black Panther Party's Oakland Community School

Charles E. Jones
Jonathan Gayles

Cofounded by Huey P. Newton and Bobby Seale in October 1966, the Black Panther Party (BPP) represents one of the leading protest organizations of the African American freedom struggle. During its 16-year history (1966–1982), the revolutionary nationalist organization captured the imagination particularly of Black urban youth across the nation and global sympathizers throughout the world. The Oakland-based group rapidly grew into a national organization with affiliates in 28 states and an international chapter in Algiers, Algeria. While generally recognized for its prominence as a model of radical insurgency, observers, nevertheless, often reduce the Black Panther Party to an organization of gun-toting Black zealots. This narrow depiction ignores that the "Panthers utilized a full panoply of tactics to achieve organizational objectives" (Jones & Jeffries, 1998, p. 41). Upon the founding of the BPP, Newton and Seale wrote:

> We believe in an educational system that will give to our people a knowledge of self. If a man does not have knowledge of himself and his position in society and the world, then he has little chance to relate to anything else. (Seale, 1970, p. 67)

In 1971, the vision of the two BPP cofounders materialized with the establishment of the Intercommunal Youth Institute (IYI), renamed the Oakland Community School (OCS) in 1975. The Alameda County Board of Supervisors lauded the fully accredited Oakland Community School as a model educational institution. When the OCS ceased operations in June 1982, it marked the end of the Black Panther Party. This chapter offers an analysis of the Oakland Community School, the alternative educational institution established by the Black Panther Party.

ORIGINS

While the BPP advocated the socialistic transformation of the United States political-economic system as its ultimate objective, the organization's Ten-Point Party Platform and Program contained a litany of issues confronting African Americans that warranted immediate redress. Among the critical problems identified by Newton and Seale were underemployment, economic exploitation, substandard housing, police brutality, a discriminatory judicial system, and an inadequate education process. Seale and Newton called attention to the bias of the educational system in Point Five: "We want education for our people that exposes the true nature of this decadent American society. We want education that teaches us our true history and our role in the present-day society" (Seale, 1970, p. 67).

The Black Panther Party initially institutionalized Point Five of the platform by creating liberation schools in response to a directive ordered by Chairman Bobby Seale. In November 1968, Seale announced the party's plans to launch a "serve the people" program. Seale directed all BPP affiliates to implement free breakfast programs and free health clinics, and circulate petitions required for a referendum vote to decentralize local police forces. Two months later (January 1969), party leaders added the establishment of liberation schools to the "serve the people" initiative. Seale explained, "We felt that the first thing to be implemented had to be the breakfast for children program. But at the same time we know that the kids in the schools have got to be taught about themselves, their Black history, the class system and who cheats who—not the same bullshit they get now" (Seale, 1969, p. 11).

Panther liberation schools were fashioned after the freedom schools of the Student Nonviolent Coordinating Committee (SNCC) (see Chapter 8, this volume). BPP affiliates created the vast majority of the party's liberation schools during a 6-month period between June 1969 and January 1970. Panthers in Berkeley, California, established the first liberation school on June 25, 1969. Panther liberation schools enrolled a broad cross-section of Black children from the nation's urban communities who ranged from 2 to 15 years old. Many of the BPP affiliates regularly attracted more than 50 youngsters to their respective schools.

Under the leadership of Doris Bush, the liberation school in Queens hosted 82 children at its opening on July 26, 1969. Panther liberation schools usually were housed in churches, which participated in the organization's free breakfast programs, community recreational centers, and BPP offices. In contrast to the highly skilled Freedom School instructors, community volunteers, Panther-in-training and/or full-time members staffed the BPP liberation schools' classes. In several instances, high school students instructed liberation classes, while SNCC Freedom School classes were often taught by college graduates (Foner, 1970).

While the curriculum of many of the Panther liberation schools included basic academic subjects such as reading, math, and social studies, the schools primarily sought to teach students about Panther activism, revolutionary philosophy, and Black history. BPP literature, such as the organization's newspaper, *The Black Panther*, and the Ten-Point Party Platform, undergirded the curriculum of the liberation schools. Panther trials were often the destination of school field trips, and party leaders and other political prisoners usually supplied the lyrics for class songs and skits. As a result of the primacy of the BPP doctrine in the curriculum of the liberation schools, classroom instruction regularly reflected political indoctrination sessions rather than liberatory education. Students often spouted BPP rhetoric, as the following exchange indicates:

Teacher: What is a pig?
Student: A pig is a low-down person who can be any color who beats us
   up and tells lies.
Teacher: How many types of pigs are there?
Student: Four types.
Teacher: Name them.
Student: The avaricious businessman pig (who may be a landowner or a
   store owner, the teacher interjected) the police pig, the president pig,
   and the National Guard pig. (Hunter, 1969, p. 31)

INTERCOMMUNAL YOUTH INSTITUTE

In January 1971 the BPP formalized its education efforts by establishing the Intercommunal Youth Institute. One of Newton's first major initiatives following his release from prison in August 1970 directed party members to create an alternative educational institution. The name of the new school reflected the organization's ideological shift to intercommunalism (Hayes & Kiene, 1998, pp. 170–172).

Located in a north Oakland house, the inaugural 25-member IYI student body consisted mostly of BPP members' children. Ages of the students ranged from 2½ to 11 years old. "We start at the age 2½ because we do believe a child doesn't have to be 5 in order to form concepts. So, they learn a lot of things at an early age," explained Ericka Huggins, the longtime director of the school (1974–1981) (*Black Panther*, 1974g). Early architects of the IYI curriculum were BPP members Gloria Smith, a University of California Berkley student, and Brenda Bay, a New York Panther who served as IYI's first director. Administrators of the school selected the motto "The world is a child's classroom" as a key organizing principle of the alternative education institution. Brenda Bay noted, "We try to expose the children to a great deal of information and direct experience with the world so they can receive a more realistic view of the world" (*Black Panther*, 1973c).

Contrary to the Panther liberation schools, the IYI placed greater emphasis on traditional subject matter and developing academic skills rather than transmitting BPP doctrine. Its initial curriculum included mathematics, language arts, history, and science. In keeping with the schools' motto, all of the subject matter was enhanced by the regular Wednesday student field trips. IYI officials latter expanded the curriculum in 1973 by adding four new subjects: political education, physical education, people's art, and music. Emory Douglass, the school's art instructor and minister of culture of the BPP, explained, "People's art is art that reflects the Black community and expresses the reality of our situation as a whole. It deals with all emotions and all things that affect the Black community" (*Black Panther*, 1974b, p. 4). Another core tenet evident throughout the 11-year history of the BPP's school was its "each one teach one" principle. Instructors and students worked collectively "in order to develop an understanding of solidarity and camaraderie in a practical way" (Newton, n.d.a). Advanced students in particular subject areas often assisted their fellow classmates.

During the 1972–1973 academic year, the BPP named the IYI in honor of Samuel L. Napier, a party comrade slain during intrafactional organizational conflict. Student enrollment in the Samuel L. Napier Intercommunal Youth Institute increased from 25 to 42 pupils. The school diversified its student body by admitting a greater number of children whose parents were not members of the BPP. During its third year of existence (1973–1974), the IYI relocated to larger facilities in east Oakland to meet student demand. Ericka Huggins recalled:

> Children beg to come here. You should see them some days. It's so sad. They're supposed to be in their own schools, but they come here and peek into the classroom doors. Some come here just to go up to our library and read. (Hoffman, 1975)

New school facilities included a curriculum center, art room, eight classrooms, a fully equipped kitchen with a large cafeteria, and a 350-seat auditorium.

The school's new setting was part of a converted church complex that also housed the Oakland Community Learning Center (OCLC) of the Black Panther Party. In addition to the IYI, the BPP implemented educational, social, and cultural outreach programs under the auspices of the Oakland Community Learning Center. OCLC sponsored adult education programming, a free medical clinic, legal aid services, employment counseling, a monthly film series, teen programs, and community forums.

BPP leaders formed the Educational Opportunities Corporation (EOC), a nonprofit, community-based 501(c)3 entity, to administer the IYI and other OCLC programs. Phyllis Jackson, a party member from Tacoma, Washington, was chief administrator of the EOC staff. Joan Kelly directed special services and Norma Armour coordinated financial matters. Elaine Brown, the leader of the BPP from August 1974 to July 1977, recalled that "as for the management of the party's increasing income, Norma Armour was maintaining a tight rein. She meticulously accounted for every penny we raised or spent" (Brown, 1992, p. 411). Rollins Reid, the director of building maintenance, occupied the final EOC staff position.

Its relocation to a larger venue allowed the school to expand the size of the student body. During 1974–1975, school enrollment increased from 42 to 110 students. Panther officials renamed the IYI the Oakland Community School in 1975. Ericka Huggins explained: "We wanted to be appealing to people. People were not going to understand the Intercommunal Youth Institute. It sounded exclusive" (Huggins, 1993).

FREIRIAN CONCEPTUAL AND CURRICULAR LINKAGES

Paulo Freire's work is a useful tool for analyzing the educational philosophy of the party. In his body of scholarship, Freire constructs for the reader many oppositions, including banking versus problem-posing education, liberatory versus domination-oriented education, narration versus dialogue, and domestication versus liberation. We employ the broad descriptor "liberatory education" that encapsulates the essence of Freire's educational contributions. Across the breadth of his work, Freire offers many descriptions of liberatory education. Freire characterizes liberatory education by three core components: (1) it fosters a critical awareness, (2) it includes dialogue (rather than narration), and (3) it is transformative in nature. Before considering the BPP's educational program, we explore each of these components in greater conceptual detail (Freire, 1998 [1973]; Freire & Shor, 1987).

Perhaps the most dominant aspect of Freire's educational philosophy is the importance of critical thinking, awareness, and consciousness. In fact, critical awareness provides an intersecting theme between the core components of liberatory education. It acknowledges the innate ability of people *to know* independently *and* in a way that reflects their lived experiences rather than an externally imparted perspective. In this sense, active participation is characterized by challenge, examination, and dialogue. "We should not submit to the text or be submissive in front of the text." Rather, he asserts that we must "fight with the text, even though loving it, no?" (Freire, 1973, p. 11).

The development of critical awareness through educational programming is achieved through dialogue—not narration. Freire describes dialogue as "a horizontal relationship between persons" in which students and teachers must be "critical agents in the act of knowing" (Freire, 1973, p. 11). In this regard, Freire offers harsh critique of the banking concept of education in which knowledge is "deposited" into the minds of students. This approach reflects narration and dictation rather than dialogue. Without dialogue, teachers deliver information to students in a manner that does not include their reality, or any reality, for that matter. Conversely, dialogue fosters liberatory education in that the learner is an active and able participant.

Finally, a truly liberatory education culminates in transformative action. Freire's notion of praxis proves instructive in that "liberation is praxis: the action and reflection of men and women upon their world in order to *transform it*" (Freire, 1973, p. 79). Therefore, liberatory education is inextricably bound to action. As a result, "people develop their power to perceive critically the way they exist in the world in which they find themselves. Indeed, they come to see the world not as a static reality, but as a reality in process, *in transformation*" [our emphasis] (Freire, 1973, p. 83). This transformation reflects the action of people who are aware and conscious of their ability to impact their world. Liberatory education then extends far beyond increasing one's knowledge of general information. Instead, liberatory education seeks awareness that culminates in change.

Huey P. Newton, who first mandated the establishment of an alternative educational institution by the Black Panther Party, perhaps best frames the philosophy underpinning the OCS:

> The Intercommunal Youth Institute's primary task, then, is not so much to transmit a received doctrine from past experience as to provide the young with the ability and technical training that will make it possible for them to evaluate their heritage for themselves; to translate what is known into their own experiences and thus discover more reality their own. (Newton, 1974, p. 9)

In his narrative, Newton mirrored the Freirian core concepts of liberatory education that anchored the educational program of the OCS. Like Freire, Newton underscored the distinction between vertical/narrative instruction and horizontal/dialogical instruction. Newton notes that "it is not, I believe,

our duty to impose our limited interpretation of this past on the next generation" (Newton, 1974, p. 9). Teaching, from Newton's perspective, is not
driven by the ability of instructors to impart their knowledge or interpretations of the world onto students. Instead, he asserts that students must come
to "evaluate their heritage for themselves; to translate what is known into
their own experiences" (Newton, 1974, p. 9). Newton further suggests that
teaching should seek to develop student critical awareness based on their
experiences and environment. Students, situated as actors rather than subjects, coincide with Freirian liberatory education.

A guiding principle of the school's educational approach answered
Freire's call for student acquisition of critical thinking skills. The OCS *Instructors Handbook* noted that "a basic tenet of our school philosophy is to
show how and not what to do. We know that if a child does not know how
she or he arrived at an 'answer' then the child does not understand the concept that is being learned" (Newton, n.d.b). Consequently, the OCS staff was
expected to promote active student learning in which dialogue rather than
dictation prevailed. In short, the OCS pedagogical approach empowered
students to critically engage the content of the subject matter. The current
contentious debate around high-stakes testing and federally mandated curricula reflects the persisting tension between delivering information *onto*
students directly and delivering information *through* students in a manner
that allows them to engage information from their lived experience. Clearly,
the OCS philosophy is aligned with the latter approach.

Learning bound to action in the world outside of the classroom remained
a consistent OCS curricular theme. Math instruction, for example, sought
to "remove the mystique typically attached to the discipline of mathematics. Children are taught that, like language, math is a tool that will help them
survive from day to day" (*Black Panther*, 1977d, p. 14).

Classroom instruction was supplemented with extensive field trips and
extracurricular activities, which furthered enhanced critical awareness among
OCS students. School field trips had a decidedly political tone. OCS pupils
regularly attended political trials, including the "San Quentin 6" trial, to
acquire "direct exposure to the inadequacies of the American judicial system for Black and other minority people" (*Black Panther*, 1974g, p. 4). In
keeping with school's motto, OCS field trips sought to expose contradictions
within the students' immediate community. This learning objective dates back
to the earlier field trips of the Panther liberation schools. "We take them out
on Prospect Avenue to a block of dilapidated houses to check out genocide.
We show them exposed lead pipes where they can get lead poisoning and
TB," explained a liberation school instructor (Hunter, 1969).

Instead of school performances of the standard canonical theatrical titles,
OCS student plays were overtly political. OCS student theatrical productions

embraced philosophical principles of the BPP. *Huey Newton's Life* included reenactments of the racism the party's cofounder experienced in school and his involvement in forming the Black Panther Party. *A Brighter Tomorrow* was a dramatic presentation of Soweto student protest in South Africa while *"Buy-centennial"* criticized consumerism and the commercialization of the nation's 200th birthday (*Black Panther*, 1977b; 1975b; 1975a; 1975d; 1974l; Newton, n.d.c).

Perhaps the most compelling evidence of OCS commitment to liberatory education was its Youth Committee (YC). The YC represented a powerful conceptual affirmation of liberatory education by serving as a mechanism for independent critical thought and participation by OCS students. Its membership included a representative from each of the group levels elected by the student body. The YC undertook the following activities: the operation of an in-school youth store; the publication of a bimonthly newsletter edited and written by students; hosting KIDS, a children's radio program; and conducting the Justice Board, "a body which handles the children's interrelations and their student understanding of school rules" (*Black Panther*, 1974l, p. 4; 1975d, p. 4; Newton, n.d.c).

From calling assemblies in order to hear suggestions and criticisms from students, to voting to establish a tutoring program for students in need of assistance, the YC served as an authentic expression of a "horizontal relationship" between OCS students and teachers. Further, the YC provided students with a mechanism to reflect critically and independently on their OCS experiences. Amar Casey, the school's department head of social sciences, explained: "We try to encourage their development through the Youth Committee by first of all allowing the children to make their own decisions and in some cases their own mistakes." Further, because of their participation in YC activities, OCS students learned to "base their decisions on correctness and not emotions and favoritism" (*Black Panther*, 1974l, p. 4).

Beginning with the 1974–1975 academic year, OCS averaged between 16 and 20 full-time instructors, and an additional 12 to 14 volunteer staff members for much of its existence. After Brenda Bay's stint as the school's inaugural director, Ericka Huggins assumed the OCS directorship in 1974, a position she held for 7 years, until 1981. Another veteran party member, Donna Howell of the Boston BPP chapter, served as the school's assistant director for several years. Unlike the Panther liberation schools, the qualifications of the highly skilled OCS teaching staff arguably matched or exceeded those of the talented instructors of the SNCC Freedom Schools.

During the early years of OCS, Bill Moore, who earned a Ph.D. in the History of Consciousness program from the University of California at Santa Cruz, served as the coordinator of the school's curriculum committee. The six department heads and volunteer instructors comprised the curriculum committee. Steve McCutchen, the head of the physical education department, is yet another example of the school's talented instructors. McCutchen, a veteran rank-and-file member from the Baltimore chapter of the BPP and holder of a Tae Kwon Do black belt, also directed the martial arts program sponsored by the Oakland Community Learning Center. McCutchen's students won state and regional karate tournaments, and the team was featured in *Black Belt* (*Black Panther*, 1975c, p. 23).

Similarly, exceptional instructors staffed the performing arts curricular offerings (dance and music). Legendary drummer and jazz master Charles Moffett directed the school's Intercommunal Youth Band and the OCLC music program. The student band won several music competitions under Moffett's directorship. In an interview with the noted educator Herb Kohl, Moffett remarked: "Music is making the children aware of their feelings and helps them to read at the same time. They are putting out their feelings into a mathematical concept. Together that is how we are integrating basic educational skills with a 'music education'" (*Black Panther*, 1974d, p. 4). The school's band played throughout the San Francisco Bay area, including a Sunday weekly performance held at the school. He further commented that the school's band "played at a Christmas party in San Francisco, and we play here every Sunday. We play for different fraternity and sorority affairs, for style shows and special concerts of our own. Some of the children have had experience in television" (*Black Panther*, 1974d, p. 4).

In short, the dedicated OCS staff proved critical to the school's success. During the final years of the BPP (1977–1982), many of its members, like Ericka Huggins, chose to remain in the organization out of the loyalty to the school's children. Angela LeBlanc-Ernest, the former director of the Black Panther Research Project at Stanford University, noted that "Huggins attributed her decision to remain a Panther, in spite of Newton's erratic and criminal behavior, to her commitment to the students of the OCS" (Leblanc-Ernest, 1998, p. 324). The unwavering dedication of Huggins and other OCS staffers helped to overcome the absence of tuition-driven income, a financial situation that placed greater reliance on vital auxiliary assistance.

AUXILIARY SUPPORT

Unlike traditional private schools, OCS did not rely on student tuition as a major revenue stream. The school only charged a nominal, non-mandatory $25 tuition. Since it cost approximately $22,000 per month to operate the school, OCS was heavily dependent upon critical auxiliary support. OCS utilized a broad array of tactics to compensate for its lack of tuition-driven income, including grants, fund-raising activities, and private donations. Third

World Foundation, the Vanguard Foundation, the Alameda County Foundation, and the California Arts Council all funded OCS programs. The school also received substantial grant monies from governmental sources. For example, the Office of Child Development and the Office of Child Nutritional Services, both located in the state's Department of Education, awarded over $300,000 per year to assist the school's Child Development Center and free lunch program. "Joan Kelley was deftly weaving a financial blanket from the yields of her proposal writings which was sheltering our social programs," remembered Elaine Brown, the then leader of the Black Panther Party (LeBlanc-Earnest, 1998, p. 324). In addition, grant support came from the Episcopal Diocese of New York.

Cosponsored with Oakland Bay area radio stations, the school's radio-thon was one of its most successful fundraising activities. OCS radio-thons consisted of local music acts with cameo appearances from public officials, dignitaries, and educators broadcasted from the grounds of the Oakland Community Learning Center. In 1976, a radio-thon cosponsored with KDIA (1310AM) raised over $13,000. In the subsequent year, the "Beautiful Get Together" radio-thon, cosponsored with KRE (1400AM and 103FM), garnered $10,000 for OCLC programs.

OCS also sponsored benefit concerts to raise funds. Prominent entertainers volunteered to headline concerts, such as the two performances by the late Oscar Brown Jr. in March 1974, which more than 1,000 people attended. John Lee Hooker, the acclaimed blues musician, also performed in a 1976 benefit concert for the school. Community festivals, monthly raffle drawings, and "Each One Teach One" tuition club also garnered monies for OCS. (For examples of financial support, see Brown, 1992, p. 410; *Black Panther*, 1975d, 1977g, 1977c, 1977h, 1977e; Milstein, 1985; Williams, 1982; Williams & Ayres, 1982.)

Parents of OCS students lent critical fund-raising assistance. Members of the Parents Advisory Board (PAB) sold tickets for the raffle donation drive, cohosted cocktail party receptions, and held frequent bake sales. Community residents frequently attended OSC fundraising events, purchased raffle tickets, and made financial donations to the school. Community organizations such as La Peña, a Latino restaurant and cultural center, hosted a well-attended fund-raising benefit. Most importantly, OCS fund-raisers cultivated financial commitments from several wealthy benefactors. Bert Schneider, producer of the acclaimed movie *Easy Rider*, was one of generous donors who supported the Oakland Community School. Don Cornelius, producer and host of the popular *Soul Train* television program, also made substantial donations (*Black Panther*, 1976a, p. 14).

From the school's inception, community volunteerism provided vital support. Individuals throughout the Oakland Bay area donated their time and expertise, which allowed the school to maximize its limited funds. Students from the University of California at Berkeley, San Francisco State University, Mills College, California State University at Hayward, Merritt and Laney Junior colleges, as well as other institutions of higher learning frequently volunteered as OCS tutors and teachers' aides. Two members of the Black Nurses Association in Oakland volunteered as school nurses. The Parent Advisory Board also assisted all aspects of school operations. In lieu of tuition, OCS parents volunteered 12 hours per month assisting school functions and programs. For instance, parents regularly volunteered as teacher aides on Wednesday, thereby permitting teachers to attend the weekly staff meeting.

A final yet equally important resource cultivated by the OCS staff is found in the school's many distinguished visitors. Throughout the history of the OCS, a broad spectrum of state, national, and international dignitaries regularly toured the alternative education institution. Notable visitors to the Oakland Community School included musicians such as Pharoah Sanders and Ornette Coleman; politicians like Senator Alan Cranston, Governor Jerry Brown, and Congressman Ron Dellums; educators like Herbert Kohl; and various sports celebrities, such as Willie Mays and Bill Walton.

LEGACY

The highly acclaimed Oakland Community School significantly enhanced the educational opportunities of Black and disadvantaged children residing in Oakland, California. OCS officials proudly declared that "children enrolled in the school consistently perform 3 to 4 years in advance of their public peers" (Huggins, 1978, 1993; *Black Panther*, 1977d; OCS Weekly Report, 1978). During the "In Celebration of Knowledge" program sponsored by the Oakland Community Learning Center on June 16, 1974, Deborah Williams, the lone member of OCS's first graduating class, reflected on her experience at the BPP's alternative education institution during her commencement address before an audience of more than 400 people:

> I enjoyed the classes here because we learn methods and how to work problems. I think method is important because it is a tool that helps me solve all problems and not just find the answers to a few. I like mathematics because it is challenging. I enjoy reading also, finding new words and meanings. Here the classroom is not a locked-up classroom. Our school motto says, "The world is the children's classroom." Every Wednesday at the Institute we would go on field trips to places which would help us learn how to put into practice many of the ideas we learn in class. I think that I will miss those kinds of Wednesdays. (*Black Panther*, 1974j, p. 2)

OCS students excelled in the schools' nurturing environment as evidenced by their numerous academic awards and honors. OCS won distinction for its display of an exhibit at the Western regional meeting of Black Engineers and Scientists. In 1974, the Intercommunal Youth Band, under the directorship of the jazz master Charles Moffett, won first place in the North American Zone Far West Region competition. In addition, several students from the school's martial arts program won karate tournaments (*Black Panther*, 1974k, 1975c, 1976a; Hoffman, 1975; McCutchen, 1992).

In 1976, the Alameda County Board of Supervisors honored the school for its outstanding contribution to the education of poor and disadvantaged youth. Ericka Huggins's election to the Alameda County Board of Education also denoted the OCS's influential role in Oakland. Sworn in on July 1, 1976, Huggins was the first African American to sit on the county's board of education. The party's alternative school received laudatory praise from the California state legislature. On August 18, 1977, 10 years after the BPP's infamous protest of the Mulford Act on the floor of the General Assembly in Sacramento on May 2, 1967, party members were formally invited to a capitol steps ceremony to receive a commendation for its school. State legislators passed a resolution applauding the OCS for its exemplary service to the children of Oakland: "Resolved, that the highest commendations be extended to the Oakland Community School for its outstanding record of dedicated and highly effective service in educating children of the community of East Oakland" (*Black Panther*, 1977f). Huey Newton, who had recently returned from his 3-year exile in Cuba to avoid criminal charges, officially represented the BPP, along with Elaine Brown and Ericka Huggins, at the Sacramento ceremony.

Newton's resumption of the party's leadership mantle proved disastrous for the school's fortunes. Upon Newton's return from Cuba, the Oakland Community School had become the cornerstone of the party's few remaining survival programs. During its final 5 years (1977–1982), the BPP membership significantly dwindled, to fewer than 50 individuals. Consequently, the organization lacked the resources and personnel to sponsor its full complement of survival programs. David Hilliard, the party's chief of staff, who returned to Oakland after his release from prison for his role in the April 16, 1968, police shootout, recalled that "for one thing the Party is completely different. The paper still appears, and the school—the Oakland Community Learning Center, led by Ericka Huggins is now highly regarded, but other survival programs have disappeared" (Hilliard & Cole, 1992, p. 383).

During the 1977–1978 school year, OCS enrolled 160 pupils, its largest student body. Indeed, from 1974 to 1980, OCS enrolled approximately 137 students per academic year. The school created vital positive publicity needed to offset Newton's unprincipled behavior. More importantly, OCS funding constituted the party's primary source of revenue, a fact not overlooked by Newton. The party enjoyed substantial grant largesse from both the city of Oakland and the state of California. Shortly after his return to power in the BPP, Newton began to embezzle grant funds. In November 1977, Oakland city officials alleged that Newton misappropriated funds from a $110,000 manpower grant, which led to the termination of city funding to the EOC. California's Department of Justice later charged Newton with embezzling monies from grants that supported the school's free lunch program and its Child Development Center. As a result, "the state Department of Education canceled grants totaling more than $800,000 a year and the school closed in the summer of 1982" (Milstein, 1985).

When the doors of the OCS closed in June 1982, it marked the formal demise of the Black Panther Party, arguably one of the most prominent organizations of the Black liberation struggle. Community service was a central aspect of the BPP's illustrious legacy. The Oakland Community School, the party's 11-year alternative institution, flourished as a model of educational excellence.

PART IV

Sankofa: Looking Back to Look Forward— Contemporary Expressions of Education for Liberation

Around 1965 there began to develop a great deal of questioning about what is the role of women in the struggle. Out of it came a concept that Black women had to bolster the ego of the male. This implied that the Black male had been treated in such a manner as to have been emasculated both by the White society and Black women because the female was head of the household. We began to deal with the question of the need of Black women to play the subordinate role. I personally have never thought of this as being valid because it raises the question as to whether the Black man is going to try to be a man on the basis of his capacity to deal with issues and situations rather than be a man because he has some people around him who claim him to be a man by taking subordinate roles.

—Ella Baker

Gender is one issue on which contemporary activists and educators should be more conscious than their predecessors from the 1960s. Understanding its salience is one thing, however; figuring out how to get young people to question something they've been socialized to understand as natural isn't easy.

Nonetheless, Susan Wilcox demonstrates in her discussion of New York's Brotherhood Sister Sol that when we can do it, the effects can be powerful. Getting young men to say they will struggle against sexism and getting young women to understand the struggles of their mothers as women are major victories.

At first glance, the Sunflower County Freedom Project appears to be a perfect contemporary exemplar of SNCC's Freedom Schools. It represents an heroic effort by one young teacher, a White male, to build an institution that speaks to the needs of some of the country's most neglected youngsters. (In good SNCC tradition, Chris Myers Asch, in the dialogue that follows, understates his role in creating the project.) Community-based programs that make a 6-year commitment to each student are few and far between. Simply funding a project like this is an enormous undertaking, all the more so, since funders are often reluctant to offer long-term funding to any one project, no matter how effective, unless it is constantly growing (which may undermine whatever made the program effective in the first place).

Still, is it really a *Freedom* School? How explicitly political does a school have to be to be considered a "Freedom School?" Remember the question from Fannie Rushing's essay (Chapter 9): Are we talking about a better life for individuals or better life chances for the group? In the jointly authored essay that follows (Chapter 12), Chris Meyers Asch debates some of these issues with educator-activist Bill Ayers.

A long-standing cliché in Black militant circles treats Christianity as the religion of the servile and cowardly, a position that fails to give slaves enough credit. We know that slaves largely refashioned Christianity into an instrument of struggle (and saying that does not deny that Christianity was simultaneously being used by others to reinforce racism). We know that slaves were particularly invested in the deliverance of the Hebrews from bondage, that Moses the Deliverer appeared more frequently in their songs than did Jesus (Levine, 1977). The Old Testament was the first Freedom School curriculum, and from it, the enslaved took both a vision of freedom and a promise of deliverance:

> My Lord delivered Daniel, Daniel, Daniel,
> My Lord delivered Daniel, then why not every one?

In the 1990s in Chicago, two young ministers posed that question again, fashioning a program that used Daniel's enslavement as a metaphor for the condition of contemporary African American boys. Displaying the syncretism typical of many programs, they also made use of more contemporary methods for framing African American consciousness, including the Nguzo Saba, the seven guiding principles found in many African-centered educational initiatives.

Education that involves social critique may be becoming more common in public schools, but few of these programs are old enough to let us judge their staying power. The experience of the Bushwick School for

Social Justice suggests that such initiatives would do well to ally themselves with a vigorous community organization, not only to do battle with the bureaucrats, but to make sure that the social justice component does not get swallowed up by the routines and cultures of school. The history of the Bushwick School (Chapter 14) again reminds us how race can be embedded in every step of the process, from conceptualization to implementation. Even the language is racialized; it says something that this is a "social justice" school, not a "liberation" school.

The young people who formed the Black Student Leadership Network (Chapter 15) in the early 1990s "wanted to complete the unfinished business of the civil rights movement." It is interesting to compare their feistiness to that of the Young Negroes Cooperative League. Coming out of community organizing, anti-apartheid work, educational reform groups and other youth-based movements, they built a movement around the Freedom School model and won accolades from many sources for the high quality of their work. Given their head, they would have tried to use the schools as the basis for multi-issue organizing, but before that could happen they got into a series of conflicts with the adults with whom they were working, who, predictably, had different understandings of what should be going on. There was no one to play the role that Ella Baker played in the SNCC's early years, the smoother of paths, the bridge-builder.

The split notwithstanding, the schools continued to prosper under the Children's Defense Fund. In the summer of 2006, they trained more than 800 servant-leaders who went on to work with more than 7,000 children in 49 cities. David Levine argued that by incorporating the rhythms of praise houses like Morning Star Hall into their work, Highlander activists demonstrated their respect for the people with whom they were working and made them feel that the movement was their own. In the same way, Children's Defense Fund Freedom Schools incorporate the rhythms of urban youth into their work, much of it through what they call "chanting." Indeed, *chanting* is a poor word for what they do, which is part dance, part rap, part rhythmic clapping and stomping, part call-and-response ritual, part Saturday night house party. It may involve 10 people or 1,000, and students cannot seem to get enough of it. Some veterans of the 1960s movement see the chants as this generation's Freedom Songs, energizing, building solidarity, connecting the movement to the day-to-day culture of the people it serves. Gale Seiler's essay (Chapter 16) captures the exuberance and significance of chanting for children in a Baltimore Freedom School.

Randolph Potts (Chapter 17) brings together two intellectual traditions: community psychology, that branch of psychology concerned with the relationships between individuals and their environments, and African-centered education, which is centrally concerned with strengthening the identity of Black children as Africans. A much-used metaphor among African-centered educators is that of Sankofa, the bird that looks back to go forward. Potts explains the philosophical underpinnings of African-centered education and describes a successful program built on its principles. Chapter 18 by Carol D. Lee conveys a sense of what it takes to build and sustain an institution in the African-centered tradition. In its current manifestation as a public charter school, Betty Shabazz International Charter school is among the best schools in the city of Chicago, but it represents 3 decades of struggle and sacrifice.

Whatever forms education for liberation takes in the future, the soundtrack for much of it will be hip-hop. Even some critics of hip-hop recognize this, but they are less likely to understand its connection with similar currents in popular youth culture in other parts of the African diaspora. Juxtaposing socially conscious hip-hop with "roots" reggae, Ernest Morrell (Chapter 19) shows that across the diaspora, "rebel musics" have the capacity to be sources of critical literacy—to say nothing of academic literacy—for a new generation.

CHAPTER 11

My Sister, My Brother, Myself

Critical Exploration of Sexism and Misogyny at the Brotherhood/Sister Sol

Susan Wilcox

A sister does not let her brothers go astray nor does she let her sisters go astray. We as a family need to undo the nonsense that has been instilled in our minds.

—Sister Sol member

In the beginning, 1994, it was The Brotherhood, cofounded in Providence, Rhode Island, by Khary Lazarre-White and Jason Warwin when they were seniors at Brown University. Young brothers explored their developing manhood with support from their immediate male elders. With the creation of Sister Sol 4 years later, the organization expanded to become The Brotherhood/Sister Sol (BHSS). Our staff was now coeducational as I joined Khary and Jason as the third codirector. Like our male members before, young women would have guidance from their immediate female elders. Both would see women and men in a position of leadership.

BHSS is first and foremost a family of youth and adults, and according to our members, a second home (Castle & Arella, 2003).[1] We are a Harlem-based community organization serving 200 Black and Latino/a youth ages 6–19. Daily programs and periodic Saturday activities take place in our brownstone and at local schools and recreational centers. We use New York City, the metropolitan area and eastern seaboard, and Africa and Latin America as learning grounds during cultural outings, wilderness retreats, college tours, and international study. Our members receive holistic support and participate in single-sex and coeducational programs. Thirteen members of our staff of 16, including five alumni members and the Directors Circle, work directly with youth. An active Board of Directors and other volunteers provide additional support, advice, and resources to the organization.

At BHSS we seek to change the way young Blacks and Latinos view and handle themselves in a world in which oppression of every sort—racism, sexism, homophobia, ageism—informs their everyday experiences, relationships and self-perceptions. The cofounders believed that helping young men direct their lives, some of which were on the edges of educational, financial, and emotional neglect, depended on how well they could read and reshape the landscape of their lives. They understood how crucial it was for young men to examine masculinity as a way of life when the code of manhood leaves them without fathers or important male guides, and as they learn to respond with indifference or violence in fear of showing weakness. The plan was to extend the work to young women, knowing females are bombarded with messages about femininity suggesting our bodies, rather than our minds, are our greatest assets and always up for criticism. With brothers and sisters in the same room, we could fully explore how each sex absorbs messages about gender role expectations.

Over 12 years, we have facilitated enough programming to see impressive impacts and have learned valuable lessons about how to guide young people toward self-discovery. We have also learned just how much helping them explore issues of gender and solidarity competes with deeply ingrained influences of family upbringing, schooling, mass media, political structures, and history that define and reinforce experiences of power and privilege. These are the deeply felt influences we hope to help our members make sense of in the relatively short time we have with them.

OUR DIASPORA

Our members are from the African diaspora: Black American, Puerto Rican, Haitian, Dominican, Jamaican, Ghanaian, Antiguan, Honduran, Guyanese. Our cultural traditions and history are the basis for solidarity building, though not because our members are from the "inner city" and "disadvantaged." BHSS is where they can see themselves and each other beyond stereotypes or as rivals in the race for the American dream. We agree with Lorde that "Divide and conquer, in our world, must become define and empower" (1981, p. 100). Writing about our move into our brownstone, a member says, "[This building] is where we can help take care of the community. It's a chance for us to show everyone that Blacks and Latinos . . . are positive and trying to maintain that way."[2]

We are well aware that Blacks and Latinos have many differences that matter a great deal. As much as I do not want to lump us together as others often do, the scope of this chapter does not allow me to discuss these differences. BHSS was, however, born of the experiences of Black people in America that have impacted the experiences of all people of color. Our work is rooted in traditions of African American education that was necessarily an act of resistance. The line from our front door winds back to the school Mary McLeod Bethune created for Black girls and young women with the motto "Self-respect, self-reliance, self-pride"; to the Black Panther Party and Young Lords Party that sought to politicize their communities while providing a free breakfast and facilitating community schools and activism based on their 10-point platforms; and to single-sex or single-race public schools created to meet the special needs of Black males or females. We have studied history for inspiration and to learn from past mistakes. Twenty-five years ago, BHSS would have been described as a nationalist organization, but we reject the sexism, homophobia, and other forms of silencing that were allowed to flourish in nationalist organizations of the 1960s and 1970s.

Our practice comes from regarding our community as a village and our responsibility, and the aims of education as being about acquiring factual knowledge *and* achieving a personal and social transformation. During the critical developmental years of our members' lives, we connect them to mentors, teachers, and friends who, as a member writes, "experienced the same things as we did . . . [and] had to overcome the same obstacles," creating a foundation for building together.

THE LANDSCAPE OF OUR MEMBERS' LIVES

The world our members live in says much about why and how we do this work. Of the many experiences and conditions contributing to their development, their 'hoods and hip-hop (and popular culture more generally) have a significant impact on their experiences with and understanding of gender, sexism, and feminism.

Our members are economically diverse, but primarily live in communities associated with urban blight and inattention, at least up until the recent wave of gentrification. Their neighborhoods are among the seven in New York City contributing about two thirds of the state prison population, with women becoming the fastest-growing segment. More young Black men in these neighborhoods are graduating *into* the New York State penal system than *from* the State University of New York. In their communities it can be easy to confuse manhood and womanhood with the "rites of passage" that gangbangin' and serving time have become. And though stereotyped as criminals, Black and Latino youth are more likely to be victims of violence, including of hate crimes and police brutality.

BHSS members range from "A" students and recipients of the Posse Award (which comes with a full 4-year college scholarship), to students struggling to stay in school due to lack of effort or a learning disability. They attend public schools where access to basic resources and quality teaching is limited. (Our brownstone is located in the district that has the most over-crowded elementary school classrooms in the borough of Manhattan.) Learning from a curriculum that relegates the history of Blacks to slavery, the civil rights movement, and a few key figures, while overlooking the vast contributions and experiences of women and people of color, our members are seldom exposed to ideas that build knowledge and skills for analyzing issues of race, class, gender, and sexuality.

Hip-hop's "ubiquity," which has "created a common ground and common vernacular for Black folk from 18 to 50 worldwide" (Tate, 2005, p. 32), offers constant commentary on these very issues. At its best, hip-hop gives voice to young people's realities, fears, and dreams. Many youth (including members of our Lyrical Circle who have won national recognition) rhyme, write poetry, and do spoken word stirred to pen their ideas, believing their words can effect positive change.

At its worst, hip-hop is tremendously demeaning and limiting to women and men. Even if young people say they just like the beat, they rap along with the lyrics. How many times can they repeat the word *bitch* or the phrase *Put it in my mouth*[3] before the message acquires meaning, or before they become desensitized to its meaning? Some young women sing these words louder than males, flaunting their sexual desires but failing to recognize their image as sexual objects. Young women are constantly seeing images of what they inevitably measure themselves against, of what many young men presumably desire. An alumni Brotherhood member asked me if I had heard the lyrics female artists were now singing, but could not quite bring himself to repeat them out of his respect for me. I finally got that the songs were about women performing oral sex on men. This brother appreciates women being sexual, but thinks the line has been crossed into deep disrespect of self. That our youngest members have easy access to music, videos, and magazines promoting women as sexual objects only means that pejorative messages about gender are seeping in at an earlier age. A 10-year-old member discussing the portrayal of women in music videos argues that if women wanted respect, then why be in the video?

Hip-hop has a homoerotic edge as well that is rarely discussed, but which clearly gets at the inherent link between sexism and homophobia. Male rappers show off their bare, hard abs in music videos in a display of machismo that is ultimately about men impressing men, a demonstration of who is the "baddest" man.

Sexism thrives everywhere, but in Black and Latino communities there is a lack of public and widespread discussion about it or feminism. Feminism—the movement—is associated with White middle-class women, tending to lose its appeal in our communities. Feminism—the concept—is recognized in so far as most people do not publicly deny that men and women should not have equal rights, though the reality of relationships between men and women is frequently less than just.

Moreover, many of our members are developing ideas about gender from having mothers and grandmothers as caregivers, with fathers leaving an impression in which their absence is making its mark. The example of strong, hardworking females offers a positive model of dedication to family through thick and thin. One young woman says her mother gives her "strength and courage to go on." Mothers are role models to young men, too, embodying the ideal woman raised on a pedestal. A young brother writes, "I'll treat my wife as I would my Mom, with the utmost respect, showing her as much affection as possible."

Mothers are often the sole voice of authority, and therefore, they also, and conversely, symbolize repression to males who likely transfer their notions about the stereotypical nagging woman to other females in their lives. And with few examples of men providing emotional and financial support to their children, even when the relationship with the mother falls apart, a young brother reflects: "I lack a father figure in my house. Khary and Jason are my father figures. They've taught me things my mother can't teach me." Many of our young women grow up not thinking much of fathers, or men, seeing them as unreliable or undeserving of their love. A young sister says, "[My father] hasn't earned my trust."

Sexism and misogyny disconnect our hearts from our minds, making it difficult to act on what we know to be right. Young women who do not feel empowered to consent or decline sex become vulnerable to contracting STDs, having unwanted pregnancies, or being in abusive relationships. Young men who mistake strength for control over others do not recognize how they are acting as the oppressor even while being oppressed. "Down low" brothers, who don't feel liberated to accept their homo- or bisexuality, put themselves and their sexual partners at physical and psychological risk.

bell hooks describes "Black male selfhood" as embodying "images of the brute—untamed, uncivilized, unthinking, and unfeeling"(2004, p. xii). Cherrie Moraga writes:

> We are afraid to look at how we have failed each other. We are afraid to see how we have taken the values of our oppressor into our hearts and turned them against ourselves and one another. We are afraid to admit how deeply "the man's" words have been ingrained in us. (1981, p. 32)

Moraga and hooks are speaking to the need for each of us to examine societal messages about gender roles and then to define *manhood* and *womanhood* for ourselves. Does the role I'm expected to play as a woman fit in with my decision not to have children? Does expressing my joy of sex mean I'm promiscuous? Does my attraction to other men mean I am less than a man? Does the fact that I cry? These are the questions BHSS is helping young people answer as we engage them in ongoing critical reflection and foster empathetic connections within and across sexes.

ANTI-SEXIST CURRICULUM

BHSS infuses values of brotherhood and sisterhood, community, and leadership across our five programs, though it is within the Rites of Passage Program (ROP) that our anti-sexist work is most intense. ROP comprises single-sex chapters established at public secondary schools and in our community that stay together for 4 to 6 years. Chapters have weekly workshops; go on wilderness retreats, college tours, and cultural outings; and participate in other BHSS programs. Workshop and enrichment activities center on our 10 Curriculum Focus Issues:

1. Mind, Body, and Spirit
2. Leadership Development
3. Pan African and Latino History
4. Sexism and Misogyny
5. Sexual Education and Responsibility
6. Drugs and Substance Abuse
7. Conflict Resolution and Bias Reduction
8. Political Education and Social Justice
9. Educational Achievement
10. Community Service and Responsibility

With the support and guidance of two chapter leaders, each chapter spends several years exploring critical social issues. We use literature, the arts, reflective writing, current news, videos, and film to teach history and help our members deconstruct contemporary social messages; imagine their lives in the future; consider the viewpoints of others; and express their own ideas in word and imagery. The experiences of Blacks, Latinos, women, gays, and lesbians are integrated naturally. A group might read the memoir *The Prisoner's Wife* by Asha Bandele over several weeks, using it to examine the issues of prison industrial complex, sexual assault, and devoted love that are raised by the author. We incorporate Oríkí, the traditional Nigerian practice of storytelling, by inviting elders to talk about their life journey. A member writes:

In Sister Sol you'll learn a lot about Hispanic . . . Caribbean and African cultures. If you take the time to learn about these things you'll notice you're learning about yourself, your ancestors, and your friends.

The following workshop summary is one approach to exploring anti-sexism. (See *Brother, Sister, Leader: The Official Curriculum of The Brotherhood/Sister Sol*, a compilation of 50 workshops with strategies for chapter building, and activity sheets.)

Gender, Sexism, and Feminism is a two-part workshop (about 2½ hours for each session) beginning with a large group discussion on:

- What attributes we value as a society
- Which attributes are "male" or "female"
- Where our ideas about female versus male come from

Working in small groups, young people are given information about a gender-related topic (e.g., Afghanistan and the Taliban, Hatshepsut and ancient Egypt, female genital mutilation) from which to develop a presentation. The objective is to highlight the scope of sexism through time and across geography, as well as bring out our members' understanding of gender, sexism, and feminism.

In the follow-up session, a scenario is distributed for the group to read together. It is about a nondescriptive "executive" and the people s/he encounters during her/his workday. Encouraged to not self-censor or overthink, the group is asked to identify the sex of each person in the scenario. Their comments lead to a discussion on how ideas about gender affect us, and either advance or limit our experiences and opportunities. The session continues with a discussion about the concept of *nature versus nurture*. Hoping to push the group's thinking, chapter leaders ask, "Who is a feminist?" The ensuing discussion explores how our members see themselves as upholding and/or practicing feminist versus sexist ideals. By grappling with sex/gender expectations, youth are helped to identify their allies, advocates and oppressors. A reflective writing assignment generally closes out the activity, with volunteers offering to share their pieces.

RITES OF PASSAGE

Aside from workshops, ROP activities help deepen our members' understanding of their multiple identities, identify personal commitments, and foster unity. In the first year, chapters create a collective *Mission Statement, Definitions for Brother/Man/Leader or Sister/Woman/Leader*, and a chapter name. As our members work on their statements, we challenge them with questions such as:

- What is the source of these values? How easy or difficult will it be to live up to these values, and why?
- Is it necessary to have blood ties with or be someone's best friend in order to be their *sister* or *brother*?
- If being a *man* means you have to financially support your family, are you no longer a man if you lose your job?
- Does a female have to be married or have children in order to be a *woman*?
- Does being a *leader* mean you have to have followers or people you influence, or can you just be a role model?
- How do we build as a community so as not to divide and conquer? Who are our allies and enemies?

It is a difficult process of consensus-building, incorporating workshop lessons and personal experience, but ultimately it is rewarding, as one young woman recalls that the "laughter and the seriousness in the room was really incredible. I didn't know that we could get so close to females the way I have."

The statements become the guiding words each chapter strives to live by. Excerpts of *Mission Statements* and *Definitions* from across our programs convey a sense of solidarity within and across genders and the importance of trust, respect, and self-determination:

A Man . . .

Takes care of his responsibilities, takes care of his own problems, and helps others with theirs to the best of his ability
Never walks out of a child's life
Never physically or mentally abuses a woman
  —*Knowledge of Self Chapter*, 12th grade

A Sister, Woman, Leader Is:

. . . proud of herself and is no one's object. She will rise together with other women, accepts their differences and the ties that bind them as one. She will become the woman that other woman look up to and admire.
  —*Eleloli: The Pages Chapter*, 9th grade

Being a Brother

Brothers respect each other.
No matter what happens, they are always by your side.
We trust each other, we help each other, and make a commitment to
be friends.
More than friends but a family member.
 —*Young Brothers Group*, ages 7–12

Being a Sister

You don't have to be blood related, but you have to treat others like
family and with love and respect.
Sisters care for one another, accept each other for who they are, and
help one another when they are down.
Sisters are supportive, dependable, and trustworthy when times are
tough.
 —*Young Sisters Group*, ages 7–12

During a chapter's third year, each member writes an *Oath of Dedication* about his or her personal beliefs, aspirations, and commitments. Because they express high hopes and anticipate having to overcome many obstacles, oaths are strong in their conviction. One young woman writes, "I promise not to tolerate sexism. There will be no living soul to tell me that I cannot do anything because of my gender." Another sister asks, "Why can't I be recognized as a person equal to Whites and men, instead of being seen as a person who has to struggle to be equal?" A young brother writes:

My dream in this life is to be a supportive father to my children. To be a provider for them financially and emotionally. I want to ensure them a life where they will be nurtured and loved. I want to pass on to them what The Brotherhood has taught me. To be a Brother, Leader, and a Man. . . . As the Freedom Fighter George Jackson said, "They will never count me among the broken men."

Like rites of passage traditions of the African diaspora, we publicly celebrate completion of the *Mission Statement*, *Definitions*, and *Oaths of Dedication*. We frame and hang them above our first-floor fireplace mantel, keeping our members' core principles at center and providing constant reminders to them of their own words.

CREATING A CULTURE OF RESPECT

Everything we do is educational. A young person may not remember a lesson, but will not forget the example an adult set (good or bad) or the time she or he took to listen. Our staff makes intentional choices about seemingly small issues, hoping that, like repetitious lyrics, our messages wind their way into our members' thinking and actions. Most important to us is maintaining a limited membership and low member-to-staff ratio because intimacy supports relationship-building. Our staff also goes through a rigorous screening process, and once involved, continuously explores our curriculum issues.

We remind members and others to use the full name of the organization, or Bro/Sis for short. It may be a small battle, but one that means the sisters are not excluded. Throughout our brownstone and in our newsletter are words and images depicting, for example, physically strong women or representing opinions of gay members.

One of our core tenets is that we do not allow our members to use the words *nigger*, *bitch*, or *faggot* while participating in Bro/Sis activities, and we facilitate workshops on the origins of these words and their endurance today. Some of our members come away dedicated to removing these words from their conversation, others with new knowledge but unconvinced that the words are negative, especially *nigger*. We understand that it is a process, and continue to challenge their thinking. "No homo" (slang used to make clear that a physical touch between people of the same sex is not sexual) is met with: What do you mean by that? How do you feel knowing your words may be hurtful to someone in our space? Admittedly, our members do not want their casual words to carry so much meaning, but we want to interrupt the soundtracks and images in their minds and have them consciously examine what has become the norm so as to no longer be observed. More than that, we want them to rewrite the script.

A 15-year-old sister from Lyrical Circle came to the brownstone one day. She was frustrated that her teachers only taught about Betsy Ross's role in the American Revolution as flag maker and asked, "Where were the women warriors?" Her teacher told her there are not many women leaders in history, and that they are not in the history books. The sister asked a staffperson if this was true, and rather than give her an answer, together they compiled a list of names for her to research in our library. Her findings became a poem she later read on *Decipher* (WPFW 89.3FM, Washington, DC) during a show about women revolutionaries.

THE JOURNEY IS WHAT MATTERS

Sister Sol members are defining a womanhood that is independent, strong, and about self-respect and sisterhood. During a Sister Sol retreat with the theme "Will the real women please stand up?", they share appreciation for having several women in their life to whom they look up. In time they may walk in similar paths, as one writes, while becoming her own woman. A member reflects, "our chapter leaders [are] teaching us the numerous, countless ways to be a sister but they are [also] teaching us how to spread and share sisterhood."

Young sisters are therefore beginning to see other females as allies. One member says, "I changed my attitude toward girls. I didn't like girls. I didn't get along with girls. Sister Sol helped me be friendly with girls." We are seeing an impact on one of the most difficult female-to-female relationships, mothers and daughters: "Hearing about these stories and being here without my mother made me realize that I have to lighten up on my relationship with my mother." They are also taking to heart lessons about gender privilege and understanding how females support sexism. A member admits, "I was not a feminist before joining the program because if someone used the 'b' word I wouldn't have said anything." Another says, "Being in Sister Sol [I know] those words are meant to disrespect you when it comes to gender." The young women are also learning to be more comfortable with their fathers through talking to Brotherhood staff.

Here there is a space for young women to honestly and confidentially explore their sexuality. Young gay women have felt safe to come out. Only one Sister Sol member has become a parent before graduating from high school, but others have said that without Sister Sol they would have been pregnant with a child and not gone to college. They are therefore making decisions about how they use and enjoy their bodies, and are creating self-determined lives.

Brotherhood members sit around a campfire during their retreats and freely express their most private thoughts to each other. They cry without shame and embrace a manhood that is vulnerable and empathetic. A brother reflects, "I felt that when everyone spoke they recited words that came directly from the heart. The level of respect, humor, and love made the heartfelt tears feel more comfortable." Khary remembers a particular subway ride with 15 of his chapter members. They enter the train and he sees the facial and body language of many riders immediately get tight. But as members depart at their separate stations and say good-bye and "I love you" to each other, the riders no longer know what to think because, just moments before, our members' presence had instilled fear in them.

Our young men are fully aware that we live in a sexist world and that they largely benefit from the privilege of being male. They are accepting that boys and men must do anti-sexist work. Their *Mission Statements*, *Definitions*, and *Oaths* speak to this awareness, as do their writings. "While my mother has taught me to respect women, the message was even more powerful from [Brotherhood]," a member writes. Brothers are thoughtful about how they treat girls and women of all ages, and are careful not to use their physical strength over females. They talk about finding a "strong woman who respects herself," as they describe it. They know that violence—whether physical or verbal and especially against females—is not acceptable, and they must find nonaggressive ways to resolve conflict.

It is incredibly meaningful for young men to bond with their immediate elders. One member writes, "I have been given two wise men that came as gifts of how to be a man and brothers that give love." Young men who are now fathers are honoring their responsibility and rejecting sexist norms. This might be the lesson BHSS has passed on to them best, that men must care for their children, that women should not be the sole providers.

There is also space within BHSS for gay or questioning brothers. A Brotherhood staff remembers how protective a particular chapter was of its gay members, all of whom felt comfortable participating in sleepover activities together. Many young men would object to having to share a room with someone who is gay.

MY SISTER/MY BROTHER/MYSELF

Our single-sex space was most definitely enhanced with our expansion into a coeducational organization. Young brothers and sisters come face-to-face to confront their ideas about gender, sexuality, and double standards rather than perceive them as only abstract concepts. Through bonding with the opposite sex, they are learning how to create respectful and loving cross-gender relationships. They are forced to come to terms with their ideas about gender because clichés—a sexually active girl is a "freak" or "niggas ain't shit"—cannot be held up, because here are young people who are struggling to live by their *Definitions*.

Here also are adults of both sexes expressing respect, commitment, and caring. Our members share with staff of the opposite sex secrets that have filled their lives with shame. Young brothers talk of admiring the leadership and fearlessness of Sister Sol staff and appreciate just being able to chill with them. Young sisters see examples of dedication and nurturance in Brotherhood staff. They see that confronting sexism and misogyny is not "women's work," no more than addressing racism is the work of people of color alone—but instead is the work of everyone who cares about social justice.

We have obviously also had our struggles. When Sister Sol was created, we worked hard to change our materials so that "he" would not simply be replaced with "she." There was much forethought put into defining young women's specific needs and interests. But the Brotherhood set the tone for rites of passage activities. When young women did not go through the experience as quickly as the brothers—to sisters, *Mission Statements* and *Definitions* are like statements of achievement, whereas to brothers, they are a goal—it was a struggle to collectively appreciate the women's process.

Whether the members are youth or staff, female or male, BHSS's objective is to create a "participatory space for the sharing of knowledge" about how sexism and misogyny are experienced and reinforced (hooks, 1994, p. 15), observing these issues broadly in society and up close in our personal lives and being critical of our beliefs and actions. BHSS is where young people are free to speak their truths and acknowledge their mistakes. A Brotherhood chapter leader says our members should at least be saying to themselves: "I'm trying to do my best. This is what I think and I'm trying to understand why." As it should be, our members have the final word:

> I kept climbing [the mountain] and it got harder, but Cidra [associate director/chapter leader] was singing and so were the other girls. That motivated me and encouraged me to keep going. And finally when I reached the top it was a sense of worth and accomplishment. I can compare climbing a mountain to life because I set goals for myself and reaching my goals haven't and will not be easy. I set a goal for myself a long time ago and now I'm graduating from high school, despite all the negativity and obstacles. Sisterhood keeps me going, God keeps me going, and I keep me going.
> —Sister Sol member

> I will not let fear, guilt, laziness, or anything else hold me. I will do what I need to do for me, my family, and all my brothers and sisters that are not blood. I will be mentally strong, physically strong, and spiritually strong. I will be a man.
> —Brotherhood member

NOTES

For more information on The Brotherhood/Sister Sol, log onto www.Brotherhood-SisterSol.org or call 212.283.7044.

1. Findings from a comprehensive evaluation of The Brotherhood/Sister Sol (Castle & Arella, 2003) show that our members describe the organization as "like a family" and a "second home."

2. Most of the quoted remarks from Bro/Sis members, unless otherwise noted, can be found in Lazarre-White (2001).

3. Akinyele [Crystal Johnson]. 1996. "Put It In My Mouth" on *Put It In My Mouth*. Volcano Records.

CHAPTER 12

And Who Gets
to Define "Freedom"?

An Exchange on the Sunflower County
Freedom Project—May–June 2005

William Ayers
Chris Myers Asch

The first part of the following chapter is a description of the Sunflower County Freedom Project written by Chris Myers Asch. It is followed by an exchange of letters between Asch and Bill Ayers.

FREEDOM PROJECT HISTORY

Sunflower County, Mississippi, was home to both Fannie Lou Hamer, the legendary civil rights leader, and Senator James O. Eastland, the spiritual leader of the segregationists. In 1962, the Student Nonviolent Coordinating Committee (SNCC) began to organize there. SNCC worker Charles McLaurin, a native Mississippian, traveled the rural backroads to get poor, Black sharecroppers to register to vote. One of his most important recruits was Fannie Lou Hamer. In August 1962, she and more than a dozen other Blacks went to the courthouse in Indianola to register, but they were denied. That night, Hamer's boss learned about her registration attempt and urged her to withdraw her application, but Hamer refused. In retaliation, he evicted her the next day.

Sunflower County schools were not integrated until after the Civil Rights Act of 1964 tied federal funding to desegregation. The first Black students to attend formerly all-White schools in the county were the eight children of Mae Bertha Carter, whose incredible story is recounted in *Silver Rights* (Curry, 1995). Once they realized the Black students were not going to be intimidated out of the schools, White families organized private academies for their children. To this day, these academies remain more than 95% White and cater to nearly all the White children in the county.

Founded in 1998 by a group of parents, students, and teachers, the Sunflower County Freedom Project was created to improve education and develop leadership among young people in Sunflower County. The founders were frustrated with the low academic achievement, high dropout rates, and other problems in the local schools. Taking the Freedom Schools of the 1960s as a model, they developed an academic program that used the history and spirit of the 1960s freedom struggle to inspire young people to become capable and compassionate leaders in their communities.

The Freedom Project began slowly, initially offering a 5-week, full-day academic enrichment program to 30 middle-school students in the summer of 1999. Held at Mississippi Delta Community College in Moorhead, that first Freedom School was such a success that the parents and grandparents on the board of directors demanded that it be expanded for the summer of 2000. In early June 2000, the Freedom Project began a 7-week program with more than 50 middle schoolers, including 20 who had participated in the first summer; the next year, it continued to expand.

After Freedom School 2001, the Freedom Project staff, students, and directors began to reassess the future. They recognized their limitations. No matter how intensive the Freedom School was, it remained a summer program; until they provided such programs year-round, students would continue to face overwhelming obstacles without enough support and guidance. They decided to make a long-term, year-round commitment to excellence with the Freedom Fellowship.

Beginning in 2002, the Freedom School became the cornerstone of the year-round Freedom Fellowship, including weekday study sessions, Saturday School, and educational field trips. This fellowship will ensure that all Freedom Project students graduate from high school on time and enter college by providing academic enrichment, mentoring, community service, and martial arts training all year long. Freedom Project students will become recognized, respected young leaders whose efforts will inspire positive changes in their schools and communities.

On joining the Fellowship, students sign the following commitment:

1. I commit to LOVE.
   a. I will love and respect myself, my teachers, and other Freedom Fellows.
   b. I will consider the consequences of my actions as they affect the Freedom Fellowship and future Freedom Fellows.

2. I commit to EDUCATION.
   a. I will attend at least one weekday study session with the Freedom Project every week and I will attend Saturday Freedom School every time it is offered. I will participate in the Freedom Fellowship's annual summer enrichment programs.
   b. I will have my parents and teachers sign all necessary papers for the Freedom Fellowship.
   c. I will do everything in my power to excel academically. I will assign myself homework even if my teachers do not give me any, and I will do it in a TV-free place.
3. I commit to personal and social ACTION.
   a. I will dress appropriately, participate in class every day, and bring all necessary materials to school and all Freedom Fellowship activities.
   b. I will participate in community service projects and field trips as part of the Freedom Fellowship.
   c. I will do everything in my power to represent the Freedom Fellowship well.
4. I commit to Freedom Fellowship DISCIPLINE.
   a. I will not curse, fight, or engage in any disrespectful behavior. I understand that such behavior will lead to my losing the privilege of being a Freedom Fellow.
   b. I will never use my martial arts training in an aggressive way. I will solve conflicts peacefully.
   c. I will do everything in my power to show self-control and make the Freedom Fellowship the best program it can be.

The best way to get a sense of what the Sunflower County Freedom Project is is to meet one of its students, Carl Parker. A native of Sunflower (population 800), Carl joined the SCFP in the summer of 2000 as a 13-year-old rising seventh grader. Sunflower is not the best place to be a kid. Carl joined the SCFP, as many of its students do, because there simply was not anything else to do in Sunflower, particularly during the summertime. Lacking educational or economic outlets, the area suffers from rampant teen crime, a teenage pregnancy rate 30% higher than the state average, and a graduation rate that hovers around 60%. Children who do graduate generally are unprepared to enter college—the average ACT score for county students is a 15 (equivalent to less than 700 on the SAT). When Carl signed up, the SCFP was solely a summer program. That first summer, Carl took classes that remain the core of the SCFP's first-year program: a reading class that emphasized the civil rights movement, math and writing classes that stressed basic skill development, an oral history course in which he conducted his own interviews with local people, a public speaking class to break him of his painful shyness, and so forth. At the end of the summer, he and his class-mates took a civil rights tour around the South, visiting important sites and meeting movement activists.

By Carl's third summer, the SCFP had expanded into a year-round pro-gram that now requires students and their parents to sign a contract agree-ing to the Commitment to LEAD—Love, Education, Action, Discipline. Students develop these qualities of leadership throughout a three-part aca-demic program:

1. Summer Freedom School, which has grown to 6 weeks and includes an extended stay at the University of Mississippi. After 3 years in the Freedom School, students spread their wings beyond Sunflower County and enjoy programs that Carl and his cohorts pioneered. As a fourth-year student, he spent a summer in Washington, DC, working as an intern for the Brady Center to Prevent Handgun Violence; the follow-ing year, he spent the summer taking classes at Sidwell Friends School. In his sixth year, he was hired by the SCFP to serve as a summer staffer and martial arts instructor.
2. Saturday School, held for 4 hours each week throughout the school year; and
3. Study Sessions, held for 2 hours on weeknights during the school year (students are expected to come at least once a week)

In addition to the intensive academic commitment, Carl and other SCFP students also participate in several important extracurricular programs, including:

1. LEAD Martial Arts: Students engage in mandatory Tae Kwon Do training, which not only offers students a physical outlet for their energy, but also reinforces the self-discipline emphasized in the aca-demic program. After a summer of training, Carl earned his gold belt; 3 years later, he earned his black belt.
2. Sunflower Freedom Troupe: The troupe performs a variety of origi-nal plays about the movement in Mississippi, including performances about the life of Fannie Lou Hamer, the death of Emmett Till, and the struggle to desegregate schools. With the drama troupe, Carl has traveled all over the South teaching audiences about the movement.
3. Media Production: Students on the Media Production Team learn to manipulate technology to create recruitment videos, documentaries, and websites.

By following the same set of students from seventh grade through high school, the Freedom Project aims to ensure that each of its students graduates from high school on time and enters college. With a 6-year record of academic achievement, drama performances, and martial arts proficiency, Carl has become one of the academically capable, socially conscious, and mentally disciplined young leaders whom the organization strives to develop. He is now a student at Berea College in Kentucky, where he won a full scholarship and the 2007 Carter G. Woodson Award for service on campus.

CHRIS AND BILL'S CORRESPONDENCE

Dear Chris,

Reading your materials on The Freedom Project in Sunflower County was, for me, a dissociating experience. I found the accounts of the project inspiring and discouraging at once—both bold and overcautious, promising and pessimistic. I was divided, ambivalent, and I'll try here to begin to sort out those discordant reactions.

Your project names the civil rights movement of the 1960s as progenitor. The original "Prospectus for a Summer Freedom School Program," written by Charlie Cobb in 1963, claimed that while the Black children of Mississippi were deprived of many things, the fundamental injury was "a complete absence of academic freedom, and students are forced to live in an environment that is geared to squashing intellectual curiosity, and different thinking." Cobb concluded that "If we are concerned with breaking the power structure, then we have to be concerned with building up our own institutions to replace the old, unjust, decadent ones which make up the existing power structure."

This is a proud lineage to be sure, a heritage worth claiming, and, of course, an inspirational moment to celebrate. But perhaps this is where I begin to lose the thread of your efforts, for celebration is not emulation. SNCC organizers understood that all education is political, that there is no such thing as a neutral education. Education stands *for* something and *against* something else. SNCC was educating for the uprooting of an oppressive system, and they said so.

The curriculum included an academic component as well as arts, recreation, and cultural activities, but the core was what they called the "Citizenship Curriculum," a sustained inquiry into politics and society. How prominent was this core aspect? In the published version, the academic part takes up two pages, the citizenship section 25 pages.

The "Citizenship Curriculum" is a question-asking, problem-posing affair:

1. Why are we (teachers, students) in Freedom Schools?
2. What is the Freedom Movement?
3. What alternatives does the Freedom Movement offer us?

The Sunflower County Freedom Project looks to the original Freedom Schools as "a model of motivational education"; they offer "an academic program that used the history and spirit of the 1960s freedom struggle to inspire young people to become capable and compassionate leaders in their communities." Worthy goals perhaps, but if the original Freedom Schools had followed that logic, they would have been isolated from any larger social movements or any critical and transformative goals, urging students to conform to the existing social order and drawing inspiration, not from the wrongs apparent in front of their eyes, nor from social and political upheaval swirling around them, but from looking backward at, for example, post–Civil War Reconstruction.

The 1964 Freedom School Curriculum was based on dialogue—teachers listened, asked questions, assumed that their students were the real experts on their own lives: Why? What's the problem? What's the evidence? How do you know? Is that fair or right? What are you going to do about it? It was a pedagogy of lived experience with the goal of allowing people to collectively question and then challenge their circumstances and situations.

The problems we face today are unique in some ways, but perhaps we can learn from the stance of the movement as it encouraged students (including community members) to come together to identify obstacles to their full humanity, to examine the world—social, political, cultural, historical, and even economic dimensions—naming those aspects in need of repair, and to mobilize to act on behalf of what their newfound knowledge demands.

I can see the academic emphasis in your project, Chris, but where is the social action aspect? I can see the deep desire for individuals to better themselves through learning, but where is the naming of a system that stands in the way?

Sincerely,

Bill [Ayers]

* * *

Dear Bill,

As I think about how to respond to your ideas, I recognize both the strengths and weaknesses of our organization, as well as the opportunities and limitations of the context in which we operate. I offer in response some thoughts on what "freedom" means at the SCFP.

You are right to note that the SCFP celebrates and takes inspiration from the civil rights movement in general and the Student Nonviolent Coordinating Committee in particular. We want our kids to know the whos and the whats and, most importantly, the whys of the movement. We want our young people to hear the voices of older people who made the movement real, people in their own communities and their own families who took risks and hastened revolutionary changes in Sunflower County and the rest of Mississippi. We want them to understand the obstacles that people in the movement faced and to recognize that the movement's success was not foreordained but required patient, often dangerous, usually tedious work. During their first summer in the program, students read Anne Moody's *Coming of Age in Mississippi*, they conduct oral history interviews with community members involved in the movement, and they take a trip to visit key sites such as Selma, Montgomery, Birmingham, and Memphis. Students in our Media Production class are currently in the process of planning and creating an interactive website that will include videotaped interviews, a movement map, and a narrative history of the struggle in Sunflower County. Our drama troupe has a collection of four original plays about the Mississippi movement.

But the knowledge of the history is just a beginning, a way to give kids a vocabulary of freedom and an appreciation of the movement's impact. We want our kids to know about the struggles that came before them not so that they can spout names and dates but so that they can be inspired to make changes in their own lives and communities today. We do not hope to re-create the original Freedom Schools, which arose in response to a specific set of circumstances, nor do we seek only to look backward at a bygone era.

We operate in a different context from the original Freedom Schools. Today, there is no unified, discernible mass social movement that has captured the national imagination; without vivid enemies such as Bull Connor or James Eastland, there is less clarity about whom or what to fight; there are any number of worthy causes, from environmentalism to AIDS prevention, that demand our attention. In such a context, the SCFP can appear to be one exceedingly small, community-based organization in one rural county, isolated from other organizations and focused on apolitical academics.

Despite the lack of a mass movement, however, the SCFP is indeed part of a political effort to change the nature of education in this country. Along with national organizations such as Teach for America, nationwide programs such as Bob Moses' Algebra Project, and the Knowledge Is Power Program schools, we seek to use education as a lever of social change, a means of leveling the playing field to give all children a real chance to achieve their version of success.

Education, as you note, can never be neutral, and we use it to promote a particular vision of the world, a world where citizens have the educational foundation necessary to think freely, participate politically, advocate for themselves, and make informed decisions about the course of their lives.

The core of our academic program is reading. In each of the 6 years that students are in our program, they read five novels from a book list designed both to expose them to some of the best literature in the English language and to get them to question the assumptions of their society and their lives. First- and second-year students read books such as George Orwell's *Animal Farm* and Chinua Achebe's *Things Fall Apart*; third- and fourth-years read, among other books, Mark Twain's *Adventures of Huckleberry Finn* and Lorraine Hansberry's *Raisin in the Sun*; fifth- and sixth-years read from a list that includes *The Autobiography of Malcolm X* and Shakespeare's *Macbeth*. In addition to reading, we focus on the other two "Rs"—'riting and 'rithmetic—and we offer project-based classes such as public speaking and media production. Our writing class emphasizes current events—students debate issues from the Palestinian-Israeli conflict to affirmative action, and they analyze news articles, political cartoons, and televised debates. Far from being "backward-looking," our kids spend more time discussing Baghdad than Selma.

The teaching methods we use in these classes are similar to those you described from the original Freedom Schools—an emphasis on dialogue and discussion (though with a stronger writing component), constant Socratic questioning, consistent comparisons and contrasts to students' lived experience. This approach forces students not only to read and comprehend the books or news articles—essential academic skills—but also to relate the material to themselves and their everyday lives.

So we are *for* using education to raise academic achievement and build students' critical thinking skills, but what are we *against*? Sadly, we are against the same kind of educational culture that Charlie Cobb wrote about and that still reigns dominant in the Mississippi Delta and elsewhere in America. As Cobb noted, the segregated culture of Mississippi in the 1960s extended far beyond simply the school system and included everything from television to newspapers to politics, all of which sought to prepare young Black students for a second-class life. Similarly, the SCFP challenges a larger culture that patronizes Black children and encourages them to accept and even seek out limited achievement.

But our students' lived experience reveals that the nature of the culture against which they must struggle has changed markedly. It is no longer the Ku Klux Klan or the Citizens Council that are killing Black youth—it is the Gangsta Disciples and other gangs that have infiltrated Black neighborhoods, rural and urban. It is no longer racist White school officials who seek to limit Black academic success—Black superintendents, principals, and teachers often run schools that tolerate, rationalize, and even promote low achievement among Black students. It is no longer a segregated admissions policy that keeps Black kids out of college—it is students' woeful underpreparation, which is itself a product both of poor public schools and a negative peer culture.

What is this culture? It is a culture of complacency and consumerism, one that glorifies anti-intellectualism and mocks academic achievement. Black students who push themselves academically face a barrage of negative attacks on their motives, their abilities, and their racial sincerity in the halls of their schools. The fact that these charges come from fellow Black students (and even adults!) only makes the struggle more difficult, because any challenge to them brings more charges of race betrayal.

Where is the social action, you ask? In a world that consistently expects Black students to do poorly, academic achievement *is* social action. Giving kids solid academic skills *is* promoting social change, because academically capable, socially conscious, and mentally disciplined young people are what our communities need to effect long-term change.

The SCFP is a small but sustained effort to create the leadership base for lasting change. The original Freedom Schools were extraordinary, but they were also short-lived—a few schools managed to live on through the summer of 1965, but not beyond that. We are still here long after our first summer, and we follow kids through the ups and downs of the school year and their school careers. We are doing the tedious "spadework" akin to organizing. It may not be glamorous, perhaps, but it is necessary.

Sincerely,

Chris

*   *   *

Dear Chris,

I agree that the civil rights movement in general and SNCC in particular provide important lessons and powerful inspiration for those of us engaged in struggles for freedom and justice today. Just what those lessons are and how they might instruct us in our contemporary contexts is, however, necessarily contested space—the movement itself was, after all, contentious and conflicted, even though the official story is often sanitized and defanged.

It's true that the work of organizing (and teaching) is mostly patient, step-by-step, and day-by-day. Glamour is neither a goal nor a particularly favorable circumstance in most cases, but rather an affliction attached to some good work after the myth-makers and the icon-builders have got hold of it.

I agree that while the children of poor and disadvantaged or oppressed communities—whether in the Mississippi Delta, the west side of Chicago, the South Bronx, or the Navajo Nation—are deprived of many things, the most profound loss is the deprivation of the right to think. The assault on think-ing—on being able to look at the world through one's own eyes, to name it, to decide for oneself what is fair and just and true, to question one's circumstances, to wonder about alternatives—is the deepest and most lasting injury.

And I admire what I understand to be the core of your academic pro-gram. Reading important books, conversation with committed and passion-ate teachers, writing and speaking, comparing and contrasting—all of this strikes me as necessary and valuable.

That said, I don't think that academic achievement is social action, nor that giving kids solid academic skills is in itself promoting social change. It depends.

For one thing, this implies a theory of social change that is a bit anemic. For another, we have before us example after example of academically tal-ented people who do terrible things in the world. In an earlier time, Henry Kissinger was a poster boy of sorts for an intellectual giant who was at once a moral midget, a big brain with a shriveled heart. And today we have the touching stories of Condoleeza Rice, Colin Powell, Clarence Thomas, and Alberto Gonzales, each a story of humble beginnings and real obstacles over-come in a march toward huge achievements. Their stories, however, don't point even tangentially toward social justice.

A struggle for justice is always in part a process of identifying overt or hidden structures of oppression—including law, institutional regularities and practices, power, bureaucratic inertia—and then organizing collective oppo-sition to those structures. People may internalize all kinds of oppressive ideas and embody a range of oppressive behaviors, and these ideas and behaviors may warrant attention and action, but absent a central focus on the *structures* of oppression, that attention tends to blame the victims, and tacitly, then, to support the status quo. Conversely, challenging the structures of oppression opens an imaginative space for an expanding sense of possibility.

I'm unconvinced by your discussion of a pervasive "negative peer cul-ture," an approach that strikes me as one-sided and borrowing too heavily on the received wisdom of the moment. Of course society always envies, worships, despises, and idolizes youth. In Shakespeare, a character bemoans the ages from 10 to 3 and 20, for there is nothing in between, he claims, except getting girls pregnant, fighting, and insulting the elders. Youth culture itself is always a contested space, and in Chicago, for example, the smartest youth organizers I know have tapped into that culture as it rejects the values of mainstream society, mobilizing youth to create their own public spaces, their own arts and culture centers, their own campaigns to fight for jobs, decent schools, and justice.

In any case, gangs are not a new phenomenon in poor communities, nor are the corrosive components of gang culture. Complacency, consumerism, low expectations and low achievement enforced by members of the op-pressed community itself—none of this is new. These were among the con-ditions faced by SNCC, the Black Panthers, and every other freedom struggle I know.

Racism still exists, still stands poised like a dagger at the heart of Ameri-can democracy. The schools are still segregated, and still terrible for poor kids of color. Large numbers of Black people are still disenfranchised in Mississippi and elsewhere. Black youth are overrepresented in juvenile court and youth detention, Black men are entangled in the justice system and the prisons at astronomical rates, chronic unemployment impacts Black fami-lies disproportionately. So what *is* new?

What's new is that legal segregation has been dismantled—a huge and important victory paid for with the courage, blood, sacrifice, steady effort, and hard work of countless people and whole communities over decades. It's right to honor that legacy; it's essential to build upon it. And building upon it includes examining the structural obstacles to freedom today, bring-ing them to light, mobilizing people to resist, confront, overcome.

One final note: the so-called Sixties is largely a myth—a collection of clichés—handed down as a brake on contemporary activists and today's struggles. What could be more depressing than longing for a ship that long ago left the shore? The received wisdom includes the notion that political struggle was wildly popular, the fantasy that everything—enemies, goals—was clear-cut, the illusion that the path forward was obvious. As you point out, Chris, nothing was foreordained. All that unanimity is imposed *ex post facto*. Internal disagreements were intense, goals murky and contested. Martin Luther King Jr.'s "Letter from a Birmingham Jail" was addressed to his fel-low clergy who did not support the struggle. King's speeches from 1965 to 1968 are neither triumphalist nor optimistic; they are the words of an angry and oft-defeated pilgrim calling for revolution. Revolution is still what we need. A revolution in values, as King advocated again and again, a revolu-tion against war and racism and consumerism, a revolution for peace, com-munity, and a world in balance.

Sincerely,

Bill

*   *   *

Bill,

Thanks for another compelling assessment of the SCFP. I appreciate your perspective and your suggestions, and I already find myself thinking more broadly and deeply about what it is that we do here at the SCFP. Let me now endeavor to address some of your concerns.

We agree that education alone is not sufficient for social justice. You note many brilliant but blind leaders, highly credentialed people who probably could score well on today's ubiquitous standardized tests yet could not muster the courage to fight blatant injustice in their hometowns. I also would point out the flip side—"uneducated" people who let neither their lack of schooling nor their unlettered grammar deter them from pushing for positive social changes in their communities. In Mississippi, of course, Fannie Lou Hamer stands out as a prime example.

Yet, while we may agree that academic achievement is not sufficient, I would argue that it *is* necessary, not simply laudable. The world in which our students are growing up is vastly different from the one that Hamer faced, and not solely because legal segregation has been dismantled. In Hamer's time, young people growing up in impoverished areas could expect to make a living—harsh, to be sure, but a living nonetheless—doing field work, domestic labor, or industrial jobs that required little or no formal education. Those opportunities are long gone. "Freedom" is meaningless if people do not have the ability to provide for themselves and their families.

You may agree with this assessment of our students' future prospects. Where we likely disagree is in our diagnosis of the primary source of future obstacles. Racism, you write, "stands poised like a dagger at the heart of American democracy," and you identify various structural obstacles, from law to bureaucratic inertia, as key barriers that require collective action to overcome. As we see it at the SCFP, the dagger pointed at the heart of our kids' America is not just external racism (an amorphous, catch-all phrase that explicates little) but internal apathy and underachievement. This diagnosis is not "borrowed" from the "received wisdom of the moment" (another catchy phrase that obscures more than it illuminates); it derives instead from our students' experiences in their schools and their daily lives.

Our different diagnoses of what is ailing our students lead us to different conclusions on what measures would be best to combat the problems. "Absent a central focus on the *structures* of oppression," you argue, a program such as ours that emphasizes academics and directly addresses the anti-intellectual, self-destructive mentality that undermines academic achievement in the Delta will wind up "blaming the victim" and upholding the status quo. Musing about the nature of academic success or what it means to be an American is no substitute for skill development; discussing the connections between Hanoi and Sunflower can be edifying, but such talks alone cannot sustain a program for any significant length of time or produce the kind of long-term social changes we both envision.

While I may be attracted to your kind of questioning, I nonetheless recognize the practical limitations of an ideological approach to education. The SCFP often attracts well-intentioned, even radical students who arrive in

Sunflower ready to teach kids how to fight institutional racism, how to discern bias in mainstream media, how to challenge the "received wisdom" of our leaders. Then, they arrive in the classroom and face the reality of kids who can barely read a newspaper article. Sometimes, in their ideological zeal, they refuse to alter their basic approach, and they seek to indoctrinate students into their way of thinking through heavy-handed methods and leading questions. The more effective teachers, however, learn to work with students where they are.

The SCFP emphasizes old-fashioned academic achievement because we believe that it provides a solid foundation on which a constructive life of community engagement, civic leadership, and responsible parenting can be built. Long-term social change requires capable citizens able not simply to advocate and "resist" but to create and build. We do not want our students to become "activists" per se, but we do want them to be contributing citizens—people who vote, who raise honorable children, who voluntarily pick up litter in the streets, who help out at the local library, who coach Little League, who look out for neighborhood kids as they would their own. We want to teach them the solid values that rural Mississippi taught generations of young children—respect for elders, family, and community; perseverance in the face of adversity; faith in oneself, one's country, and one's creator. To demand that poor children in Mississippi work hard, achieve academically, respect themselves and their communities, and show self-discipline is not "blaming" them; on the contrary, it honors their humanity by holding them to high standards.

A key assumption in our effort, a dirty little secret that may not be fashionable in certain circles, is really quite simple: Opportunity exists in this country, for poor kids as well as rich, for Black kids as well as White, for rural kids as well as urban. Forty years ago, White mobs rioted to prevent the integration of the University of Mississippi; today, Ole Miss bends over backward to provide scholarships and access for Black students. Forty years ago, Black applicants had little hope of landing a job that paid more than subsistence wages; today, companies crave a diverse workforce (even if only for PR purposes) and battle each other for the right to hire qualified Black employees. Forty years ago, Black Mississippians could only dream of controlling the basic institutions and levers of power in their communities; today, Black officials run countless towns, public school systems, and courtrooms throughout the state. Denying the multitude of opportunities available to young Black Mississippians today not only belittles the power and impact of the civil rights movement, it also cripples young people with a mentality of powerlessness.

By no means do I intend to imply that the movement won, the struggle is over, and America is indeed the colorblind land of opportunity that its leaders often profess it to be. Far from it—if I believed that, I would not have spent most of my adult life working to improve education in rural Mississippi. I recognize, as you surely do, that major, seemingly insurmountable barriers still exist, and they loom higher the lower you go on the economic ladder. In our daily work with students, we do not deny or dismiss the presence of societal barriers; instead we use those barriers as motivation. Perhaps it's simply a matter of emphasis—we emphasize opportunity over oppression, diligence over discrimination, self-discipline over self-pity.

I can hear the sighs and see saddened heads shaking. The original Freedom Schools, as you accurately observe, consciously sought to undermine an oppressive system and overthrow a social order. They were part of a revolution! The SCFP and other groups like us, alas, seem so small, so limited, even bourgeois by comparison. As inspiring as we may find the movement, we do not believe that SNCC leaders had all the answers and we do not defer to activists of another time and place. The "freedom struggle" is not static; its means and ends shift over time as contexts change and people adapt to new circumstances.

One lesson in particular that we have internalized is that the turn to radicalism in the late 1960s, while perhaps understandable given the implacability of powerholders and their continued resistance to change, nonetheless was a self-destructive tangent from which many on the left have yet to return. In their attacks on capitalism, their physical assaults on individuals and institutions, and their self-righteous rejection of American ideals, some radical activists alienated many of the very people they hoped to unite for the revolution. Aaron Henry, a native Mississippian who remained active in local politics long after movement leaders left the state, expressed frustration that activists refused to recognize that most Blacks in Mississippi did not want, as he put it, "to destroy the middle class but rather to join it and be like them, to share in the comforts conferred by that status" (Henry & Curry, 2000, p. 202).

Henry spoke of aspiring to be "middle-class" and achieving "the American dream"—words that led him to be branded a "Tom" and still might elicit mocking laughter in many activist circles even today. Yet that is precisely what we hope to give our students—a real chance to achieve the American dream. In some ways, this approach does indeed hark back to activists of another era—the activists of the 1950s and early 1960s who sought inclusion into American society, not a rejection of it. It was out of this culture of activism, not the one that followed, that the sit-in movement and Freedom Schools grew. Like those determined citizens who courageously waved the American flag and sought to make this country live out the true meaning of its creed, the SCFP seeks liberation not *from* America but *for* America.

This discussion of ours reminds me of a sharp exchange I witnessed between two aging SNCC veterans at the 40th anniversary of the founding of the organization. A young Black man, a senior at Shaw University, asked what he could do, upon graduation, to contribute to "the movement." The first SNCC member encouraged him to pursue graduate work or to begin some productive career, make a decent living, buy a house, raise a strong family, and become a solid citizen in the community. That, the civil rights activist assured, would be the most important contribution to the movement today. From the back of the room came a piercing cry of "No!" from a silver-haired SNCC veteran who proceeded to outline all the reasons why America was too corrupt a society for such an approach. What was needed, he insisted, was a revolution that would tear down the institutional barriers to Black achievement in this country.

The young man was left bewildered, as was I. What to make of such advice? Was the second SNCCer—a highly respected activist—arguing that to work hard and achieve success was akin to selling out or preserving the status quo? If so, what alternatives would he suggest? Do we not want qualified Black doctors and scientists and Secretaries of State? Is that not progress, even if not the ideal world we wish to see?

Chris

* * *

Dear Chris,

There's really no point in repeating that SCFP is small and limited—with what seems, incidentally, like an unwarranted defensiveness. I certainly have no problem with small or limited. In fact, every great work I can think of in history—the American Revolution, emancipation, suffrage for women—was small, marginal, and limited at its inception. Indeed, Martin Luther King Jr.'s organization was small, SNCC was tiny, and the Highlander Folk School a couple of little buildings on an insignificant hill in Tennessee. You may be arguing with someone else on this question of small and limited, but you'll get no criticism from me for your modest size.

Further, students need academic skills, and again, we have no argument about this. We need to set high standards for all of our students, and make them aware of the language of power that opens many of the doors of opportunity. Youngsters need to learn to read widely and well, and to write and speak with clarity and courage; they need to become confident masters of the language of mathematics; they need to learn to think for themselves and to have minds of their own. All of this is critical for full and active participation in the world as we find it, as well as for the world that will necessarily be created by the coming generation. As the blues legend Willie Dixon sang, "We need to know better in order to do better."

I don't see a contradiction, as you seem to, between asking deep, critical, and probing questions of the world and teaching academic skills. Posing powerful questions and pursuing them to their furthest limits does not have to be mere musing—a dreamy kind of waste of time—nor does it have to compete with or become a substitute for skill-building. Indeed, the best teachers tend to tackle the latter with energy and commitment in light of the former. I know a group of fifth graders in Chicago, for example, who decided with their teacher to investigate the dilapidated condition of their school building; they approached the inquiry with investment and passion, and 9 months later, when they were given a civic leadership award, they could also note with pride that each had learned to write better; to do sustained library research; to get a range of information from the Internet; to analyze statistics and present findings with charts and graphs; to speak with clarity to a variety of audiences, including the press, the school board, and the mayor's staff. I know another group of students in California—high school kids—who combed the press every day with their teacher in search of stories they wanted to pursue further; one such exercise led from a seemingly insignificant obituary of a teenager in the Oakland *Tribune* to a study that unearthed the largest illegal smuggling ring of indentured servants in California history—those kids also learned a wealth of skills along the way. We have to teach skills in light of something; why not in light of looking critically at our shared world and then asking questions of the taken-for-granted?

I think you're right to criticize and warn against the kind of sectarianism, dogmatism, and splitism that we engaged in during the 1960s. We should today search diligently for unity among progressive people and forces, and we should build it and tend to it with care and hope. But I think you're mistaken to pick out a single activist (Aaron Henry) whose choices you approve as somehow embodying all the right things to have done at that critical historic moment. Here was the situation: Racism—not an amorphous term really—was morphing once again into new forms but with the same ugly consequences; a foreign war that the majority of Americans opposed continued unabated at the cost of thousands of people murdered every week. What to do? People who lived through that time and believe that they made all the right moves are delusional. Anyone who doesn't have some serious self-criticism is not paying attention.

The sharp exchange you describe between SNCC veterans in response to the Shaw University student's seeking advice might have been more illuminating had someone in that room had the presence to invoke what I think of as the quintessential teacherly response: "What do *you yourself* think, given all you've heard and experienced and thought about, would make a contribution?" That response would have at least taken him seriously as a person with a mind and a heart. "What is the movement today, anyway? In fact, why don't we take a moment and ask every student in the room to describe what the movement is now, and make a list of five ways you might like to make a contribution to it; let's have that guide the rest of our discussion here today." That might even have led to some greater depth and some productive debate, a deeper understanding and a wider range of options. But apparently no one asked these questions, no one engaged the wisdom in the room, and consequently the teachable moment was lost, you left bewildered, and we'll never know.

I don't follow your attack on "an ideological approach to education." I've known many well-intentioned idealists who are terrible teachers, but I've advocated neither indoctrination nor rigid methods nor dogmatic blinders of any kind—quite the contrary. I think much of what masquerades as education in our country is really nothing more than propaganda—top-down, unidirectional, insistent, shrill. If that's what you mean by ideology, I'm against it.

But if by ideology you mean a set of guiding ideas and assumptions, then show me an example of an educational project that's entirely free of ideology. You profess a belief in the American dream, a desire for a level playing field so that winners will be determined more fairly, a sense that opportunity exists for poor, Black, rural kids, and that internal apathy is the primary obstacle to Sunflower County students' success. Isn't that an ideology? If I disagree with you on one or another point, and you accuse me, then, of the sin of being ideological, aren't you assuming that the American dream, the level playing field, and all the rest are just obvious, the kinds of things that every right-thinking person adheres to? Doesn't this end any chance of dialogue, of give and take, of learning?

It took me a long time to realize that the other person's orthodoxy is always glaringly obvious in its gaudy obtuseness, whereas our own dogma has the comforting odor of common sense.
Sincerely,
Bill

*   *   *

Dear Bill,

Amen! Though we certainly have our disagreements, your last letter reveals to me quite a bit of the common ground that underlies our discussion—our shared wariness of dogmatism, our mutual devotion to critical intellectual inquiry, our respect for the complexity and messiness of everyday choices. You may be right to observe that in some ways I am taking issue not with you, Bill Ayers, *per se*, but with some of the strains within progressive education circles.

I would like to comment on your reference to my "defensiveness" about the SCFP's small size and limited scope. The pressure (much of it well intentioned) to serve as a "replicable" model and to expand our operations comes from a variety of places—researchers, funders, activists, our dominant culture. A program is worthy, it seems, only if it can be replicated, franchised, or expanded, as if a community-based organization in itself has little value. Mind you, I do not reject the idea of replication in itself. I am flattered when people ask us for advice on how to create strong, sustainable programs for teenagers, and I believe that we have built our program on essential principles that could apply in a variety of situations. But the current "replication" push seems driven by a desire to find the right formula, the perfect "business model" that can be plopped full-grown into an existing community without having to struggle to figure out a way of one's own. That approach defies the spirit of our effort, which seeks to build on the particular strengths of our community and staff while targeting the specific needs of our particular community. The key is flexibility—as circumstances and students have changed over the years, so have we. We are free to experiment with new ideas, and we do so constantly. This past year, for example, we began an exchange program with a school in Los Angeles to bring L.A. kids to Mississippi for 2 weeks, followed by our kids going to California for a fortnight. If the kids respond to an idea well, we do it again; if the idea falls flat, we try something different. So when people ask if they could set up a "Freedom Project" in their communities, I encourage them to do so, but caution them against merely trying to re-create what we have done in Sunflower County.

Now to your larger arguments. First, you suggest that I see a contradiction between asking probing questions and building academic skills. I certainly hope there is no such contradiction—I might be out of a job! This past spring, our Media Production Team created an interactive video documentary project that is now linked to our website. Entitled "Sankofa," the project tells the story of the civil rights movement in Sunflower County and applies the lessons learned to what young people can do (and are doing) in the area today. The effort required students to conduct primary and secondary research (including several oral history interviews), write concise and accurate text for the web page, and speak confidently to a variety of audiences, from local activists to conference-goers in Cleveland, Ohio. Our drama troupe conducts two tours each year, performing original plays about the movement in Mississippi. In the process of practicing and performing, students become the resident experts on the history they are teaching their audiences. Our last production, "Thirty Years From Now," addressed the dicey topic of school integration (which for all intents and purposes has yet to happen in Sunflower County), and our students performed in front of audiences that included not only sympathetic parents, teachers, and activists, but also a significant number of wealthy community members whose children attend private schools and who even helped establish the White academies that were the subject of the play.

Nonetheless, I will confess to a certain degree of skepticism about the dedication of some progressive educators to pushing high academic achievement. My skepticism emerges not simply from the fact that many progressive educators have spent considerable time and energy combating the push for accountability and higher standards for low-achieving schools, or that their agenda seems to reflect a greater concern for lowering college admission standards than on increasing achievement. Instead, it is has grown from my personal experience with schools and organizations that patronize minority students by refusing to expect them to behave and achieve as decent citizens.

If there is a conceit on the left, it tends toward the romanticization of radicalism and the reification of revolution. Historical figures who worked within "the system" or advocated gradual change are ridiculed as sellouts while their radical counterparts are glorified. On college campuses in particular I find that activists often try to outdo one another in their radicalism, conveying a "more activist than thou" attitude that can turn committed, socially conscious people away from progressive causes. Programs, such the Freedom Project, that advocate academic achievement and other traditional goals get belittled or dismissed as "mainstream."

Finally, you argue that the SCFP, like all educational endeavors, is itself ideological. Indeed, you are right—as our exchange can attest, we have a strong sense of who we are and what we hope to instill in our students, and we certainly have a guiding set of assumptions and ideas. By "ideological," I meant a more colloquial (and pejorative) definition that approximates propaganda. If we may agree that much of what "masquerades" as education in America is "top-down, unidirectional, insistent, shrill," I might add that much of what slides by as "progressive" could be dismissed as naïve, unstructured, dogmatic, and ineffective.

And that is where I would like to return to our common ground. I hope that one thing you and I share is a preference for action over rhetoric. One of many "lessons" we have taken from the movement and that we emphasize with our students is the question that SNCC members often asked of Americans in general (and Dr. King in particular, if unfairly): "Where is your body?" Where are you—are you working for the changes you advocate, or are you simply criticizing others' work? Are you on the front lines of change or are you in the rear taking potshots?

My general inclination, and I suspect yours as well, is to respect those folks who are out there working in their own ways to create the world they wish to see. I may not necessarily agree with their strategies, and I may find their approaches ineffective at times, but I honor their efforts. The Freedom Project often winds up on the receiving end of criticism for a variety of apparent shortcomings—we are an organization that works with Black kids but we are run by a White man; we claim to be inspired by the original Freedom Schools but we were not ourselves involved with SNCC; we are not "revolutionary" enough; we read too many books by "dead White men"; and so on. Some of the criticisms are legitimate, and we seek valuable feedback that can help us improve our program—your critique has been quite helpful. But often the criticism seems unproductive, intent only on tearing down rather than building up. At the end of the day, I come back to SNCC's question: Where are you? Are you willing to roll up your sleeves and join us? Are you willing to move to Sunflower County and work with our kids? If not, what are you doing in your own community? Do you know of a better way? Are you pursuing it? If so, in what ways can we learn from one another? If not, why not?

Our students often ask, as they learn about the movement's past, "Where is the movement today?" We answer, in ways both explicit and implicit, in the words of Charles McLaurin, a former SNCC field secretary who still lives in Sunflower County and has served on our board since our inception: "It is in you."

Chris

CHAPTER 13

Project Daniel

A Church-Based Program of Liberation for African American Boys

Michael G. Hayes

Back in 1990, I was a student at the University of Chicago Divinity School while I served in various ministerial capacities at the Apostolic Faith Church located in the Grand Boulevard neighborhood on Chicago's South Side. Because of that combination of occupations, I enjoyed the rare opportunity of peering into two worlds, that of an elite private American university and that of an ailing ghetto. I saw the social isolation that sociologist William Julius Wilson maintains is typical of neighborhoods populated by no one but the permanent underclass (Wilson, 1987). It seemed as though the people of Grand Boulevard might as well have lived in another country, alienated as they were from the mainstream of Chicago life. It was against this backdrop that the story of Daniel's life as told in the book of Daniel spoke to me as the basis for an educational program that would develop the "critical consciousness" of Black boys (Freire, 1973/1998).

When Project Daniel™ was first launched in the summer of 1990, the Grand Boulevard neighborhood of Chicago was a devastated slum. None of the gentrification of recent years was yet under way. It was plausible, walking through the neighborhood in those days, to suppose that some foreign army had taken many of the residents captive in a military campaign. Houses with broken-out windows resembled skulls with empty eye sockets. I often wondered where all the people could have gone to cause so many houses and apartments to be vacant, dilapidated, or destroyed. On 47th Street, once-thriving businesses and department stores from bygone days were barely left standing. Gutted out, these buildings were the largest trash receptacles in Chicago. Many years' accumulation of waste and liquor bottles sat among the rubble in many storefronts. At 2:00 p.m. on a summer day, I used to notice the adults out on the street to catch a breeze. Seemingly, they had nothing better to do.

My aim in using the book of Daniel as the inspiration for a summer-enrichment program was to connect the boys of our community with Daniel and the other Jewish boys, youth in similar circumstances who rose to the challenge of their situation by maintaining their integrity before the Lord. Project Daniel operated from 8:30 a.m. to 3:30 p.m., Monday through Thursday, for 7 weeks during the summer of 1990. It was a summer-enrichment program operated at the Liberty Baptist Church. Sponsors of the program included Apostolic Faith Church and Liberty Baptist, the Chicago Urban League, the Theta Lambda Chapter of the Alpha Phi Alpha Fraternity, as well as local businesses and individual donors. Boys from age 8 to 13 from Liberty Baptist, Apostolic Faith Church, and the neighborhood participated.

The central metaphor of the program was the example of Daniel, which students and counselors studied together during daily devotions. The book of Daniel relates a saga about four young Jewish youths whose lives provide some remarkable parallels to the lives of inner-city Black boys. Bible scholars place the book of Daniel in the literary category of apocalyptic eschatology, a type of literature that typically uses a specific formula: God reveals to a sage or hero the terrible moment when he will end the evil course of human history (the Apocalypse). In its place, God will institute a new epoch in which his righteous, divine order will reign. God will overturn the current corrupt social order to vindicate the oppressed. The way Daniel in the saga receives visions of the Apocalypse is a classic example of the role of the sage in this type of literature. Throughout history, social apocalyptic movements tend to appear as disillusioned groups cry out that the society is crumbling beneath the weight of its own injustice and oppression. Some biblical scholars—notably André LaCocque among them—argue that the book of Daniel was written to encourage Jews to resist assimilation into Greek culture in the second century B.C.E. (LaCocque, 1988). The book is set at the time when the city of Jerusalem was besieged by Nebuchadnezzar's powerful Babylonian army. Nebuchadnezzar captured prisoners from the upper classes and stole sacred vessels from the Temple. Later, because Israel refused to pay tribute to Babylon, Nebuchadnezzar besieged Jerusalem again. This time he burned down the Temple, killed indiscriminately, and took many of the able-bodied into captivity to be slave labor for the empire (Hanson, 1975; LaCocque, 1979). The book's moral is that if God's people remain faithful and do not defile themselves through assimilation, God will use supernatural means to protect them.

As the program's designated curriculum developer, I can say that our daily lessons were developed by intentionally asking the book of Daniel to speak to our present context as males of African descent in America. As I dialogued with the text, certain important themes emerged, which we highlighted week-by-week. I aimed to interweave these themes in an interdisciplinary fashion so that we could follow the theme from subject to subject throughout the day. Devotions were the first activity of the day and were usually half an hour long. Students took turns reading verses of scripture from passages in Daniel. The boys liked the devotions because of the stories of adventure and heroism that fill the book's pages. At times, instead of reading the scriptures, the boys would act them out on the spot.

What follows is a list of devotion synopses with scripture references and the complementary interdisciplinary activities and studies.

WEEK 1: "THE IMPERIAL PROGRAM"

We read an outline of Nebuchadnezzar's program to assimilate and control the captured Jewish youths (cf. Dan 1:1–7). From this, we considered the sociopolitical forces African Americans have had to face as a foreign racial group in American society. While we investigated Daniel's capture and exile into Babylon, we held a simulation of a slave hunt. The counselors "captured" the boys, put them in the hold of a ship, and carried them to the New World to be sold as slaves. After they arrived in the new land, the counselors let them form themselves into small groups. The reason for the exercise was to show the importance of belonging to a community of mutual support. Each tribe, as the groups called themselves, chose an Afrocentric name, designed its own flag, and elected its own leaders for the duration of the program.

During that first week, the boys took in a forum on the topic of racial and gender-role scripting in the American context. As it relates to Black boys, the presentation asserted that the experience of slavery has violated the Black male's gender-role script because he was neither able to protect the Black community as a whole, nor the Black female in particular, from oppression at the hands of White males.

WEEK 2: "REFUSE TO EAT THE KING'S MEAT"

We looked at health in a comprehensive way—physically, mentally, and spiritually—as we read of how the Jewish youths determined that they would only eat healthy kosher foods (cf. 1:5–16). We coupled the devotion discussion about diet and covenant with our own discussion of health. We invited a toxicologist in to speak to us about different substances and their effects on the body. We also discussed maintaining our purity by resisting negative images that bombard us daily through the media. One day we asked the boys to bring in recordings of their favorite popular songs and then together we analyzed them. The most animated discussion surrounded Digital Underground's hit single "The Humpty Dance." The boys shared their feelings about the song's ethic of machismo, expressed in the rapper's cavalier attitude about sex.

WEEK 3: "DEFIANT SPIRITUALITY"

We read about Daniel's defiant spirituality and discussed the importance of maintaining a daily devotion with the Lord despite negative peer pressure (cf. Chapter 6, the Book of Daniel). When Daniel decided to keep a regular hour of devotion, jealous Chaldeans used his religious practice as a snare to get him thrown into the lion's den. Through this episode, we explored the topics of resisting gang pressure and doing the right thing in the face of opposition. We watched a film entitled *Cadillac Dreams* about a young man who sold drugs to capitalize a legitimate business venture, one that he dreamed he might someday launch. The youth in the film got involved in dealing drugs but did not want his younger brother entangled in this lifestyle. After watching the film, one of the boys spoke up and told us about how a gang in his neighborhood was trying to recruit him, and that he resisted only because he did not want his younger brother to follow his example. The film so moved the boys that they decided to adapt it into a play and present it to their parents.

WEEK 4: "WE ONLY BOW TO GOD"

We read and discussed the importance of standing up for one's convictions in spite of unpopularity (cf. Chapter 3, the Book of Daniel). We took this theme from the story of the other Jewish youths, Hananiah, Mishael, and Azariah—better known as Shadrach, Meshach, and Abed-Nego—and their refusal to bow to the golden image that King Nebuchadnezzar had set up in Babylon (cf. Chapter 3, the Book of Daniel). Embedded in this story is a lesson about the attitude the Jewish youths had when they faced unjust opposition. These youths decided that they were not going to bow before the golden statue erected on the plain of Dura, not because by obeying Yahweh they obligated him to protect them, but merely because it was the right thing to do. They told the king that they were confident that God could rescue them from his execution, but if he chose not to do so, they were still not going to bow to the idol. This story complemented the principle of self-determination, which we were studying. We read poetry by African American authors that week. We discussed Langston Hughes's poem "I, Too, Am America," in detail. The poem is about a Black servant who receives ridicule from his White employers because of his inferior social status. The Whites do not know this, but he laughs to himself because he is quietly pursuing a program of self-determination, becoming stronger nourished by the food he eats in the kitchen.

WEEK 5: "TO WHOM MUCH IS GIVEN ... "

We read and discussed the gifts God gave the Jewish youths for keeping themselves ritually pure (cf. 1:17–20). To coincide with the devotional topic of the fifth week, we talked about how we should act because we have an attitude of excellence (cf. 1:17). We discussed the issue of sitting in the front of the room in school, looking at it as a right and a responsibility. We looked at it from a historical perspective that there once was a time when the law did not recognize Black people as equal. We shared the interpretation that "separate but equal" is actually a doctrine of inequality.

WEEK 6: "FAVOR"

For the sixth week, we discussed and defined the biblical term translated as "favor" in the King James translation of the text (cf. 1:9). As the story goes, Daniel receives a reprieve from the royal decree to eat the king's rations because he obtains favor from the royal steward who was responsible for his welfare. In the program, we discussed the importance of presenting oneself in a positive light and how that presentation affects the treatment we receive from others. We used mock employment interviews as an exercise to give ourselves experience in presentation.

While on the topic of presentation, we also looked at language as a medium for performance in the Black cultural idiom. We let everyone take the stage, sharing examples of the various forms of public performance. We talked about another speech act peculiar to Black culture—playing the dozens.[1] We discussed the positive and negative effects of playing the dozens (Smitherman, 1977, p. 82).

WEEK 7: "EXCELLENT SPIRIT"

We reviewed all the attributes that made the Jewish youths the best of their generation (cf. Chapters 1–6, the Book of Daniel). The seventh week was the end of the program, and we used it to review the contents of the other 6 weeks. We summarized the positive behaviors and attitudes of the program in one phrase, "excellent spirit." Several times the text refers to Daniel as a man with an excellent spirit. We tried to coin our own definition of that phrase by saying that it means that whatever obstacle came Daniel's way, he had a spirit to excel above it. We used all these attributes to construct a definition of *manhood* based on the biblical example of Daniel's integrity.

Throughout the program, we studied the Nguzo Saba, what most African Americans know as the seven principles of Kwanzaa. Since there are seven principles, it was convenient to highlight a different principle each week as a focal point of discussion and activities. (The seven principles of the Nguzo Saba are listed in Table 13.1.)

Although we devoted a week to each one of the principles of the Nguzo Saba, Umoja received more attention during the program than the rest. To drive home the importance of unity, we juxtaposed two passages in Daniel to heighten the contrast between the behavior of jealous government officials (cf. Chapter 6) and the behavior depicted by Daniel and his companions (cf. Chapter 2). In Chapter 6, the government officials resent Daniel's rank and authority in the empire. Finding nothing to discredit in his exemplary performance, they conspire to discredit his Jewish faith. They decide to trick King Darius into signing a decree prohibiting worship of any God for 30 days. After Darius signs the decree, the officials easily catch Daniel continuing his daily practice of praying to Yahweh in his chamber. They denounce him before the king for having broken "the unalterable law of the Medes and Persians," and for that transgression, the king has no choice but to throw Daniel into the lion's den.

TABLE 13.1: The Nguzo Saba

PRINCIPLE	PRONUNCIATION	MEANING
Umoja	oo-MOH-jah	Unity
Kujichagulia	koo-jee-cha-goo-LEE-aah	Self-determination
Ujima	oo-JEE-mah	Collective Work & Responsibility
Ujamaa	oo-jah-MAH-ah	Cooperative Economics
Nia	NEE-ah	Purpose
Kuumba	koo-OOM-bah	Creativity
Imani	ee-MAH-nee	Faith

In Chapter 2, Nebuchadnezzar threatens to execute all the royal wise men, including Daniel, for not interpreting his dream. Daniel then shares his predicament with his companions, and together they pray to God for the interpretation of the king's dream.

The lesson we learned from these scriptures is that people denounce someone when they feel threatened by his or her status or abilities, and when they feel inadequate about themselves. To do such a thing is what young people call "hating on" a person. By contrast, when Daniel felt threatened as he faced execution, he went *to* his companions with his problem. When they heard Daniel's story, they prayed together. The bond of brotherhood created a unity of regard and purpose as the Jewish youths entreated God for mercy to reveal the secret to Daniel and spare their lives. We applied this lesson to the program by setting aside time on a weekly basis for community praise. Every week the boys would talk about the positive actions of their companions in the program. Each week we gave special recognition to the boy whose behavior most embodied that week's Nguzo Saba principle. It was our hope that a culture of peer praise would counteract the culture of negative peer pressure. Everyone learned a great deal about Umoja or unity through several experiences of the program. Every morning and afternoon— and sometimes at other points in the day—all the participants in the program would "call all the brothers" to hold hands and join the circle. Any participant in the program had the right to call the brothers for emergencies or community grievances. In the earliest days, the counselors challenged the boys never to break the circle, meaning not to let go of their neighbor's hand for any reason. Sometime later, the saying became symbolic; if someone "broke the circle," it meant he was jeopardizing the welfare of the group for personal gain. In some cases, that person would have to apologize to the group to regain admission to the circle. This ritual took on some of the qualities of a game when the counselors would test the tenacity of the group. Counselors would try to tempt, trick, or bribe the boys to break the circle. If you broke the circle, you had damaged the group's sense of Umoja.

I would like to turn the discussion to the issue of fitting the theology of Project Daniel into the stream of African American theological reflection. What issues are at stake in Project Daniel's reading of the text? What possible confluence exists between the lives of those Jewish youths in the text and the lives of today's African American boys? The image that unites Jerusalem of old with the ghetto of today is the picture of devastation where the men have somehow disappeared from the scene. It is as if, 300 years after their foreparents came here as slaves (cf. II Chron. 36:20), most of the exiles— no longer useful to the empire—have nowhere to turn but the ghetto.

Project Daniel presented a case to the boys that spiritual purity, excellence, and moral integrity are the ingredients of liberation. In so doing, Project

Daniel follows a long-standing tradition of African American biblical interpretation. Gayraud Wilmore, a scholar of the Black religious tradition, stated that leaders of the African American church of the 19th century made some crucial decisions about how they would interpret the experience of slavery. Clergy grappled with the problem of theodicy: How could God be powerful enough to prevent Blacks' oppression, yet permit it? Either God was omnipotent and dualistic (both good and evil) or God was not omnipotent and could not actually protect his people from oppression. The formulators of the Black religious tradition rejected both of these conclusions and opted for another. They pondered the possibility that God had somehow tied their suffering to a greater destiny:

> Certainly, the Black Church of the 19th century had this sense of vocation because our foreparents had the audacity to see themselves in the pages of the Old Testament. They assumed from reading about Israel that God either had a valid reason for the affliction that was somehow related to their African past or a mysterious purpose connected with their future in America, and indeed, beyond America to the future redemption of Africa. This assumption of a vocation, related to American transformation and African redemption, won out in the debate among Black preachers about why it was that a just God permitted them to be enslaved by the very people who were supposed to be their brothers and sisters in Christ. (Wilmore, 1984)

Thus, Blacks returned the verdict that the ordeal they suffered in slavery was part of God's plan for America's redemption.

Project Daniel reflects a powerful strand of the Black religious tradition, one with radical and subversive implications. Dr. Wilmore has captured the subversive nature of the public ministry of the Black church in this observation:

> The paradox that sometimes serves to confuse the issue [about whether the Black church is radical or conservative] is that because we have always had to fight for sheer survival in this world, the Black church has been at one and the same time the most radical and the most conservative institution in our community. (Wilmore, 1984)

What did the experience of Project Daniel demonstrate about using the story of Daniel to educate young Black minds? Regrettably, Project Daniel, a small start-up effort, never developed the capacity to perform an empirical self-study to prove the positive impact that I observed in the boys, in their attitude toward themselves and their world. Nevertheless, what I observed was a group of boys brimming with confidence—boys who believed they held a meaningful stake in their future. I attribute that confidence to the book of

Daniel. The experience of using the book of Daniel reaffirms the value of an educational tool very much at home in the Black Church. Black preachers and teachers have stylized a tradition of using the scripture as a metaphorical canvas upon which to superimpose the struggles of Black people, allowing them to match present-day trials with the trials of the heroes and heroines of the faith.

NOTE

1. "Playing the Dozens" is a verbal joust popularized in the African-American community. Participants try to humiliate each other in front of onlookers by ridiculing each other's loved ones. As a speech act, playing the dozens is a complex match of wits.

CHAPTER 14

"Freedom Is a Constant Struggle"

The Story of the Bushwick School for Social Justice and Make the Road by Walking

Hollyce C. Giles

This chapter tells the story of the Bushwick School for Social Justice (BSSJ), a new small public high school opened in September, 2003 in Brooklyn, New York. In telling this story, I consider the extent to which the school can be connected to the tradition and spirit of African American education for liberation. It is my intent that the narrative of the successes and struggles of this contemporary urban public school with a mission of social justice—created not as part of a social movement, but as part of a corporate- and foundation-sponsored school reform—will be instructive to educators, community organizers, and others who hope to transform the education of economically poor students of color within public education systems. Drawing on the historic African American liberation schools as a standard for comparison offers a basis for considering ways that BSSJ might move toward offering its students an even more engaging and transforming education, within their quite different contemporary context.

The first part of the chapter's title, "Freedom Is a Constant Struggle," is the name of a protest song. The song evokes both BSSJ's connection to the aims of the Freedom Schools, and the truly constant struggle the school's leaders have experienced in working toward those aims. At the same time, the lyrics of the song, *"They say that freedom is a constant struggle, O Lord, we've struggled so long, We must be free, we must be free,"* serve as a reminder that historic African American liberation schools differ from BSSJ in an important way—these schools were deeply rooted in the unique history and struggles of African Americans. As such, the song's lyrics offer a cautionary note, a reminder to take care not to gloss over the important differences in the educational endeavors.

SETTING THE FRAME: INTRODUCTION TO THE PARTNERSHIP LINKING BSSJ TO AFRICAN AMERICAN EDUCATION FOR LIBERATION

BSSJ's differences from the African American liberation schools are clear. BSSJ's initial founders, Mark Rush, Matt Ritter, and Matt Corallo, are White teachers, from outside of the local community. Their primary mission is education. The founders of the historic African American liberation schools in most cases were Black activists, deeply involved in the freedom struggle, and while they sought to offer a strong education to their students, their primary mission was social change. Also, BSSJ's founding teachers were influenced by the contemporary model of education for social justice developed by teacher educators (Ayers, 2000; Cochran-Smith, 2004). This model, while similar to the historic tradition of African American education for liberation in its emphasis on constructivist pedagogy, critical thinking, and the inclusion of power, injustice, and activism in the curriculum, differs from that tradition in that its primary mission is education, not social change, and it is not rooted in the specific history and struggles of a particular people.

What links BSSJ to the liberation schools is that its White founding teachers chose, doggedly courted, and have sustained a strong relationship with Make the Road by Walking, a community group with an impressive record of organizing local Latinos/as to win changes in their workplaces, hospitals, clinics, and schools, as well as in immigration policies. Make the Road was founded in 1997 by its current codirectors, Oona Chatterjee, who is Asian Indian, and Andrew Friedman, who is White, both community activists who had recently graduated from law school. This group, often with little or no funding, has remained consistently and extensively involved in the life of BSSJ, frequently pulling the school back to its social justice mission. When challenged by a foundation officer about the wisdom of an organizing group being so involved in running a school, Chatterjee countered that she saw the school as a potential "movement institution." Her commitment to this vision has been central to moving in the direction of making this a reality at BSSJ.

Another important figure in the creation and early life of BSSJ is its principal. The school's full planning team—teachers as well as parents, youth, and organizers from Make the Road—interviewed candidates and had input into the selection of the principal. The team chose Terry Byam, a Trinidadian American with many years of experience as a teacher and administrator in the New York City public school system, and a strong track record of helping Black and Latino youth to succeed in public schools. His addition to the team meant that there were two educators in the school's leadership, himself and Lorraine Gutierrez, a Latina teacher who joined the planning team in its early stages, in whom the students and families of BSSJ could see their own races and ethnicities reflected.

Gutierrez, who is Puerto Rican, grew up in Brooklyn, and was pursuing her doctorate in curriculum studies in the state of Michigan at the time BSSJ was created. Her area of specialization concerned issues of race and gender in curriculum studies. Her insight into the life experience of the Latino residents of Bushwick, and her professional expertise in issues of race and gender in the curriculum, brought an important perspective to the planning team that created the school.

I have been involved with BSSJ for over 3 years, as a professor at Brooklyn College, one of the school's community partners. I, like the initial founding teachers, am White. Our common race may have led the Whites I interviewed for this chapter to be more comfortable sharing their perspectives with me than the Black and Latino educators and students I spoke with. At the same time, I often have brought the topic of race into conversations at the school, and co-led an anti-racism workshop for staff, so the staff knows that I am interested in talking about how issues around race may affect relationships in the school. This stance around race probably led some interviewees to feel more comfortable in talking about race with me and led others to be more cautious.

In the following sections, I offer a snapshot of BSSJ and of Make the Road by Walking. I then describe the impact of the partnership between the two organizations on several dimensions of the life of the school.

THE BUSHWICK SCHOOL FOR SOCIAL JUSTICE

BSSJ opened its doors in 2003, as a new small school created as part of a citywide reform to replace several existing large, low-performing high schools with theme-based small schools. The school's mission is to "provide a rigorous college preparatory curriculum that empowers students to succeed in future academic and professional endeavors and to be informed and active citizens" and to "prepare students to take an informed and active role in the social, cultural, and political life of their communities, their country, and their world" (Bushwick School for Social Justice, 2003).

Bushwick, the neighborhood in which the school is located, received widespread publicity for the extensive arson and theft that it suffered during the New York City blackout in 1977, and the flight of many of its White and middle-class residents in the period afterward. Most students who attend BSSJ live in Bushwick. The neighborhood's current residents are mostly Latino, primarily from the Dominican Republic and Puerto Rico, with 40%

identified as being from immigrant households. The community struggles economically, with 33.6% living below the poverty level, and many residents working multiple jobs for minimum wage or less (New York City Housing and Neighborhood Information System, 2000). At the same time, the neighborhood has a strong history of activism and advocacy, with ongoing vibrant networks and coalitions of activist community organizing groups, churches, and labor unions that work to address issues impacting residents' lives.

Building toward a target enrollment of 400 students in grades nine through 12, BSSJ will add a cohort of approximately 100 ninth graders in each of its first 4 years. In its second year, the school had 238 students, two-thirds Latino, and one-third Black. The 21 full-time teachers were 70% White, 20% Black, and 10% Latina, with a guidance staff of five who were all Latina. Of the six members of the support staff, two were Latino and three were Black. As noted earlier, the principal, Terry Byam, is Trinidadian American.

Traditional indicators of academic success show impressive achievement in BSSJ's first year. Ninety percent of the ninth graders were promoted to the 10th grade. By way of comparison, at the large high school BSSJ is replacing, Bushwick High School, only 7% of the freshmen who entered in 1998–1999 made it to the 11th grade (New York City Board of Education, 2001). In BSSJ's second year, 29 10th graders passed the Math A Regents' Exam 6 months early, an accomplishment that had a rippling effect on other students' academic motivation. According to Matt Corallo, one of the school's founding teachers,

> We have another 50% of our students kicking themselves because they did not take the math exam in January and I think that's also a victory, because you have kids saying, "God, what if I could have passed that exam 6 months shy of another semester of math? I think that's great when you can get kids excited and really aware of what expectations are, and how to really carve out their own success, that's great.

By the end of the year, 78% of the BSSJ 10th graders had passed the exam, as compared to 50% of their 10th-grade peers at Bushwick High School (New York City Department of Education, 2005).

As impressive as these academic achievements are for a school so new, the most striking accomplishment of the school, and one certainly linked to students' academic success, is the generally strong and trusting relationships between students and their teachers. The school staff, community partners, and students attribute the strength of the relationships largely to the advisory system, in which a small group of 12–15 students meets with their advisor for 45 minutes every day. The advisories function as students' home base, where they share their joys and struggles with each other and with their advisors. The advisories also do social action projects together, discuss relevant health and social issues, and learn how to prepare and apply for college. Adilka Pimentel, a 10th grader, spoke warmly about the school and her advisory:

> Because it's small you get the attention you need that you wouldn't get in a regular high school. The difference is that you can talk to your teachers, like my advisor, believe me, he knows a lot, so I could sit down with him and just tell him my problems. If I'm having a bad day, like I'm having a bad day today, and he sat me down in advisory and he spoke to me. At other schools, they wouldn't do that. They'd just suspend you for being mad at somebody else, they wouldn't let you sit down and explain what happened.
>
> Don't get me wrong, when they need to be strict to get you to do work, they'll do it. They're going to make sure we got to pass and meet with all the standards. But they also know things . . . because we're teenagers, so they always have time to joke around also.

Another noteworthy accomplishment for the school is that it has made significant headway in integrating the theme of social justice into the curriculum. The day I spent attending classes at BSSJ with ninth grader Jorge Sequeira, I saw ample evidence of the social justice theme. For example, in the English Language Arts class, taught by Lorraine Gutierrez, the walls of the room were covered with posters with social justice themes, such as:

Guiding Questions

1. Which characters in the text have power?
2. Which characters in the text do not have power?
3. Do the characters who have power use it fairly?
4. Do you see examples of power in the characters who you believe may not have power?

In the same class, a poster read "Complacent = Complicit."

In the math class taught by Audrey Federman, a poster with an image of Angela Davis had the words, "Sister, you are welcome in this house," and another said "If you have come to help me, you are wasting your time, but if you have come because your liberation is bound up with mine, then let us work together." In the Social Studies class, taught by Tabora Johnson, students were studying the divide-and-conquer concept as manifested in the politics of the tribes of Nigeria.

Gutierrez spoke to how students' response to the social justice aspects of the curriculum had changed over time:

> At the beginning, they didn't understand what they were being asked. "Like what? Why am I supposed to care about this? I don't care!" At the beginning, it was like "they have power because they're the White man, that's it! They have power." And they had a really simplistic kind of response. I think that making the connections between issues of social justice and where they come from is a painful process, because it forces them to look at what's going on around them in a way that's uncomfortable. Even now, I still have kids who really can't do that. At the same time, I think that more of the students are capable of doing that, of recognizing that there are some issues in the communities and neighborhoods, but at the same time there are a lot of things in those communities and neighborhoods that are amazing and really powerful. And that as young people they can make it even more powerful.

Gutierrez went on to describe the oral history project that her class was doing as a project intended to help students figure out how to make their communities more powerful. Students chose topics that included security scanning at the high school, the immigrant experience, and the New York City blackout in 1977. Gutierrez observed,

> That's what the oral history project is. It's not just negative things, but it's "look how far we've come." So for the blackout and how it affected Bushwick in 1977—it's not just that a lot of people moved and left, the community came together and the community survived, it's still here. And that survival is part of what they need to understand as well. So I think that now, they can make the connections and they can respond to it in a way that they couldn't in the beginning.

Evidence from students themselves that they have internalized the concept of social justice surfaced in my interview with the three 10th graders, Adilka Pimentel, Freddy Mitchell, and Eddy Polanco. I had not asked them explicitly about social justice at the school, but when I asked whether there was anything else that they wanted to say about the school at the end of our interview, Mitchell kicked off a vigorous debate among the three of them about whether the school offers social justice classes. The conversation ranged from whether advisory counted as a social justice class, to the social action projects their advisories did, to the slowness of their student government to take action, to the importance of knowing your rights, and how Make the Road by Walking helps them with their rights. Their discussion, essentially an interrogation of the validity of the school's basis for calling itself a school for social justice, suggests that they know that their voices are valued, and that they are comfortable with questioning the authorities at their school, even their beloved advisors.

MAKE THE ROAD BY WALKING

A 5-minute walk from BSSJ, Make the Road is located in a storefront office on a street of multi-unit brick residential dwellings. A 1,100-member, multi-issue community organizing group, Make the Road "builds power through organizing; develops leadership through education; and promotes justice through the provision of legal and other services" to its members (Make the Road by Walking 2004, preface). The group organizes around education, health care, environmental and housing justice, workplace and economic issues, and youth issues, and includes GLOBE, formed to "combat institutional homophobia and the harassment, isolation, and invisibility of lesbian, gay, bisexual, and transgendered people in Bushwick" (Make the Road by Walking, 2004, p. 5). Some of Make the Road's recent victories include coalition organizing work that resulted in New York City investing over 70 million new dollars in the prevention of childhood lead poisoning, local hospitals and outpatient clinics signing an agreement to offer interpretation and translation services to limited–English proficient patients, a successful boycott of a Bushwick area retailer to improve the employer's treatment of workers, and organizing that resulted in the removal of an unresponsive and ineffective principal of a local middle school, where 90% of students were reading and doing math below grade level (Make the Road by Walking, 2004).

The first time I visited Make the Road, I was struck when I entered the office by the presence of an attractively dressed, transgendered Latina, talking with an older Latino gentleman near the front desk. I immediately had a sense of a diverse, welcoming, and inclusive atmosphere. I later came to know the Latina as Dee Perez, the founder of GLOBE, and Make the Road's office manager. Another woman was cooking something that smelled good in a large pot on the stove in an open cooking area not far from the reception desk. Then, and every time I have visited Make the Road since, the meeting rooms and offices have seemed at maximum occupancy, with children, youth, and adults working on organizing campaigns, or learning English, or discussing legal rights around housing violations, immigration, and other issues, as well as many other activities. With such a strong sense of community, hospitality, and "something happening," I can understand the appeal of the place for BSSJ students.

Make the Road's work with BSSJ students, parents, and faculty has been extensive. With students, much of Make the Road's involvement has focused on helping the advisories to choose and develop social action projects, and take turns presenting them at the school's weekly Town Hall meeting. Every advisory visits Make the Road, so that all students have a firsthand familiarity with the office and staff. The staff arranges for activist speakers to meet with students, during the Social Justice Day they sponsor at the school, and at Town Hall meetings. For example, a former Black Panther recently spoke at Town Hall. To prepare for that visit, students read about the Black Panther Party in their advisories. Students also have used articles from *Word on the Street*, the quarterly newspaper written by members of Make the Road's youth organizing group, Youth Power, as a text for their advisories. The 20 or so BSSJ students who regularly participate in Youth Power's organizing activities take what they learn there, including social analyses and organizing strategies, back into conversations with peers in their advisories. Chatterjee is helping to facilitate BSSJ's newly formed student government. Through Youth Power's participation in the Urban Youth Collaborative, a citywide coalition of youth organizing groups addressing education issues, students from BSSJ will be able to experience the power of joining with youth from other neighborhoods to create social change on a larger scale.

The three 10th-grade students I interviewed described their experience with Make the Road:

Adilka: Make the Road helps us with our rights.
Freddy: They make constant trips to our school, because we're in partnership with them. And they let us know what's going on, protests.
[What do you protest?]
Freddy: In the winter we did something on heat. There was no heat in any of the buildings, yet in like 30 degree weather and it was cold.
Eddy: I don't even know if it worked, but I had fun doing it. And there was something about homeless people, the city spending more money on houses, on shelters—instead they use it for prisons and stadiums and stuff like that.

Though most of Make the Road's involvement is with students, members of its staff also participate in decision-making bodies at BSSJ, and work with parents. Make the Road has collaborated with BSSJ's parent coordinator, Dinorka Ogando, to develop the Parents' Association, and offers workshops for parents on legal rights and classes in ESL. Make the Road also has worked with Ogando and me, to organize BSSJ's twice-annual Community Walk, during which small teams from BSSJ visit with parents in their homes to get to know each other and share their hopes and concerns for the school.

THE IMPACT OF THE PARTNERSHIP ON BSSJ'S SOCIAL JUSTICE MISSION: THE BENEFITS OF HAVING A HOME IN THE COMMUNITY

Our participation [in designing the proposal for the School for Social Justice] has offered Make the Road's staff and members the opportunity to do two hope-inspiring things: imagine what is possible through the creation of this school, and learn to believe that our voices, wisdom, and ideas are vital to its success. The project has captured the hearts and minds of our youngest members—8-year-olds who have come to see themselves as future graduates of BSSJ—and has galvanized parents and grandparents to pour into the proposal all of their dreams and ambitions.

—Oona Chatterjee, from a letter of support
to the Committee Selecting
the New Small Schools

Most schools in poor neighborhoods typically have little sense of place, or community allies who can lend their power to challenge policies and practices from the education bureaucracy that they believe undermine their efforts to educate students (Warren, 2005). After initial skepticism, and an intense period of courtship by the founding teachers, Make the Road offered BSSJ a home in Bushwick.

To be fair, the reform from which BSSJ emerged created both new opportunities as well as daunting problems. The design of the reform legitimated partnerships between schools and community organizations by requiring that the teams proposing new schools have at least one community partner, as well as an administrator, teacher, parent, and student. At the same time, leaders of the reform reinforced communities' basic alienation and suspicion of the New York City Department of Education instilled by repeated past failed reforms; by offering little, if any, information about which large high schools would be phased out; and by making it difficult for residents to have any say in what the new small schools in their neighborhoods would look like, or even whether they wanted them at all (Anyon, 2005, p. 186; Make the Road by Walking, 2002). Perhaps most unsettling was that the design of the reform introduced a strong dynamic of haves and have-nots into a community by housing the new small schools with their typically young, enthusiastic teachers and significant additional resources inside the same building with the large, underfunded, struggling high school that was being phased out. The small schools created through the New Century reform process receive $1,000 per student in addition to the usual funding allocated to a start-up school by the Department of Education, giving each new school approximately $100,000 of additional funding per year of their first 4 years.

It was in this context that three idealistic young White teachers—Matt Corallo, Matt Ritter, and Mark Rush—decided to form a team to try to create a new school. At the time, they were teaching in a small alternative school in Brooklyn that they characterize as a "little big school," small in size, but driven by the values and practices, and plagued by the problems, of a traditional large high school. Passionate about teaching and committed to their students, but distressed by the dysfunctional culture of the little big school, when a colleague told one of them about a new reform inviting teams to develop proposals for start-up schools, they jumped on the opportunity. They began to work on a proposal for a new school that would be a small school in practice as well as in theory, where, according to Rush, "a kid goes from one excellent experience to another all 4 years."

Matt Ritter describes how they chose the theme of social justice for their school:

> I'd been reading a book William Ayers (2000) edited, *A Simple Justice*—about school reform and small schools. . . . I went to a meeting and said why don't we just be a school for social justice, because it's something that we are committed to—well it's the one thing the three of us are sitting here meeting and talking about all the time without even realizing it sometimes, like the work we want to do is an act of social justice and social change. It totally resonated.

The team expanded to include Brooklyn College through Rush's relationship with his former education professor there, Peter Taubman, and Lorraine Gutierrez, another former student of Taubman's who had done her student teaching with Rush at the "little big school."

At the same time that this new team was gathering to create a small school in Bushwick as part of the citywide reform initiative, Make the Road was organizing Bushwick residents to challenge the reform. As part of the newly formed Community Coalition for Bushwick High School that included parents, students, teachers, and neighborhood churches and community-based organizations, representing more than 8,000 Bushwick residents, Make the Road was holding press conferences that demanded that the Department of Education include residents of Bushwick in decision making about what would happen to the existing Bushwick High School, and to determine exactly which new schools would be located in their community. The coalition was also preparing a report, *Ask Us! Towards a Bushwick Community Vision for High School Education,* that summarized the priorities of more than 300 Bushwick residents for high school reform in their neighborhood.

To meet the reform requirement that they have a community partner on their team, the BSSJ founders turned to the Internet to search for a community organization in Bushwick that was engaged in social justice work. Make the Road by Walking emerged as the clear favorite, and Rush, completely unaware of Make the Road's position and organizing around the reform, called up Oona Chatterjee the codirector, to ask whether Make the Road would be the community partner for their new small school. At first, Chatterjee and her codirector, Andrew Friedman, said no to the group's offer, but the planning team persisted, and Make the Road decided to let the planning team present its ideas for the school to the organization's membership. As Chatterjee remembers,

> They kept calling us. Finally we had a meeting and all the students and parents at Make the Road were really excited about creating a school and so we decided to work with them.

Though BSSJ's founding educators initially had no idea that they were entering into a relationship with a community group that was questioning the justice of the Department of Education's process for the reform, by doing so, their school was able to have more integrity in its formation and greater solidarity with community residents than other small schools forming through the same troubling process. From its earliest days, BSSJ was accountable to its community, and through long conversations and many meetings with members and staff of Make the Road, and close study of the *Ask Us!* document, BSSJ came to know the concerns and priorities of community residents. These priorities played an important role in shaping the guiding philosophy and design of the new school.

Another important way that Make the Road by Walking helped BSSJ to develop an ethic of justice in a process with inequitable dimensions, was by continuing their organizing and long-standing relationships with students at the original Bushwick High School while, at the same time, working to help develop BSSJ. By engaging youth from both Bushwick High School and BSSJ in their afterschool organizing group, Make the Road helped to mitigate the divisiveness of the dynamic of haves and have-nots in the schools. Make the Road's stance of engaging in the reform process so that it benefited students in the community, while remaining critical of its injustice for some residents, and taking action to address those issues, helped students to develop their own critical analysis of a complex and contradictory situation, and to sustain relationships with their neighbors despite the divisiveness of the reform.

THE FIGHT FOR SOCIAL JUSTICE IN THE CURRICULUM: "GIVING TO CAESAR WHAT IS CAESAR'S WITHOUT BETRAYING WHAT IS THE KIDS'"

The planning team's conception of BSSJ's social justice mission, as articulated by Matt Ritter, was

> to make sure the kids learn the skills and become aware of the issues that directly affect them. And not only that, but learn how to address those issues, become agents of change themselves, and understand that as part of their own identity.

Major bureaucratic obstacles to realizing this mission presented themselves in the arena of the curriculum early in the life of the school. In an apt metaphor, Matt Corallo suggested that effectively dealing with these obstacles called for "giving to Caesar what is Caesar's without betraying what is the kids'." Indeed, the teaching staff was savvy and persistent in its efforts to satisfy bureaucratic mandates without betraying their mission or the students.

A central principle of the reform process was that teachers in the new small schools would have significant latitude in shaping their curriculum, as long as it prepared students to pass New York State's standardized graduation exams. Taking reform leaders at their word, the summer before the school opened, teachers on the planning team, with the help of faculty at Brooklyn College, spent many hours creating an innovative interdisciplinary humanities curriculum called "Revolution and Rebellion," which focused on people's struggles against oppressive forces throughout history.

The team learned in August, 3 weeks before the school was scheduled to open, that they would not be allowed to teach the curriculum they had created. Instead, they would be required to teach a heavily scripted, standardized curriculum called "Ramp Up," which all New York City high schools with a certain percentage of students reading below grade level were mandated to teach. The team was devastated. The school district's decision dealt a near-fatal blow to the founding teachers' belief that their ideals and values were going to be integral to the life of the school.

One important consequence of the mandate to do the standardized curriculum was that teachers, at their own discretion, would have to find a way to weave social justice ideas into the prescribed curriculum. As such, the only location left in the curriculum for a full and direct infusion of social justice content was the advisories. Make the Road would play a central role in bringing the social justice theme to the advisories. As Rush explains it,

Ramp Up changed how we were going to think about social justice. What happened probably a lot less consciously than we'd like to say is that advisory and Town Hall became the space for that because we didn't have any other space except how teachers could bring social justice into the curriculum themselves. There was no other space for it. Luckily we had Oona and Brinda [Make the Road's liaisons to the school] and teachers who were really committed to make it work, and who were committed to the idea of a school for social justice. Even though at that point we were wondering, where is the social justice?

Over time, the daily, 45-minute advisory, and the weekly Town Hall meetings during which advisories took turns presenting their social action projects, became the place that the social justice theme was most clearly articulated. Make the Road, particularly Oona Chatterjee and Brinda Maira, would be central to providing the scaffolding needed by students and teachers to implement this mission in the curriculum during the first year. As informed and articulate as the educators on the planning team were about social justice, and as committed as they were to the students, they did not have the knowledge and firsthand experience of activism needed to show their students how to become agents of social change. Also, teachers had their hands full with other aspects of the curriculum and the extensive, exhausting work of starting a new school.

Mark Rush describes the general plan for the social action projects and how staff from Make the Road worked with him and his students to develop his advisory's first-year project, called "Bathroom Justice," which targeted the unsanitary, basically unusable, bathrooms at the school:

> We'd decided we'd do social action projects, mini-projects at the beginning of the year, and they would evolve, or be the jumping-off point for bigger projects and would be presented in Town Hall. Brinda from Make the Road was coming in and helping that happen. For example, in my advisory, when I came to her with the idea for my advisory's project [Bathroom Justice], she came in and went through the model for organizing, like identifying targets and collecting data and getting pictures and writing letters, and we shared that with the staff. That's how Bathroom Justice happened, because we had the connection with Make the Road.

Adilka Pimentel participated in the project as one of the students in Rush's advisory. She describes their project:

We did potty power last year. See, because our bathrooms are unsanitary. So we went on the radio, and we put on a play in Town Hall. We had meetings with the principals of the other schools, and actually they did paint over it [the bathrooms], and put soap and stuff in the bathrooms.

Other advisory projects and Town Hall presentations have addressed issues such as obtaining adequate space for BSSJ in the building; sexual harassment; racial profiling in the school, community, and larger society; and creating a safe and welcoming environment for lesbians, gays, bisexual, and transgendered students and teachers. Though some tensions have emerged in this collaboration between organizers and advisors, seemingly related to the different primary missions of Make the Road (social change) and BSSJ (education), school leaders have developed strategies to address the tensions to reduce any adverse impact on their work with students.

In addition to their direct work with students, Make the Road's staff also have played an important role of holding BSSJ accountable for maintaining the social justice mission in the midst of bureaucratic and societal contexts that have other values and priorities. As Chatterjee put it, "We're a little reminder of social justice to the school." For example, she noted that this past year's advisory projects tended a little more in the direction of good works or charity than that of social change. Mark Rush shared Chatterjee's sense that the school needs to work to expand teachers' use of the social change model next year:

> Not everyone's using [the social change model]. That's what we want to do with the staff next year—make sure that it's much more explicit—that everyone has a model to work with.

Through its curricular and extracurricular work with students, Make the Road by Walking has offered BSSJ's students an experience on the same continuum as that of students in the Freedom Schools in Mississippi. As Payne describes students' experience,

> Young people going to Freedom Schools were surrounded by activists who genuinely believed that they could change the flow of history. Such confidence must have been magnetic. They grew up wanting to be SNCC [Student Nonviolent Coordinating Committee] field secretaries. We would need to think very carefully [in adapting the Freedom School model to our time] about how to give young people some comparable sense of their own potency and comparably clear models for actualizing it. (Payne, 2000, p. 75)

Students at BSSJ have not yet experienced the intensity or immersion in a movement that Freedom School students did, but BSSJ students have been exposed to a powerful social change model at Make the Road by Walking. They have developed relationships with adults and other youth from the neighborhood who have had significant victories in organizing to change public policies and practices harmful to residents of BSSJ. Youth from the school have played an important role in these campaigns as well, experiencing their own potency to effect social change.

Without Make the Road's involvement in the advisories, its infusion of an organizing ethos into BSSJ through its other activities, and its vigilance about staff alignment around social justice, BSSJ's curriculum probably would look quite different. Students most likely would be learning the concept of social justice in their courses, but not internalizing it by witnessing others engaged in social action and engaging in it themselves, as many of them have been able to do at BSSJ and Make the Road by Walking.

CREATING SPACES FOR "HARD SOCIAL JUSTICE CONVERSATIONS"

BSSJ has faced two significant challenges in its efforts to create a democratic, inclusive culture: developing a governance structure that represents the voices of all members of the school community and, at the same time, allows decisions to be made efficiently; and creating the conditions for healthy interpersonal and group dynamics, that is, relationships that do not reproduce the problematic values and power relations of the larger society, such as a command-and-control culture as opposed to a more relational culture based on conversation and dialogue. Members of the BSSJ community have learned through trial and error that both the formal organizational structure and the informal culture of the school need to allow for spaces where people can talk directly with each other about issues and dynamics that are creating problems among them, for what one teacher I interviewed called "hard social justice conversations."

Make the Road by Walking has played a central role in encouraging and teaching BSSJ faculty, staff, and community partners how to dialogue and make decisions as part of a diverse collective. Based on its experience with democratic decision making in its own organization, Make the Road proposed including a "collective" composed of representatives of all of the school's constituencies as part of the school's governance structure. The structure that BSSJ eventually settled on consists of a cabinet composed of several BSSJ staff members, with whom the principal consults day-to-day as well as on larger decisions, and a collective composed of teachers, parents, students, and community partners, which gives feedback to the cabinet regarding the larger decisions in the life of the school. This structure allows for wide-ranging discussions about the life of the school, including hard social justice conversations.

Creating an informal culture that supports the school's social justice mission of developing local community leaders has proven to be both less tangible and more difficult than developing the formal governance structure. The school's leaders have faced the challenge of figuring out how to meet the onerous demands of running a new school in a demanding bureaucracy, while nurturing the skills and leadership of educators, students, and parents collaborating with them—in some instances, individuals from groups typically marginalized in American society.

This challenge has been faced by many organizations with a democratic, inclusive mission, and staff with diverse levels of education and experience, including the organizers of the Mississippi Freedom Movement. The organizers of the Freedom Movement struggled to meet the demands of running a social movement while developing the skills and leadership of their local colleagues, who tended to have less formal education and experience than they did. Payne quotes a local Mississippi woman, Mary Lane, describing this issue,

> There were local people that were holding positions in SNCC [the Student Nonviolent Coordinating Committee] before the summer of '64. And you know, after these [summer volunteers] came in, you could see it every day, the man moving up a little more, you know. And he knew more. And he had it, where maybe you didn't. But you [had been] learning. . . . You sit down and work with them everyday and you find out that they can do a much better job of it than you could (Payne, 1995, p. 336).

The challenge for the organizers in the Freedom Movement over 40 years ago, and for the leaders of BSSJ now, is to provide good training to colleagues, students, and parents, and then to step back and let them take on important responsibilities and learn by doing, so that they can build confidence in their own abilities and leadership, and participate in the life of the school in a powerful way.

CALLING ON PARENTS AS SCHOOL AND COMMUNITY LEADERS

Their rhetoric notwithstanding, public schools tend to focus most of their energy with regard to parents on getting them to support the academic achievement of their individual children, and minimizing their participation in decision making that affects the school as a whole. BSSJ's goal of engaging parents in addressing issues that affect the whole school reflects a paradigm shift in relations between educators and parents, particularly in economically struggling neighborhoods (Giles, 1998; Mediratta & Fruchter, 2003). Make the Road's experience in training and organizing parents and other residents in BSSJ has made the group a powerful ally in working toward this cultural shift in the role of parents at the school.

To engage parents in relationships that support the school as a whole, Make the Road by Walking and Brooklyn College have collaborated with BSSJ to hold one to two Community Walks each year (Shirley, 1997). At the Community Walk, the school's principal, teachers, and parent leaders, Make the Road staff, and university faculty and students gather at the school and then go out in small teams of two to three to visit with students' parents in their homes. During the 20-minute-long visits, parents and team members get to know each other, and share their hopes, concerns, and ideas for the school and students. At the end of each visit, the teams invite parents to the next Parents' Association meeting, and to meetings at Make the Road that are relevant to issues parents have raised, such as their other children's struggles at the local middle school, and problems on their jobs. At the end of the Walk, the teams gather back at the school to have dinner together, evaluate the Walk, and report on issues of concern identified by parents, such as safety, the need for afterschool tutoring and extracurricular activities, and parents' desire to learn English. The goal, only partially realized as of yet, is for the school's Parents' Association to organize its members to take action to address the issues identified during the Walk.

BSSJ has made some progress toward shifting the paradigm of parent-school relations toward more active engagement and leadership by parents. It is one more area in which greater staff alignment around the meaning of social justice will be important.

CONCLUSION

The White teachers who first conceived of BSSJ have expanded beyond their initial focus on the quality of teaching, and their somewhat limited connection to the community, and, together with the school's Black principal, have developed a vibrant partnership with a community organizing group, opening up the school to the transforming involvement of this group. It is this partnership that links the school with the tradition and spirit of African American education for liberation. This kind of partnership and extensive involvement of a community organizing group *inside* of a public school is rare—but possible.

It is also possible for contemporary schools such as BSSJ to learn from the struggles and failures of the schools in the tradition of African American education for liberation. These schools eventually lost sight of their mission and their strong sense of community, as changes occurred in their contexts—such as media's increased focus on movement leaders and government agencies' involvement in funding and controlling movement educational organizations (Payne, 1995, pp. 338–390). BSSJ faces some similar dynamics. Can the school learn from history—in this instance, that keeping sight of one's mission and a strong sense of community are key to the survival of education for liberation?

Creating the kind of school culture that will allow the racially diverse yet White-dominant teaching staff at BSSJ to sustain their mission of social justice, and sense of community, will require the development of "holding environments" (Winnicott, 1960). In the context of BSSJ, such environments would be safe enough spaces where teachers could have frank discussions about taboo, conflict-laden issues, such as patterns of injustice within the school itself, and their links to larger historical, social, and political realities. Through such conversations, teachers can develop the fluency and courage to discuss and address these issues with their students. As it has in many other dimensions of the life of the school, Make the Road by Walking will be a crucial partner in this effort.

CHAPTER 15

The Black Student Leadership Network's Summer Freedom School Program

Sekou M. Franklin

A major organizing initiative adopted by student and youth-based movement organizations has been the development of Freedom Schools, or community-based educational institutions designed to offer assistance to poor children, the unemployed, adult learners, union activists, and workers. Scholars generally refer to these types of schools as alternative or "parallel institutions" because they perform functions similar to those of mainstream institutions, but usually do so in autonomous or semiautonomous settings (Lee, 1999; Ramanathan, 1965; Butler, 2000, p. 131). Parallel institutions or Freedom Schools are further used to organize aggrieved and neglected communities around social justice issues and critical pedagogy.

In the 1930s and 1940s, the Southern Negro Youth Congress (SNYC) organized labor schools in Nashville, Tennessee; New Orleans, Louisiana; and Birmingham and Fairfield, Alabama. The labor schools educated Black workers and local union leaders "on the present problems of the labor movement, as well as of techniques for improving the effectiveness of their particular union meetings and procedures."[1] Besides the labor schools, the SNYC set up citizenship schools and organized leadership development seminars for youth activists. During its first year in operation, the SNYC organized a "Youth Leadership Seminar" in Kings Mountain, North Carolina, which conducted sessions on "History of the Youth Movement," "Cooperation with Adult Agencies," "Conducting Youth Campaigns," and "Developing Youth Leadership" (Richards, 1987, p. 44).

The Mississippi Freedom School program of the 1960s is one of the most influential examples of parallel institutionalism, inspiring many similar initiatives. This chapter outlines the history of one such initiative, the summer Freedom School program established by the Black Student Leadership Network (BSLN), a national organization that operated from 1991 to 1996.

When the Black Student Leadership Network was first created, its core leadership wanted to train and develop a cadre of young social and political activists in movement-building and social change activities, and then immerse them into grassroots and community-organizing initiatives. They also wanted to strengthen intergenerational linkages between activists and advocates who came of age during the modern civil rights era of the 1950s and 1960s, and young people who came of age after this period.

During its short life span, the BSLN introduced hundreds of college-age Blacks to direct action advocacy, community organizing, social-movement-building, child advocacy, and critical pedagogy. It developed Freedom Schools in dozens of rural and urban locales throughout the country, which linked educational initiatives with locally directed, grassroots organizing campaigns.

In examining the BSLN's Freedom Schools, I give particular attention to the origins of the BSLN and the Freedom Schools, as well as the internal debates over the operations and direction of the program between the BSLN's leadership cadre and its parent organizations, the Children's Defense Fund (CDF) and the Black Community Crusade for Children (BCCC). I also draw upon my experiences as a teaching intern/student activist in the BSLN's summer Freedom School program from 1993 to 1996.

THE ORIGINS OF THE BLACK STUDENT LEADERSHIP NETWORK

The BSLN was initiated by a collective of activists, some of whom had previous experience as community organizers in poor, urban communities, or as activists in the South African divestment movement of the mid-1980s, the Jesse Jackson presidential campaigns, and the antiracism mobilization struggles that were prevalent across college campuses and universities during the 1980s. These activists believed that the formation of a national-level, youth-based movement organization was essential to developing the leadership capacity of a new generation of young Black activists.

They also believed that a national-level, youth-based movement organization was essential to combating the conservative movement's growing influence and the range of public health epidemics (for example, community violence, high incarceration rates, unemployment and underemployment, juvenile crime, teenage pregnancy, the drug culture's dynamic influence, police brutality, and school dropouts) that had devastating effects on poor Black communities and, especially, poor Black youth in the post–civil rights era (Marable, 1991).

The BSLN actually emerged out of a national campaign called "A Crusade for Black Children," initiated by Marian Wright Edelman, the president of the Children's Defense Fund (CDF). The campaign attempted to combat Black child poverty and the right wing's assault on social welfare programs throughout the 1980s and 1990s (Children's Defense Fund, 1991a). The campaign was spearheaded by the Black Community Crusade for Children (BCCC), a network of leading Black intellectuals, policy experts, advocates, and grassroots activists that Edelman first brought together in 1989 and 1990. The BCCC resided under the CDF's organizational umbrella, and the BSLN operated as the BCCC's youth wing.

THE FORMATION OF THE BLACK STUDENT LEADERSHIP NETWORK

Despite Edelman's movement-building activities, the BCCC's national campaign began without the inclusion of young activists and students. For example, in November 1990, she brought together a group of prominent Blacks for a meeting in Leesburg, Virginia. The purpose of the meeting was to have "an overview and discussion of the crisis facing America's Black youth, steps for mobilization and an action plan within America's Black communities" (Children's Defense Fund, 1991a, p. 1). Yet this meeting occurred without the substantive input and perspectives of young adults and youth organizers, especially young people organizing in poor communities.

Edelman's concerns regarding young adult representation led her to search out Lisa Sullivan, a young activist and Yale graduate student, who, as an advisor to New Haven, Connecticut's NAACP Youth Council, became one of the principal organizers of a grassroots, youth-based movement in the city in the late 1980s. This movement pushed for educational reforms, combated community violence, and even tried to broker a truce between rival street crews in the city's ghettos, and was instrumental to helping to elect the city's first Black mayor, John Daniels (Boyce, 1990, p. A11; Finnegan, 1990; Gurwitt, 1990, pp. 29–33). The New Haven youth movement caught the attention of a number of prominent Black activists outside of the city, including Edelman, who requested a meeting with Sullivan to discuss the BCCC's objectives. This informal meeting was something of a litmus test, more so for Sullivan. Sullivan

> told Edelman she believed young African Americans genuinely want to complete the unfinished business of the civil rights movement, but they have no one to bridge the generation gap between old and young, the way Ella Baker had done during the creation of the Student Nonviolent Coordinating Committee in the 1960s. (Payne, 1996, p. 8)

This won Edelman over, and she invited Sullivan to participate in the early discussions with the BCCC members to develop a national campaign.

Before and during these discussions, Sullivan convened a series of meetings comprised of student and youth activists with the purpose of garnering support for a potential marriage between young activists and more established Black leaders. Some of these activists questioned the potential efficacy of this marriage, and viewed the BCCC's efforts with a great deal of caution, particularly considering its affiliation with the CDF, perceived to be a mainstream organization that was stocked with mostly White employees and too closely aligned with elite (and less confrontational) political circles.

Despite this skepticism, the young activists agreed to work with the incipient organization if it utilized its resources to cultivate and develop a new cadre of young leaders. They also conveyed their belief that this collaboration should concentrate on organizing and building grassroots support to deal with the problems that were central to the BCCC's concerns (Sullivan, 2000). During the early years of the campaign, Edelman repeatedly expressed a strong desire to recruit and train 1,000 new young Black leaders/advocates under the age of 30. The young activists were already organized and had been involved in a series of political battles themselves. Thus, they brought with them a sense of autonomy, independence, and political astuteness.

Matthew Countryman, who had known Sullivan since his days as a leading student activist in Yale University's divestment movement against U.S. corporate holdings in apartheid South Africa, was particularly instrumental to these early discussions and the BSLN's overall development. He was attracted to an organization like the BSLN because of the possibility that a national organization would provide resources and infrastructure support to students, something that did not happen in the divestment movement.

Countryman articulated these concerns shortly after the BSLN's founding conference in 1991. In a letter to Edelman, he stated that "The inability of student activists to effect change in national politics in recent years is testament more to the failure of progressive organizations to put essential resources and organizing skills into student mobilization than it is to student apathy and/or self-centeredness." Furthermore, he thought the prospect of a Black student-based organization that focused on working on behalf of Black children would attract a broad section of "Black student activists—liberals, leftists, entrepreneurs, and nationalists" (Countryman, 1991). Such a political formation could bridge ideological differences among Black students that tended to create difficulties in developing a student movement.

The BSLN held its founding conference at Howard University in June, 1991. Some of the 40 participants included Sullivan and Countryman; Kasey Jones, a student activist who worked with the Washington chapter of the Student Coalition Against Racism and the Concerned Black Awareness Council; Helene Fisher, who participated in the 1989 Howard University protests, spearheaded by Ras Baraka's Black Nia Force organization, which opposed Republican strategist Lee Atwater's appointment to the university's Board of Trustees; Errol James, a student at John Jay College of Criminal Justice, and a senior member of the Harlem Writing Crew; Richard Gray, a young adult advisor to the Free My People Youth Organization, which was a radical group of high school–age youth in Roxbury-Mattapan-Dorchester sections of Boston, and at the time, the co–executive director of the National Coalition of Advocates for Students (NCAS) in Boston; Leslie Watson, a Southern University student, who was instrumental in organizing the National Student Mobilization against the war in the Persian Gulf (Children's Defense Fund, 1991b); Keith Jennings, a founding member of the Georgia Progressive Black Student Association; Jeff Robinson, a recent graduate of Michigan State University, where he served as the president of the campus NAACP; Marty Rodgers and Amy Wilkins, both CDF staff employees; and Leah Williamson, a University of Maryland student who previously had served as the co-chair of the Malcolm X Leadership Summit, and was a member of the National Collegiate Black Caucus.

At the close of the meeting, they created a working committee to carry out follow-up initiatives. The Working Committee and Edelman, upon the recommendation of Sullivan, drafted Steve White of New Haven. In 1989, White served as the campaign manager for John Daniels's successful mayoral bid in New Haven, despite being only 25 years old. He had just served as a member of John Daniels's cabinet, and had assisted Daniels in his second mayoral victory in 1991. He also set up a political action committee, 21st Century Leadership, which aided the New Haven NAACP Youth Council's voter registration efforts. White accepted the offer and became the BSLN's first director by the end of 1991 (Robinson, 1991; K. Jones, 1991; Jones, 2000; Lydia, 1999).

During its short-lived history, the BSLN engaged in numerous activities: voter registration and education drives; anti-violence initiatives that addressed juvenile violence and gun crimes; and the creation of Advanced Service and Advocacy Workshops (ASAW), which were leadership development workshops that introduced young people to relevant policy debates. Its Brooklyn, New York, chapter administered a feeding program called the Peoples' Community Feeding Program, and later started Sista II Sista, a young girls'/young women's activist collective. Taj James, the head of the BSLN's Western Regional Office from 1995 to 1996, organized young people in support of a school funding initiative in the San Francisco Bay Area, and mobilized opposition to Proposition 209, California's anti–affirmative action ballot initiative (James, 1999; Black Student Leadership Network Staff, 1996, p. 33). The BSLN's Southern Regional Field Office, led by Darriel Hoy, organized a childhood hunger campaign; fought against the 1995 Balanced Budget Amendment, which targeted welfare and social programs for budget cuts; and formed a coalition with the Food Action Research Council, the North Carolina Hunger Network, and other statewide anti-hunger networks (Hoy, 1996; Hoy, 2000).

FREEDOM SCHOOLS AND THE SUMMER FOOD SERVICE PROGRAM

The BSLN's most important initiative was its Freedom School program. The program allowed the BSLN and its parent organization, the BCCC, to establish beachheads in local communities across the country. The BSLN also used the Freedom Schools to recruit hundreds of college-age Blacks into its organization.

The possibility of utilizing the BSLN's capacity to mobilize young people to coordinate a summer Freedom School program was discussed as early as 1991. CDF decided to wait, fearing logistical and fund-raising difficulties but gave the BSLN the leeway to develop a small-scale but manageable summer organizing initiative, which became a social movement school, the Ella Baker Child Policy Training Institute.

Developing the institute was an important step for the BSLN in establishing a political identity that was grounded in collective leadership and grassroots organizing. The institute provided a 2-week training session on direct action advocacy and community organizing, political education and civil rights movement history, media relations, and critical pedagogy. The BSLN named the institute after Ella Baker because it attempted to institutionalize her organizing approach, which focused on "collective" and "group-centered" leadership and participatory democracy (Mueller, 1990, p. 52; Payne, 1989, p. 896), inside of the BSLN and the summer Freedom Schools.

The BSLN members chose to have the first institute at Shaw University in Raleigh, North Carolina, and their first summer organizing initiative in North Carolina. Shaw was historically symbolic because it is where the SNCC held its founding conference. In June, the institute welcomed its first group of workers. In preparation for the summer training, Countryman developed a direct action advocacy/community-organizing training module that he adapted from the Midwest Academy/United States Student Association (USSA) Grassroots Organizing Weekends (GROW) training curriculum (Black Student Leadership Network, 1994, pp. 4–5). Sullivan incorporated the civil rights film series *Eyes on the Prize* into the training, in order "to point out how movements and people get organized" (Countryman, 2000), as well as to help the participants demystify how social change generally takes place. After the training, the 25 participants worked with local organizations throughout North Carolina.

By the end of 1992 and early 1993, the Freedom School plan was reconsidered and became much more attractive to some BCCC members, especially after Bill Clinton's presidential victory. With Clinton's victory, Edelman pursued an innovative way to merge the BSLN's mobilization efforts and the Freedom School program with the U.S. Department of Agriculture's Summer Food Service Program (SFSP).

The SFSP was an entitlement program created in 1968 that offered free and reduced-price lunches to children in poor communities. It was particularly important because many children who received free or reduced-price lunches from their schools during the academic year were left to go hungry during the summer, once they were out of school. Despite the SFSP's importance, it reached only about 2 million out of the eligible 13 million children (Johnson & Hoy, 1994, p. 1). Social advocates were convinced that the program failed to reach those who were eligible for the program because its feeding sites were poorly administered and inoperative. In some cases, families were unaware of the program, or were discouraged from sending their children to the sites because they were rumored to serve unhealthy food. Thus, to encourage hungry children and families to use the free food program, Edelman insisted that the BSLN restructure its summer organizing initiative and implement Freedom Schools that would be used as feeding sites for the USDA's program.

The BSLN's leadership cadre endorsed the Freedom School proposal for the summer of 1993, even though it forced them to abandon plans to carry out an organizing campaign similar to the one that had occurred the previous summer in North Carolina. They believed the program could replicate the SNCC's Freedom Schools from 3 decades earlier, as well as enhance the youth group's organizing efforts and expand its constituency. They received additional encouragement from Edelman, who wanted the Ella Baker Child Policy Training Institute to train more than 100 college-age young people for the 1993 summer, and to staff Freedom School sites around the country. Furthermore, the idea of linking the Department of Agriculture's food service program with the BSLN-run Freedom Schools created the opportunity to use anti-hunger policy as a vehicle for organizing residents around local issues.

The summer workers/organizers—officially called teaching interns— recruited by the BSLN, were sent to work in Freedom Schools around the country after they completed the institute's 2-week training. The summer workers and local BCCC members, in turn, recruited children into the Freedom Schools, and informed eligible residents within the schools' communities about the food service program.

FREEDOM SCHOOLS AND DIVERGING VIEWPOINTS
WITHIN THE BCCC-BSLN COALITION

Although the BSLN members enthusiastically endorsed the Freedom School program, they also expressed some concerns about the overall direction and operations of the Freedom Schools. The BSLN's leadership cadre feared that some BCCC members wanted to shape the program as a service-based initiative that de-emphasized community organizing and political engagement. Such an initiative could serve as a model program for others across the nation, and perhaps garner support among public officials and liberal allies. However, given their extensive backgrounds as social and political activists, the BSLN's influential leaders insisted upon establishing a Freedom School program that would organize poor Black communities around progressive policies. National BSLN director Steve White believed that such a program would attract progressive students who might have otherwise been "turned off by just solely working on children's issues" (White, 2000).

To formalize their concerns, Countryman and Sullivan developed a Freedom School program curriculum rooted in community organizing and direct action advocacy. It was a step-by-step, full-scale community-organizing plan, which was to be implemented by the summer workers in 1993. It was designed to have the summer workers, as well as the children and teenagers who participated in the program, organize local communities to evaluate the USDA feeding sites through surveys and parental evaluations. Other components of the curriculum involved door-to-door outreach efforts and meetings with editorial boards of newspapers and elected officials, both of which were to bring attention to the problems of the feeding sites, and to encourage more families to use the food service program (Countryman, 2000).

The curriculum was ambitious, and would have been difficult to implement given the demands of running a school-based program during the summer. Nonetheless, it would have been effective in accommodating the BCCC's interests of developing a model program that could be duplicated across the nation. At the same time, the curriculum would have engaged the summer workers and Freedom School attendees in what Countryman called "the politics of the community" (Countryman, 2000). Unfortunately, this proposal was rejected by some BCCC members, perhaps due to the concerns that it could potentially expose the USDA's poor administration of the feeding sites, and give conservatives ammunition for introducing cutbacks to the feeding program.

The BSLN's leadership core agreed to support the Freedom School concept, despite the exclusion of its comprehensive organizing plan. As a substitute, they modified the curriculum and organizing strategy by removing the community evaluation. They focused most of the training for the summer institute on civil rights movement history, as well as community organizing and direct action advocacy. They brought in a group of educators and conflict resolution specialists who helped the summer workers with their teaching methodology, and prepared them to adjust to the daily challenges of teaching marginalized and at-risk children who made up the nucleus of the Freedom Schools.

Still, the rejection of the curriculum caused some tension between the BSLN and BCCC, and underscored what some BSLN members perceived as larger philosophical differences between the two organizations. These philosophical differences were hinted at in a 1993 essay by Steve White, Lisa Sullivan, and Matthew Countryman, the most influential members of the BSLN's inner circle.

The commentary derided "traditional Black politics" and the "civil rights politics" of Black leaders [the BCCC] for ignoring the concerns of alienated Black youth and for embracing strategies that were safe, that befitted a middle-class agenda, and that had no immediate or long-term impact (White, Sullivan, & Countryman, 1992–1993, pp. 6–7). It said that these leaders "impede our efforts to build effective broad-based political support in the Black community for the policies and programs that will solve the current crisis of Black youth." The authors further argued that "Rather than viewing poor and working-class members of our community as potential agents for social change, middle-class-led organizations too often see those who are poor and less educated as constituents to be served" (White, Sullivan, & Countryman, 1992–1993, p. 1). The essay indirectly targeted Edelman. As the principal advocate for the BCCC, she had an overwhelming influence on the BCCC's direction, especially in relation to the debates over the Freedom School program. BSLN members believed that she favored a more service-based-type program geared toward academic and cultural enrichment, and one that was probably more acceptable to political and foundation elites. Furthermore, a similar, yet locally based, initiative/school-based program had already been in operation in the CDF–Marlboro County Office, in her hometown of Bennettsville, South Carolina. The CDF poured resources into that program, and it experienced a great deal of success in combating child malnutrition and other public health dilemmas, which may have contributed to her belief that a successful, service-based program could be replicated nationally through the BSLN-run Freedom Schools.

The disagreement over the Freedom School curriculum reflected a national debate involving some BSLN members over the relationship between community service or volunteerism and youth-based social movements. BSLN members were critical of community-based initiatives that were entirely service-based (such as mentoring, tutoring, volunteering in homeless programs, working in soup kitchens, and so forth). These initiatives were nonconfrontational and less concerned with developing the leadership capacity of the college-age activists.

Interestingly, there were divergent viewpoints within the BCCC's leadership infrastructure about the Freedom School program that were not taken into account in the criticisms by the BSLN's leadership cadre. These viewpoints were revealed at a July 1993 BCCC retreat in Sante Fe, New Mexico. At the meeting, the BCCC's Education Committee held a similar viewpoint to that of the BSLN's leadership cadre. Drs. Ed Gordon and James Comer, both of Yale University, saw the Freedom School program as a vehicle for mobilizing local communities. Comer stated that the Freedom Schools had the "potential to serve as a focal point for mobilizing the Black community," particularly around educational and economic development initiatives (Black Community Crusade for Children, 1993, p. 27). Gordon saw the Freedom School program as a "perfect vehicle for pulling youths back into the mainstream," and for bridging the growing class divide in the Black community, or, as he stated, for connecting "functioning" elements of the Black community (college students) with "nonfunctioning" segments (some economically disadvantaged children and families) (BCCC, 1993, p. 26).

After the summer of 1994, the majority of the direct action and community-organizing activities of the Ella Baker Child Policy Training Institute that were present from 1992 to 1994 were taken out; the BCCC essentially took over the institute. A Freedom School curriculum team, comprised of BSLN and BCCC members, was given the task of developing training sessions and Freedom School curricula that engaged school-age participants in academic and cultural enrichment. The BCCC also changed the age requirements for the Freedom School children. Whereas the 1993 and 1994 summer Freedom School program accepted anyone into the Freedom Schools who was under 18 years of age, beginning in 1995, the participants could be no older than 12 years old. This was an attempt to pattern the Freedom School program after a more traditional, elementary academic setting.

By the end of 1994, the BCCC began to channel the responsibilities of the development of the Freedom School curriculum to the staff of the CDF–Marlboro County Office. The staff, in turn, began to exercise control over the Freedom School program and patterned much of it after its own academic and cultural enrichment programs. By 1996, the Marlboro County Office gained virtually complete control over the design of the curriculum.

INNOVATIONS, CHALLENGES, AND DISPUTES IN THE SUMMER FREEDOM SCHOOL PROGRAM

Despite the recurring debates about the Freedom School curricula, the expansion of Freedom Schools across the country allowed the BSLN to make tremendous strides, in terms of its mobilization and outreach efforts.

With the backing of the CDF and BCCC, the BSLN opened over a dozen Freedom School sites in a number of cities and rural jurisdictions throughout the country. About 800 Black college-age young people participated in the Ella Baker Policy Training Institute and Freedom Schools between 1993 and 1996. In 1994, close to 400 young people attended the BSLN's national conference, and more than 1,200 attended its annual conference in 1996.

In addition, the Freedom Schools allowed the BSLN to recruit young people who were not as ideologically on the left as the organization's leadership, but were attracted to the program's focus on children (Chatmon, 2000). This gave the BSLN the opportunity to politicize young people who otherwise may have not been exposed to social justice issues.

Notwithstanding the tensions between the BCCC and BSLN leadership cadres, some local affiliates shaped and altered the operations of the Freedom Schools, to mirror their distinct political orientations.

For all of its positive outcomes, the Freedom School program experienced some growing pains from 1993 to 1996, all of which placed BSLN members under intense scrutiny by BCCC leadership. A major concern was that the BSLN summer organizers were overwhelmed by the variety of public health epidemics in the program (Walker, 2000). Many Freedom School children suffered from mental health problems, as well as sexual and physical abuse, and some were adversely affected by community violence.[2] Addressing these problems went beyond the scope of the Freedom School training and curriculum, and required far greater attention from health-care professionals, social workers, and counselors.

Another challenge was that the Freedom Schools were established in collaboration with local support agencies, community organizations, and churches. In some places, the summer workers received little actual assistance from sponsoring organizations. In some localities, BSLN summer workers had to compete with entrenched local organizations for the same children to participate in the program, or they clashed with sponsoring organizations over the direction of the program.

In the summer of 1993, the BSLN's Freedom Schools in Harlem, New York, were hosted by Geoffrey Canada's Rheedlen Centers. Canada was a leading figure in the BCCC and the Rheedlen Centers was widely considered one of the country's most successful urban, anti-poverty organizations. Yet disagreements surfaced between Canada and BSLN members after he expressed his discontent at having little input in the hiring and management of the Freedom School staff for Harlem's four Freedom School sites (Burrowes, 2000; Canada, 2001). BSLN organizers at the two Freedom Schools in Los Angeles and Watts during the summers of 1993 and 1994 also expressed concerns about the lack of resource support from the BCCC's local sponsoring agency, the Charles Drew Development Corporation (Taaffe, 1999;

Gavins, 2000; Greene, 2000). To make matters more complicated, the BSLN and BCCC did not have enough support from indigenous, homegrown activists, beyond the Drew organization.

Most of the summer workers were from outside of the Los Angeles area and were unaccustomed to its political culture. They were unfamiliar with the spatial reality of Los Angeles, which differed from midwestern, eastern seaboard, and Southern urban centers. Sean Greene, a native of New Haven, Connecticut, who worked in Los Angeles as a Freedom School intern and later as a community organizer with the Community Coalition, said that "the [BSLN's direct action organizing] model was developed with the East Coast in mind and that just didn't work once we got to L.A." (Greene, 2000). He described the Los Angeles area as a place where there existed "a bunch of neighborhoods linked together," yet "worlds apart." He said the lack of transportation in the vast landscape of Los Angeles made organizing extremely difficult. BSLN activists further described the Los Angeles community as "turf conscious." Local activists were wary about outsiders coming into their communities and leading programs, and competing for the same constituencies and resources, a suspicion not unique to Los Angeles.

Convincing local agencies to raise funds for the costs of the Freedom Schools and pay the summer workers was another difficult task. As the program expanded, Freedom Schools were generally limited only to communities and organizations that had the capacity and local support networks to run and help raise the funds. The irony was that between 1993 and 1996, it cost a relatively substantial amount of money to operate a Freedom School program, considering that some jurisdictions operated two or three Freedom School sites. Estimated costs of $43,000 for a program made Freedom Schools unattractive to some community organizations/agencies.

The fund-raising controversy was exemplified in the deliberations to establish Freedom Schools in Raleigh, North Carolina, in 1994. Although there was strong community interest to establish a program in Raleigh, the local organizations and agencies lacked the resources. Lisa Sullivan made an appeal to Edelman for additional monetary resources, to support local efforts to open up Freedom School sites in Raleigh. She proposed that funds be redirected from the previous year's budget to support these efforts. Edelman, on the other hand, believed that a community agency's ability to raise part of the funds was demonstrative of its willingness and commitment to run an effective program.

THE DEMOBILIZATION OF THE BSLN

Unfortunately, the BSLN collapsed in August 1996, due to recurring struggles over the BSLN's autonomy between the youth group's leadership cadre—its Steering Committee and advisors—and some of the CDF and BCCC's key leaders. The tensions fueling these debates had always existed. Yet they boiled over in the summer of 1996, after some BSLN members questioned the utility of expending their resources and energies on CDF/BCCC projects, particularly the parent organizations' efforts to defeat impending federal legislation to eliminate welfare (Personal Responsibility and Reconciliation Act, P.L. 104-93).

Although BSLN members adamantly opposed President Clinton's welfare reform legislation and understood the urgent need to defeat it, they insisted that more attention should be given to expanding their recruitment base and implementing their newly developed organizing project. This project was outlined in three proposals between 1995 and early 1996: the "One Thousand by Two Thousand" project, Citizenship 2000, and the Black Youth Vote project (Hoy, Gavins, & Walker, 1995; View, 1996). Collectively, these projects would have created a virtual army of young progressive organizers who concentrated their efforts on community organizing, education, and electoral organizing. If successful, the BSLN's leadership core believed they could create a space for young people to participate in progressive, grassroots organizing initiatives, along the same lines as the conservative movement's successful effort to recruit college students in the 1980s.

As early as February 1996, the BSLN began to mobilize support among Black and Latino youth for these initiatives. In coordination with the CDF's annual gathering in Charlotte, North Carolina, the BSLN organized a parallel conference. As a result of an extensive recruitment drive, it brought more than 1,200 Black and Latino high school and college students and young community organizers to the event. Through training sessions and workshops, the youth were introduced to topics related to advocacy, direct action organizing, and public policy (Black Student Leadership Network, 1996). Yet, notwithstanding these efforts, these initiatives were not fully implemented due to internal dissensions within the CDF/BCCC/BSLN alliance, and the ultimate collapse of the BSLN by August 1996.

CONCLUSION

Despite its short-lived history (1991–1996), the BSLN trained hundreds of youth and young adults in community organizing, child advocacy, and teaching methodology. The BSLN's flagship initiative, the summer Freedom School program, operated in dozens of locales throughout the country. The Freedom Schools gave the BSLN and its parent organizations, the Children's Defense Fund and the Black Community Crusade for Children, the opportunity to immerse young people in on-the-ground organizing campaigns, and to cultivate relationships with indigenous activists at the local levels.

The disputes over optimum strategies—organizing against welfare re-form or developing a comprehensive grassroots organizing campaign—underscored larger tensions over the BSLN's autonomy. These tensions were exacerbated by the BSLN's reliance upon the CDF and BCCC for infrastruc-ture and financial support. The CDF and BCCC's leadership believed that since it provided the BSLN with resources that were critical to its mainte-nance and survival, the youth group should endorse their initiatives.

The break-up of the CDF/BCCC/BSLN was unfortunate and, perhaps, avoidable. Yet, despite the nature of the BSLN's collapse, its leadership and constituents acknowledged the significance of their alliance with the CDF and BCCC. The parent groups provided mentorship and infrastructure to the BSLN. Without these resources, the BSLN would not have blossomed into a full-fledged, social movement organization. Marian Wright Edelman created an intergenerational bridge between the assortment of activists in-volved in BSLN's formation, and pulled together the resources that were essential to the overall development of the summer Freedom School program.

Notwithstanding the BSLN's collapse, the summer Freedom School pro-gram continued to remain in operation. After 1996, the Children's Defense Fund's Student Leadership Network for Children (SLNC) replaced the BSLN and staffed the summer Freedom School program. (The student activists who remained affiliated with the CDF/BCCC morphed into the SLNC.) Currently, the CDF supervises the Freedom Schools and still recruits students (also called interns) to staff the program.

These efforts demonstrate the continued importance of parallel institu-tionalism in the Black community. For the BSLN, the Freedom School pro-gram served as vehicle for introducing young people to grassroots activism and community organizing. It further served as a tool for connecting young people to indigenous leaders and seasoned activists, many of whom cut their teeth in the civil rights movement.

NOTES

1. This information is based on my three dozen interviews with BSLN and BCCC activists, as well as my participant observation as a summer Freedom School intern between 1993 and 1996.

2. This information is based on my experience as a Freedom School organizer for four summers (1993–1996) in Oakland, California, as well as my numerous conversations with Freedom School organizers. I also worked as a teaching intern/organizer for the Mason-Butler-Hobson Freedom School.

CHAPTER 16

The P-O-W-E-R of Children's Defense Fund Freedom Schools

Gale Seiler

"I Can and Must Make a Difference" is the guiding theme of the Children's Defense Fund (CDF) Freedom Schools.® Across the country at more than 80 Freedom Schools in the summer of 2005, this theme encouraged and empowered African American children to make a difference in themselves, as well as in their families, communities, country, and world. Modeled after the Mississippi Freedom Schools founded by members of the Student Nonviolent Coordinating Committee in the 1960s, the current CDF Freedom Schools summer program arose from the work of the Black Student Leadership Network in the 1990s, as described in Chapter 15. As in the 1960s, the danger is still real; an African American male has one chance in 9,900 to earn a Ph.D. in math, but a one in three chance of being under the control of the penal system (Children's Defense Fund, 2006). Like the original Freedom Schools, the current initiative aims to provide youth with both roots and wings, arming them with social, cultural, and historical awareness. With a nationally recognized reading curriculum, African American youth discover a connection between literacy and liberation as they read texts that reflect positive and empowering images of themselves.

As summer programs of 5 to 6 weeks duration, Freedom Schools offer something that traditional public schools usually do not—they connect with the culture of the African American attendees and create in these young people the desire to participate as valued members of a community that both reaffirms and develops their identities, an approach that many educators have identified as key in reversing the failure of schools to educate African American children (see, for example, Ladson-Billings, 1995; Murrell, 2001).

THE SUCCESS AND GROWTH OF CHILDREN'S DEFENSE FUND FREEDOM SCHOOLS

The current CDF Freedom Schools initiative has grown since the mid-1990s, both in the number of sites and the number of children served. Many individual sites have swelled from 50 to 200 attendees; in some cities the number of sites has expanded from one to 10 or more. Kansas City Freedom Schools recently received funding from the Ewing Marion Kauffman Foundation to expand to 20 sites. In 2004 the CDF Freedom Schools won the Excellence in Summer Learning Award from the Institute for Summer Learning at Johns Hopkins University.

Anecdotal accounts of the power of Freedom Schools have accumulated over the past 10 years as scholars and servant-leaders[1] attest to the many ways that Freedom Schools have made a difference in their lives. A number of servant-leaders have "come up" through Freedom Schools, first as scholars, then as junior-servant-leaders, and then as servant-leaders. Some have become trainers at the national level (Ella Baker Trainers) or site coordinators of local Freedom Schools, and others have worked at the Children's Defense Fund's national office. Thus, they represent success in one of the Freedom Schools goals—the nurturing and development of a cadre of leaders, activists, and organizers.

THE ROLE OF SERVANT-LEADERS

The servant-leaders at Freedom Schools throughout the country are chosen to serve as "real models" for the youth who attend, to show the young scholars that people who are like them can aspire to college and careers, and can also make a commitment to serve and to lead. The Children's Defense Fund reports that between 40 and 50% of the servant-leaders who attend national training each year are returnees, that is, they have worked at Freedom Schools in previous summers.

Many servant-leaders describe working in a Freedom School as a transformational experience, in terms of their own identity and their aspirations; a number have changed their college majors and are becoming teachers. A first-year servant-leader wrote this reflection, "I was apprehensive about it at first because I never thought I was really the teaching type. I realized that I'm more of a teacher than I would ever admit."

Working at a Freedom School in Baltimore impacted the servant-leaders' feelings of responsibility to serve and to lead in the Baltimore community, as well as the way the servant-leaders understood young Black teens. An African American male servant-leader who grew up in Baltimore explains,

"Learning about the scholars' lives and their personal situations made me feel obligated to some degree to help these kids make the best decisions they could." A female servant-leader who immigrated to the United States from Nigeria when she was young, acknowledged her own growth:

> I really began to understand how our environment and experiences that we go through affect who we are. For me, I got a better understanding of the African American struggle after emancipation and how it is still affecting us today.

THE BALTIMORE FREEDOM SCHOOL

Baltimore exemplifies a city whose children and teens greatly need the culturally congruent approach found in Freedom Schools. The Baltimore City Public Schools are 88% African American, and over 50% of its students do not receive a high school diploma.

The Baltimore Freedom School summer program began in 2005 and is held at a public high school in Baltimore (however, it is not formally associated with the Baltimore public school system). It is the only Freedom School site in the country that serves high-school-age youth exclusively. During its first 2 summers, the Baltimore Freedom School had 11 servant-leaders; six were male, and two were White. Four attended Morgan State University, a historically Black College/University (HBCU) in Baltimore; three attended the University of Maryland; and the others attended college out of state though they were from Baltimore. Three servant-leaders, along with the site coordinator, had previously worked at Freedom Schools in other states. In its first year, 94% of the scholars were African American; 35% lived with both parents; 14% had a mother with a college degree, but none had a father with a college degree.

At this site, one of the ways we measured success during the first year of operation was by how many scholars attended and completed this optional summer program. Even we were surprised at the high daily attendance rate (over 90%) although the participants had to walk or travel on public transportation from their neighborhoods throughout the city to arrive each morning. Fifteen out of 49 scholars received awards for perfect attendance. In many ways this belies common stereotypes about African American urban youth as not finding value in education.

Ninety-eight percent of the parents and guardians responding to a survey at the Baltimore site reported that scholars were more motivated to attend the Freedom School than to attend school during the year. Several described how their scholars developed a new habit in which they set the alarm clock and got themselves up, not wanting to miss or be late for Freedom School.

Nearly all parents and guardians gave testament to the positive influence of the Freedom Schools experience on their children. One said of her daughter, "She learned about self-motivation, self-awareness, and self-expression." And another recounted, "He came out of his shell and socialized in a positive way."

Nearly three fourths of the scholars at the Baltimore Freedom School in 2005 were young men. We learned in talking with their families that they had great concern for the well-being of their African American teenage males on the streets of Baltimore in the summer. The families knew the dangers of Baltimore's high rates of murder and violent crime and the high incidence of police harassment and arrests.

THE CULTURAL RELEVANCE OF FREEDOM SCHOOLS

As noted earlier, the teenage scholars at the Baltimore site attended with great regularity. But what is it about Freedom Schools that keeps the movement going and growing and makes it effective with young people of many ages? The ability of Freedom Schools to infuse the learning environment with cultural resonance seems to be key to their success and growth. In both implicit and explicit ways, the program elements are attuned with the history and culture of the participants who, in Baltimore and elsewhere, are largely African American youth.

Just outside the Baltimore Freedom School, you pass the Civil Rights Memorial Garden, composed of trees and shrubs planted on a hot summer day by scholars and servant-leaders and surrounded by flat bricks on which the names of chosen civil rights heroes and heroines are painted. Inside the building, a banner hand-painted in red, black, and green welcomes scholars and visitors to the school cafeteria. Music from the Freedom Schools CD fills the air at breakfast and lunch, and inspires scholars to sing along or break into dance. At the finale on the last day, the scholars in the processional sway to the music of Sweet Honey in the Rock singing "We Who Believe in Freedom" as they enter the auditorium, and they wear scarves of African motif fabrics draped around their necks.

HARAMBEE

Perhaps the best example of the infusion of positive cultural messages into the Freedom School ethos is the daily opening session called Harambee, which fills the halls with chants, cheers, and stomps. *Harambee* is a Kiswahili word meaning "let's pull together," and it is a time for the entire Freedom School community to come together in celebration, both individually and communally. Harambee is an upbeat, energetic, expressive interaction using music, call and response, and movement that provides an opportunity for scholars to display and share aspects of their cultural identities in a setting where they are valued.

Scholars, parents, and guardians at the Baltimore Freedom School told us that Harambee is the part of the Freedom School experience that keeps teens coming back. When asked what part of the program had the greatest impact on their child, 72% of parents and guardians responded, "Harambee," or some component of it. Parents repeatedly made comments such as, "Even being a summer program, he would go to bed at a reasonable time, just to get up on his own in the morning ready for Freedom School and that Harambee." In an open-ended survey item that read, "What I like best about Freedom School is . . .", 75% of the scholars cited Harambee or some part of it. When asked what they liked *least* about Freedom School, one scholar's response was, "When I'm late for Harambee." One response to the survey question "What would happen if you got to Freedom School and there was no Harambee that day?" summed up the emotional force that Harambee has on Freedom School scholars: "If there was no Harambee I would cry and want to go back home." Another scholar put it, "It's crunk.[2] I'm gonna miss it."

Harambee at all Freedom Schools across the country follows the same 30-minute schedule: Read-Aloud (often with a guest reader), Theme Song, Cheers/Chants, Recognitions, Moment of Silence, and Announcements. At the Baltimore Freedom School, Harambee took place in the lunchroom of the school building. As the session began with the Read-Aloud, the participants sat at the cafeteria tables and then moved to an open area of the lunchroom as the words of the theme song rose from the CD player. Scholars, staff, and guests formed a large circle facing inward, with the servant-leaders inside the circle leading the proceedings. Throughout Harambee, the scholars stood close together, side by side, sometimes entering the circle themselves to lead a cheer or make a recognition. Depending on the activity there was sometimes more than one caller, and the caller frequently changed. Participants were usually in synchrony with each other and responded on cue to callers, both orally and physically, using verbal chants, clapping, dance steps, or gestures.

Read-Aloud and Theme Song

The Read-Aloud selection sets the tone for the session and begins to focus the attention of the participants. Scholars normally sit and listen during this time, or interact with the story or reading for the day. Moving into the theme song, the participants rise, sing, and move to the song "Something Inside So Strong" by Labi Siffre, using hand and body motions that they have learned from the servant-leaders and personally stylized. The following transcript of the chorus of the song conveys the mood and involvement of the participants as they sing along.

Although the style of this song is not hip-hop, the musical genre most familiar to youth today, the inclusion of hand and body motions invites the scholars to get involved in it. Since its selection by the national program as the Freedom School theme song, it has morphed into a version that is more connected with youth. The original version contains a musical interlude after the third verse. Several years ago at national training, servant-leaders filled this musical space with a verse from a song by hip-hop artist Nas, called "I Can." With clapping and call and response, this verse is now included in the theme song.

At local sites, scholars and servant-leaders commonly personalize the motions and lyrics of the theme song by adding a new movement or a soulful "Oooooooh, ooh, ooh" to the song. For example, during the line "We're gonna do it anyway," participants usually pump their fists in the air, but at the Baltimore Freedom School, they incorporated high fives and chest bumping at this point in the song. The way in which these additions are embraced by the group and included in the performance illustrates one of the important aspects of Freedom Schools—they allow for individual expressiveness while generating solidarity.

TABLE 16.1: Freedom School Theme Song

SONG LYRICS	ACTIONS
Something inside So strong	Both hands tap the chest. Fists are clenched and both arms are bent to show a flexed bicep muscle.
I know that I can make it	Index fingers tap the temples.
'Though you're doing me wrong, so wrong	Hands are waved horizontally in front of the body.
You thought that my pride was gone	Hands cover the eyes and face.
Oh no, something inside so strong	Hands are waved horizontally in front of the body. Both hands tap the chest. Fists are clenched and both arms are bent to show a flexed bicep muscle.

Cheers and Chants

Following the theme song, Harambee intensifies as scholars and servant-leaders engage in cheers and chants. These are high-energy and engaging, involving both verbal and physical participation. The cheers and chants have evolved over the past 10 years, often being "remixed" at national training or at local sites. Like the theme song, these are learned by the servant-leaders and taught to the scholars.

A visitor to Harambee will immediately notice the call and response patterns that engage the participants, as shown in the table below. These practices are part of the African American experience, and their roots have been traced to traditions in West Africa. Although the students do not know the formal names of the traditional forms, they need no instruction in how to participate in them orally and physically.

P-O-W-E-R

By far, the favorite cheer of the scholars at the Baltimore Freedom School, the one they would break into spontaneously whenever there was a lull in

TABLE 16.2: Call and Response in Cheers and Chants

NAME OF CHEER	CALL & RESPONSE FORM	WORDS AND ACTIONS
Boom Chick-a Boom	**Neighboring** (caller initiates and responders repeat the phrase)	*Caller*: I said a boom chick-a boom. *Responder*: I said a boom chick-a boom.
Freedom School Is Where It's At	**Closed Inquiry** (caller asks a question, followed by a simple, often one-word, response)	*Caller*: Y'all tired yet? *Responder*: No. *Caller*: Y'all ready to quit? *Responder*: No.
Red Hot	**Ellipsing** (responder completes the initiator's sentence)	*Caller*: Freedom School is *Responder*: R-E-D with a little bit of H-O-T.
Gator	**Appeal and Action** (responder replies with an action)	*Caller*: Let me see you do the gator. *Responder*: Do the gator. Do, do the gator. (Imitates a gator with his/her arms.)

the chants and cheers of Harambee, was "Power" in which the word was spelled out to start the cheer:

Group: P-O-W-E-R. We got the power
    Cause we are the superstars
Individual: My name is Carmen
    And I'm first on the list
    I got my reputation
    Cause I do it like this
    (*Individual demonstrates expressive movement.*)
Group: She does it like this
    (*Group imitates individual's movement.*)

This cheer is emblematic of the culturally resonant approach used in Freedom Schools. It relies on a call and response pattern, encourages participants to use both their voices and their bodies, and develops interpersonal bonds by alternating between individual and group actions. Such cheers and chants build on and give expression to cultural dispositions shared to varying degrees by many African Americans.

Nearly 30% of the scholars listed this specific cheer as their favorite part of Freedom School. It gave them a chance to express their individuality and to have their expression repeated by the others. Some performances were "off the chain," while others were more laid back. Several scholars and interns became associated with specific moves that they performed when doing this chant, and those moves became their trademark.

The emotional level intensified as Harambee progressed from the theme song into the cheers and chants. The positive nature of the emotions generated during Harambee was evident in the smiles, laughter, and hoots and hollers of the participants, and their willingness to stand and participate for 15 to 20 minutes in the morning.

Recognitions and Moment of Silence

Building on the energy of the cheers and chants, recognitions follow. The increasing volume of both caller and responder demonstrates the energy and enthusiasm that each recognition generates:

Caller: I got a recognition!
Responders: Recognize!
Caller: I said, I got a recognition! (*louder or in another expressive style*)
Responders: Recognize! (*louder*)

Caller: I want to recognize all the scholars who got here on time this morning!

Recognitions are commonly offered to acknowledge positive behavior, for a special occasion such as a birthday, or sometimes for something trivial, such as "I wanna recognize everyone who has on a shirt with a collar today." The Moment of Silence is designed to bring the collective energy level back down, while preserving the positive feelings generated by the preceding events of Harambee. Participants are asked to reflect on how they feel at that moment and to envision how they will make a difference in their own and each other's lives during that day. During Harambee, feelings of solidarity and personal emotional energy are generated, and these positive feelings are carried away as the group breaks up and disperses into the morning literacy sessions.

FROM HARAMBEE TO THE IRC

Following Harambee, the morning session at all Freedom Schools is devoted to reading. The Integrated Reading Curriculum (IRC) is an activity-oriented curriculum designed to motivate, challenge, and inspire young readers. The goal of the curriculum is to help both readers and nonreaders develop a love for books and a desire to read. The IRC contains four levels corresponding to grades in school, and books are selected to align with weekly themes: I Can and Must Make a Difference in My: Self (Week 1), Family (Week 2), Community (Week 3), Country (Week 4), and World (Week 5).

Each year new books are chosen and new lesson plans are developed for the IRC by the CDF national office. The books are selected to be developmentally appropriate, introduce the children to people who have made a difference in the lives of others, help children explore issues related to self-esteem, and expand the children's capacity to dream and to believe they can turn their dreams into reality (Children's Defense Fund, n.d.).

The lesson plans that comprise the IRC are designed not only to develop skills in reading, but also cooperative learning, critical thinking, social action, conflict resolution, and discussion skills. They tap into scholars' multiple modes of intelligence by using drawing, diagramming, poetry and prose writing, role-playing, and other forms of expression. The intention is to engage all scholars, regardless of their reading ability. Thus, at the high school level (Level IV), the IRC includes a great deal of group work, peer reading, and summarizing chapters, so that all participants can progress through and understand the books and benefit from their important themes. This makes for lively, interactive classrooms; as in Harambee, it also creates opportunities for the scholars to express themselves individually and to cement group bonds.

At times, Harambee cheers make their way into the IRC and become resources for interpreting the readings and working together to complete the classroom activities. Perhaps the most common Freedom School chant is "Good Job" in which the words are spelled out and accompanied by clapping.

> Good job, good job.
> G-double-O-D-J-O-B
> Good job, good job.

Scholars, servant-leaders, and staff frequently use this recognition to applaud a strong effort or to offer praise or gratitude. Once someone starts it, others always join in, and then sometimes there is a remix.

In most educational settings, such spontaneous "outbursts" would not be acceptable, since the culture and experiences of African American young people are often maligned and devalued in school. Through Harambee, the IRC, and other aspects of Freedom Schools, scholars experience their cultural affinity to orality, movement, expressiveness, and communalism (Boykin, 1986) as something of value.

Music, dance, and call and response are deeply embedded in African American culture, including youth hip-hop culture. Freedom Schools recognize these historical and social threads that permeate culture. Freedom Schools succeed because, like the Freedom Schools of the Mississippi Summer Project of 1964, they are rooted in a "deep-seated understanding of African American experience, culture, and heritage and the ways that this understanding informs successful teaching of African American children" (Murrell, 2001, p. xxiii) and there is much to be learned from their success.

NOTES

1. The primary teachers and leaders in CDF Freedom Schools are college students who are called servant-leaders to honor their dual role, both to serve and to lead. The children participating in Freedom Schools are called scholars to acknowledge their intellectual capacity. These names were specially chosen by the Children's Defense Fund and are used at Freedom School sites across the country. For that reason they are used throughout this chapter.

2. *Crunk* means crazy with energy and volume.

CHAPTER 17

Emancipatory Education Versus School-Based Violence Prevention

Randolph G. Potts

School-based prevention programs have targeted problems such as substance abuse, school maladjustment, teen pregnancy, delinquency, and violence through person-centered and environmental programs (Durlak & Wells, 1997; Mason, Cauce, Robinson, & Harper, 1999). The data on school failure, violence, and substance abuse do not tell the whole story of the cultural experiences of children of African descent, nor of the structures and processes that sustain these problems. Children and adolescents of African descent only become "at-risk" under specific historical circumstances. However, in most school-based prevention programs, the only targets of change are the individual behaviors, attitudes, and interpersonal skills of children. In their review of 177 primary prevention programs for children and adolescents, Durlak and Wells (1997) found that that 150 of these interventions (84.8%) were person-centered. This focus on change at the individual level neglects the sociopolitical forces that shape people's lives. This rather superficial approach to social problems does not go undetected by participants in school-based interventions, as the following example shows.

> Part of my training as a first-year community psychology doctoral student involved conducting a substance abuse prevention program in a "behavior disorder" (BD) classroom in an elementary school near a Chicago public housing complex. The class consisted entirely of African American males. The intervention modules we were given by our community psychologist supervisors consisted of educational materials on the effects of drugs on the body, but mostly decision-making exercises calling upon the children to "stop and think" in

A version of this essay appeared as Potts, Randolph G., 2004, Emancipatory Education Versus School-Based Prevention in African American Communities, *American Journal of Community Psychology, Vol. 31*, No. 1. Reprinted with permission from Springer.

situations in which they were exposed to drugs. In the midst of one of these exercises focusing mainly on the children's cognitive skills, one of the students in the class illuminated the discussion by saying: "We're not the main people responsible for the drug problem. None of us and nobody we know flies any planes full of drugs into this country." Several other students in the class echoed these concerns that our emphasis on strategies for individuals to avoid drug use fell far short of addressing a larger social problem of which individual drug use is just one part.

These students offered a cogent critique of the person-centered perspective of this prevention program. Interventions that depoliticize social problems, define them as individual problems, and prescribe only individual changes on the part of the oppressed serve to protect and maintain the status quo (Prilleltensky & Fox, 1997). Such conceptualizations of social problems inhibit the flow of creative, liberating dialogue and social action.

Similarly, school-based violence prevention programs tend to focus on helping individuals manage their anger and resolve interpersonal conflict through enhanced communication and decision-making skills. Such interventions typically do not address the violence between social groups that has historically had a devastating impact on African American communities. African psychiatrist Frantz Fanon describes violence as a process through which the physical, social, or psychological integrity (or a combination of these) of another person or group is violated (Bulhan, 1985). Fanon described how victims of vertical (structural) violence may often unleash their anger and frustration through interpersonal ("horizontal") violence against others in their community or themselves (Bulhan, 1985). Fanon also suggested that the development of political consciousness may reduce internecine violence among the oppressed.

EMANCIPATORY EDUCATION

An emancipatory African-centered model of education is defined here as one that (1) addresses social oppression and situates community problems within historical context, (2) acknowledges students as agents for social change, and (3) affirms African cultural resources for healing and social transformation. One underlying assumption in advocating a critical Africanist pedagogy for children of African descent is that affirming a child's African identity may be associated with beneficial outcomes. A growing body of research is emerging in support of the proposition that knowledge of and respect for African culture may be positively associated with educational success and other healthy outcomes for children of African descent. For example, several studies suggest that "racial socialization" may act as a buffer against negative racial experiences and messages with which children are confronted (Stevenson, 1994, 1995). Racial socialization involves transactions with care providers through which ethnic pride and an awareness of racism in society are conveyed to the child (Bowman & Howard, 1985; Stevenson, 1994). Bowman and Howard (1985) found that racial socialization was associated with greater academic achievement among African American children.

There is additional evidence that positive regard toward one's ethnic group, as measured by scales of ethnic identity, is related to educational success and other healthy outcomes. In an ecological study of ninth-grade classroom environments, Sheets (1999) found that programs using cultural knowledge and promoting ethnic identity had higher levels of academic success. A study by Smith and others (1999) found that ethnic identity and self-esteem contribute to children's perceptions of their ability to achieve academically and other prosocial attitudes. Belgrave, Van Oss Marin, and Chambers (2000) found higher ethnic identity to be associated with less risky sexual attitudes among female African American adolescents. Similar research finds positive relationships between racial identity and drug attitudes among African American children (e.g., Townsend & Belgrave, 2000), and racial identity and other competencies among African American adolescents (e.g., Arroyo & Zigler, 1995).

Education is itself a process of cultural socialization and identity discovery. One of the most significant healthy outcomes of African-centered emancipatory education may be the student as social change agent. Within this pedagogical framework,

> Students do not learn to read and write; they read and write in order to learn. Liberatory education provides them with the heuristic tools and skills to critique ideas. . . . Liberatory education expands one's horizons and challenges the cultural hegemony of the traditional canons. (Gordon, 1995, p. 65)

Students participating in African-centered emancipatory education are invited to continue a tradition of social action by people of African descent. An underlying assumption in this approach to education is that children of African descent should not be required to adjust to an education that is maladjusted for them and their community, acquiesce to living in a community infested with drugs, or repress their indignation at structures of oppression. African American educators Carter G. Woodson and Benjamin E. Mays defined education as an empowering resource preparing the student for action against injustice. Benjamin E. Mays, the mentor of Martin Luther King Jr., saw education as being more than just acquiring skills or information. "Mays defined education in terms of social responsibility and the educated person as an instrument to bring about a positive change in society . . . to do something in the world around them to correct some of the problems, and to make it a better place in which to live" (Matthews, 1998, p. 281). Education (as opposed to "schooling") speaks directly to the urgent issues in the student's daily life, preparing the student to act upon these issues. *Praxis* is a central concept in emancipatory education. *Praxis* here means learning that is deepened by engagement in work for social change (Murrell, 1997).

The multifaceted, historical system of domination experienced by African people is described by some African scholars as the *maafa* (Ani, 1994), a Kiswahili word that means "disaster." A central feature of African-centered models of education is countering the *maafa* through reconnecting students with African and African American history, traditions, values, and principles. The Akan symbol *sankofa* represents the African teaching that knowing one's history is essential for understanding present circumstances and successfully moving forward into the future. For children of African descent, understanding both the African cultural legacy of intellectual achievement and the contemporary structures of domination are essential in preparing them to confront conditions that are destroying their communities. "Reclaiming historical memory" is an essential component of liberatory education and liberatory psychology (Martín-Baró, 1994). Providing children with the tools for deconstructing miseducation and misrepresentations of the African experience, reconstructing knowledge of African history and philosophies, and constructing a better life for the community are what Akbar (1998) identifies as three critical methods for Black psychology and education. "African indigenous pedagogy is the vision of the teacher as a selfless healer intent on inspiring, transforming, and propelling students to a higher spiritual level" (Hilliard, 1998, p. 78). Reclaiming historical memory can inspire students' own participation in social action. This has been the case in the Benjamin E. Mays Institute.

THE BENJAMIN E. MAYS INSTITUTE

The Benjamin E. Mays Institute (BEMI), founded by middle-school teacher Sadiq Ali in 1997, is a cluster of 100 male students of African descent within Fox Middle School, a public school in Hartford, Connecticut. BEMI incorporates principles from African-centered emancipatory education in its programs for students, parents, and the surrounding community. BEMI is located on Hartford's North End, a community in which two-thirds of the male students of African descent entering high school fail to reach the 12th grade.

Major components of BEMI are its rites of passage program (directed by a community elder with over 30 years of experience in rites of passage programs), parent organization, mentorship program, community workshops and conferences, African-centered curriculum, off-campus studies (e.g., visits to Yale University, Harvard University, Holy Cross College, and Trinity College), and forums involving students and community leaders addressing major issues in the community.

Evidence of the students' sense of ownership, agency, and immersion in African principles can be seen in the newspaper that they edit and publish. An article in the second issue of their newspaper identifies some of the principles the students find particularly relevant—*sankofa*, *kujicahgulia* (Kiswahili for "self-determination"), *SBA* (Kemetic term meaning "teaching, learning, wisdom, and study"), and *maat* (Kemetic term representing the integration of truth, justice, righteousness, balance, reciprocity, and harmony). Addressing this article to members of the community, the author explains, "Some of the ways your sons prosper is that we not only practice African terms, we study them, memorize them, and believe in them. This is part of the way the boys do so well not only in school but also out of school" (Morgan, 2000, p. 2).

THE PROBLEM OF VIOLENCE
AT THE BENJAMIN E. MAYS INSTITUTE

A major concern for the students in BEMI has been the problem of violence—the violence of community members against each other as well as police violence against young men of African descent. Around the same time of the fatal police shootings of Amadou Diallo and Patrick Dorismond in New York, Malik Jones in New Haven, and Franklyn Reid in New Milford, an unarmed 14-year-old named Aquan Salmon was shot to death on Hartford's North End by a White police officer. BEMI organized a community forum on this problem that was held in the school auditorium. A panel of community leaders, including students from BEMI, addressed the forum and shared ideas on what must be done to stop police violence and racial profiling. Students from BEMI engaged community leaders in discussions on this problem and suggested possible solutions. Articles have been written by BEMI students in their newspaper analyzing not only police violence but gang violence and other urgent issues impacting the community. In BEMI, reading, writing, and engagement in other academic activities are often linked with confronting the problem of violence and structures of domination. Students not only read about African history and principles but are challenged to participate in that history and live according to these principles.

VIOLENCE PREVENTION AND EMANCIPATORY EDUCATION

How else might school-based violence prevention programs be more consistent with African-centered emancipatory education? In addition to borrowing some of the approaches used by BEMI to the problem of violence noted above, there are African wisdom teachings that may be particularly relevant for violence prevention.

The wisdom teachings of the Egyptian sage Ptahhotep, written over 4,000 years ago, specifically address the problem of violence from several dimensions. In *The Teachings of Ptahhotep* (Hilliard, Williams, & Damali, 1987), the oldest surviving complete text in the world, there are 14 teachings on preventing interpersonal violence as well as violence in society as a whole. Ptahhotep taught that those in positions of power can create conditions that provoke violence, and that greed sets violence in motion at both the individual and social levels.

Presenting the teachings of Ptahhotep (re)connects students with ancestral figures from their cultural legacy while providing them with valuable insights on the nature of violence. Ptahhotep's more contextual analysis of violence, like Fanon's analysis of violence discussed earlier, is one in which the student is not singled out as the primary source of violence, yet is challenged not to contribute to *processes that harm* the community.

Violence prevention programs could include a focus on specific practices of children in the community that may be used either in the service of violence or greater community cohesion. For example, a "stop the ranking" program at BEMI involved students' examination of values expressed in verbal dueling practices that sometimes escalate into conflict. Students in this program were called upon to use the same skills in verbal repartee, critical thinking, and creativity in the service of conflict resolution and strengthening unity. Similarly, in *Signifying as a Scaffold for Literary Interpretation: The Pedagogical Implications of an African American Discourse Genre* (Lee, 1993), Dr. Safisha Madhubuti describes how similar verbal practices among African American children can serve as a vital resource for enhancing literacy development and academic achievement.

A program on violence prevention could also acknowledge spiritual, philosophical, and religious traditions of people of African descent, traditions that affirm the sacredness of human life and contain teachings against violence. Members of the community who have been able to turn away from violence through spiritual transformation may be called upon to share their experiences. This type of personal narrative from a community member was helpful for students in BEMI, and is described in an article in the students' newspaper (Collins, 2000).

Violence has had a devastating impact upon many communities of color. The Benjamin E. Mays Institute is not a violence prevention program and does not include an explicit "violence prevention" component. It is an emancipatory educational institution dedicated to uplifting young men of African descent, based on the proposition that knowledge of African culture and history may be positively associated with many beneficial outcomes. Violence and other problems are addressed within historical context, and students approach such problems as agents for change, fortified through participating in African traditions such as rites of passage.

It may come as no surprise that BEMI students have appeared stronger on measures of African identity than other students in their cohort. Using the Racial Identity Attitude Scale (Helms & Parham, 1985, cited in Gordon, 2000) and the Multigroup Ethnic Identity Measure (Phinney, 1992, cited in Gordon, 2000), Gordon (2000) found higher scores in racial and ethnic identity among BEMI students than among other students in their same middle school. But it is also important to note in closing that BEMI students have consistently outscored all other students in their school on the Connecticut Mastery Tests (CMT), and more BEMI students make the honor roll than those in any other school cluster.

CHAPTER 18

Profile of an Independent Black Institution

African-Centered Education at Work

Carol D. Lee

In the prophetic novel *Two Thousand Seasons* (2000), Ayi Kwei Armah challenges Black people to find sustenance in their origins. He calls especially on those he describes as "you hearers, seers, imaginers, thinkers, rememberers, you prophets called to communicate truths of the living way to a people fascinated unto death" (p. ix). Armah asks that Black people look beyond the confusion of the present and find ways of "linking those gone, ourselves here, those coming" (p. xiii). As he continues:

> The eyes of the seers should range far into purposes. The ears of the hearers should listen far toward origins. The utterers' voice should make knowledge of the way, of heard sounds and visions seen, the voice of utterers should make this knowledge inevitable, impossible to lose. (p. xiii)

Part of the quick-fix mentality and single-solution approach that has characterized reform efforts in American schools has focused on simplistic solutions, i.e., including African American history in the curriculum of inner-city schools will elevate the self-esteem of poor Black youth; changing the school climate to one of higher expectations will result in a safer school environment; the creation of single-sex schools for Black males will solve their disciplinary and academic problems; the appropriation of culturally nonspecific instructional models like whole language and phonics-intensive or process approaches to teaching composition skills will improve reading and writing deficiencies; reciprocal teaching or cognitive apprenticeships emphasizing critical thinking skills will teach complex thinking processes. Each of

Original version published in *Journal of Negro Education*, Vol. 61, No. 2, 1992, pp. 160–177. Reproduced with permission of Howard University.

these "remedies" has value and applicability to underachieving, ethnically diverse, and poor students as well as to so-called mainstream, middle-class students who are not competing academically in the world test market. In isolation, however, each is incomplete.

For example, the inclusion of a truthful view of American and world history that includes the contributions and perspectives of the variety of African Americans, Native Americans, Asian Americans, and Hispanic Americans— as well as those of underrepresented Eastern European groups—is vital to America's salvation and maximal development. Facing a population whose majority will soon be people of color, the United States must come to terms with the fact that two major holocausts provide the foundation on which much of American history rests: the African Holocaust, which lasted for nearly 400 years and resulted in the death or the enslavement of literally tens of millions; and the Native American Holocaust, in which entire nations of indigenous people lost their land, their autonomy, and their lives. However, the relationship between historical accuracy and self-esteem is not clear. Research on self-concept among African American youth indicates that a distinction must be made between personal self-esteem and group concept. That is, the personal self-concept of individual African American youth is likely to be high, while his or her understanding of the way in which Black people (and the physical characteristics of Black people) are valued in the society may be reflective of low self-esteem (Cross, 1985; Spencer, 1988). Additionally, Fine's (1991) research indicated that African American high school dropouts may have quite high self-esteem; and Hale-Benson (1982) has observed that many African American male children demonstrate strong and aggressive leadership qualities beginning in the primary grades.

Delpit (1986, 1988) has raised serious questions about the wholesale applicability of process approaches to teaching composition to underachieving African American children and, by implication, other open-ended models such as whole language. Delpit argues that children from politically disenfranchised ethnic groups should be explicitly taught the "rules of power" for language use, including acceptable school norms. Similar observations for bilingual populations have been made by Reyes (1991a, 1991b). The reservations articulated by these ethnically diverse researchers indicate the need for comprehensive approaches that take into account the cultural knowledge and political needs of nonmainstream student populations.

Rather than simply complain and react, the independent African-centered school movement has taken a proactive stance, defining within a community context the possibilities and gifts that Black children offer the world, and creating institutions to manifest its ideals. Institutions validate knowledge, help to shape visions, inculcate values, and provide the foundation for community stability. Over the past 35 years, New Concept Development

Center (NCDC) of Chicago, Illinois, along with other independent Black institutions (IBIs) across the country, has strived to educate and socialize African American children to assume their future roles as political, intellectual, spiritual, and economic leaders in their communities and the world. Its vision is one in which Black people are self-reliant, productive, self-defining, and firmly rooted in family and community—a vision NCDC's founders and staff hope will be impossible for its students to lose.

This profile is offered for several reasons. First, new IBIs are opening up across the country, and they often call on members of established institutions for advice. Yet, no matter how many independent schools are founded in the near future, they cannot begin to serve the majority of African American children. Thus, schools such as NCDC can also offer instructive models of development for public schools. In the last 10 years, a number of IBIs have transformed into charter schools. In Chicago, New Concept continues, but its founders have also now established three African-centered charter schools under the umbrella of the Betty Shabazz International Charter Schools. Thus, the history and principles (pedagogical, cultural, and institutional) embodied in this case history are being extended into public schools in many urban districts. The lessons of the nation's independent African-centered schools are particularly relevant for several reasons. Public school parents, students, and educators are becoming increasingly interested in culturally responsive curriculum and pedagogy. Also, the dismal failure of public education for African American students clearly indicates the need for alternative influences. In light of the expressed needs for culturally responsive and comprehensive reform, the evolution and example of independent, African-centered, community-based schools such as NCDC are highly relevant to the larger issues of public education in the United States.

EARLY BEGINNINGS

NCDC first opened its doors in 1972 in the midst of the Black Power and Black Arts movements as well as the heightened international movement for Pan-African unity. It began as a Saturday school program servicing African American children between the ages of 2 and 12. The program concept emerged from a small group of Black intellectuals who had been working with the independent Black publishing company, Third World Press, which had begun 5 years earlier, in 1967. The founding group included poets Haki Madhubuti, Johari Amini, and Sterling Plumpp; and educators Safisha Madhubuti (Carol Easton, now Carol Lee), Jabari Mahiri, Kimya Moyo, and Soyini Ricks Walton. Our goal was to develop an educational institution within Chicago's Black community that would teach African American his-

tory and culture as well as imbue the values of Black self-love and cooperation among the children it served. Moreover, it was envisioned that this institution would operate independent of resources and influences from outside
the Black community.

At its inception, NCDC was the only program under the auspices of the
Institute of Positive Education (IPE). NCDC staff constituted the initial board
of directors of the entire IPE operation. Subsequently, a cadre of full-time
workers and volunteers evolved to carry out other IPE programs, which have
included a community lecture series, a pamphlet series, *Black Books Bulletin* magazine, a typesetting operation (Hieroglyphics, Inc.), and the Ujamaa
Food Cooperative. Although membership in IPE was open, a stringent work
and study schedule was demanded of its staff. As part of a lengthy incorporation process, early members of the board collectively developed guidelines
that stipulated the rights and responsibilities of membership. They met
monthly to conduct business and at least bimonthly to study as a group. These
study sessions included focus on classic texts such as *The Destruction of Black
Civilization* by Chancellor Williams (1974/1987), Armah's *Two Thousand
Seasons* (2000), *The Mis-Education of the Negro* by Carter G. Woodson
(1933), *The Crisis of the Negro Intellectual* by Harold Cruse (1967), and
From Plan to Planet by Haki R. Madhubuti (1979), as well as readings related to diet, exercise, and health.

As IPE's program roster expanded, so did the specializations of staff
members. By the time NCDC expanded in 1974 from a Saturday tutorial
and cultural enrichment program to a full-time day school, IPE staffers had
specialized into teachers, typesetters, editorial and advertising staff, and other
specializations according to their roles in the various operations. Although,
in some instances, staff members brought related training and experience to
their jobs at IPE, many staff were apprenticed into skills for which they had
little or no prior training. Most of the early NCDC staff, although college-
trained, had little formal experience working with young children. Thus, while
we knew the end goals we wished to achieve, we had little idea how to translate our goals into developmentally appropriate learning activities for young
children. In this sense, the early years of the institution were educational ones
for both the IPE staff as well as the community we served. None of the businesses created by IPE was ever intended to make significant money for individuals. Rather, they were founded to provide needed services within the Black
community and to generate sufficient revenue to continually upgrade the
services and modestly support those who worked within them. Staff members who worked outside jobs voluntarily donated money monthly to support the business operations. As the businesses flourished and the staff grew
to 25 people, it became apparent that the original structure was too unwieldy
to manage the day-to-day operations of the expanded organization. A smaller

administrative body—democratically elected, responsive to the entire staff, and guided by African-centered values—was thus formed to manage IPE's daily operations. This first administrative body was called the *Baraza Ya Kazi* (Kiswahili for "work council").

CHALLENGES OF EXPANSION AND EVOLUTION: STAFF AND LEADERSHIP DEVELOPMENT

Working in an independent Black institution has always been an avocation of dedication. The philosophical basis of the independent school movement precludes simplistic notions of working within them as merely a "job." As long as community-based institutions with limited financial resources remain small and are staffed by highly politicized and youthful staff, the consistency of their organizational vision is generally predictable. However, as these organizations grow, they must find ways to generate new leadership and resources. The founding and early NCDC staffers consistently worked 12 to 16 hours a day, and fulfilled multiple responsibilities. As staff members aged and began to raise families and take on greater financial burdens in an increasingly inflationary economy, these expectations could not be reasonably maintained.

Training teachers to impart the appropriate cultural knowledge and ideological perspectives into their instruction at African-centered schools has not been an easy task. Mainstream university teacher training programs, on the whole, do not prepare teachers to be responsive to diverse cultural concerns in their instruction, and they certainly do not prepare them to work in schools like NCDC. A major source of continuity and reinforcement for teachers in independent schools has been the National Teacher Training Institutes of the Council of Independent Black Institutions (CIBI). Since 1975, CIBI has offered 2-week training seminars on how to develop and sustain an IBI. In recent years, the Teacher Training Institutes have expanded to provide training for public school educators and parents on African-centered curriculum.

Attempts over the years to recruit graduates from traditional teacher training institutions or to entice average public school teachers to work at NCDC have proved disastrous. For instance, years ago, as the center's first director, I was interviewing applicants for an elementary school–level position at the center. One young African American woman, a teacher education program graduate, came into the building, guardedly scrutinized its walls, which were resplendent with pictures of Black heroes and heroines, Black art, and artifacts, and asked in amazement, "Is this place *all Black?*" Without waiting for a reply, she quickly turned around and walked out.

Experience has shown that the most effective means of training new staff to engage in NCDC's culturally responsive mode of teaching is to have beginning teachers spend their first year as assistants, or apprentices, to experienced teachers. NCDC also maintains an ongoing staff development program. Teachers meet weekly by section and monthly as an entire staff to discuss programs and problems. They meet monthly for staff development sessions conducted by the school's program coordinator, university professors, and former NCDC staff with specializations in science and mathematics. These sessions have included studies in African American history and culture as well as intensive review of theories of learning, and introductions to new strategies for teaching in various content areas, and culturally responsive manipulatives and teaching units. Moreover, NCDC pays for its teachers to attend relevant seminars and workshops offered at local universities or teacher centers.

In addition to the problem of selecting, developing, and maintaining its teaching staff, NCDC also faces the challenge of developing and supporting new administrative leadership. Many independent schools have not withstood the test of time partly because of their overdependence on singular leadership. At NCDC, we do not believe a director can simply be imported from another setting (unless, of course, the candidate has had prior leadership experience in another independent school). All positions below that of the director are thus seen as training ground for future directors. To this end, all decisions related to the school program are first discussed and, if possible, resolved among the school staff themselves. Levels of decision-making responsibility are shared among the director, the assistant director, and the section heads for the preschool and primary school divisions. As of 2007, the current director is actually a graduate of the program who went on to earn undergraduate and master's degrees from Howard University.

In many respects, NCDC's evolution mimics the process of specialization one would expect to find as any business expands its scope and services. On the other hand, what is unique is the enduring spirit of unity, commitment to collective work and responsibility, and institutional and political independence that has characterized this institution since its inception 35 years ago.

PHILOSOPHICAL FOUNDATIONS OF AFRICAN-CENTERED SCHOOLS

African American culture connects with Africa and reflects not only shared history but also social relationships, belief systems, social practices, and collective responses to political and economic realities. An African-centered pedagogy must take all of this into account. As I have outlined elsewhere (Lee, Lomotey, & Shujaa, 1990), an African-centered pedagogy should fulfill the following aims:

1. Legitimize African stores of knowledge;
2. Positively exploit and scaffold productive community and cultural practices;
3. Extend and build upon the indigenous language;
4. Reinforce community ties and idealize [the concept of] service to one's family, community, nation, race, and world;
5. Promote positive social relationships;
6. Impart a world view that idealizes a positive, self-sufficient future for one's people without denying the self-worth and right to self-determination of others;
7. Support cultural continuity while promoting critical consciousness; and
8. Promote the vision of individuals and communities as producers rather than as simply consumers. (p. 50)

Karenga (1990), in his contemporary translation of the Kemetic (Egyptian) sacred text *The Book of Coming Forth by Day* (known more commonly as *The Egyptian Book of the Dead* [Budge, 1967]), describes ancient African principles of ethical character development as including the following propositions, which are encompassed in the concept of *maat*:

> 1. the divine image of humans; 2. the perfectibility of humans; 3. the teachability of humans; 4. the free will of humans; and 5. the essentiality of moral social practice in human development. (p. 26)

These moral propositions in educational terms translate into the belief that each child is capable of learning complex bodies of knowledge and problem-solving strategies, and that each child has the moral responsibility to use that knowledge for the good of his or her family and community. These two propositions provide the social foundation on which African-centered education rests. In more vivid terms, persons working within African-centered independent schools realize that, with family and community loving care and training, all African American children—from the physically aggressive young boy; to the snotty-nosed, nappy-headed, raggedly dressed young girl; to the impudent, threatening-looking teenager—have a spark of the divine within them and thus represent the possibility of perfectibility.

NCDC, like most other institutions in the independent African-centered school movement, has adopted the "Nguzo Saba" or Black Value System conceived by Maulana Karenga (1989). (Karenga is also the originator of Kwanzaa, the African American holiday celebration.) The Nguzo Saba is a nondoctrinaire, nondenominational system that promotes and supports the following principles in the African American community: (1) Umoja—unity, (2) Kujichagulia—self-determination, (3) Ujima—collective work and responsibility, (4) Ujamaa—cooperative economics, (5) Kuumba—creativity, (6) Nia—purpose, and (7) Imani—faith (in one's self, one's family, and one's people). The application of these principles as the philosophical tools for institution-building means that workers in IBIs must commit to engage in democratic decision-making processes, have faith in the possibilities of leadership that each person possesses, and dedicate themselves to serving the African American community.

Just because one is knowledgeable about Black history and culture and likes children does not mean one can effectively teach using an African-centered pedagogy. According to Lee, Lomotey, and Shujaa (1990), the implementation of an African-centered pedagogy demands teachers who advocate and are well-grounded in the following principles:

1. The social ethics of African culture as exemplified in the social philosophy of *maat* (Karenga, 1990);
2. The history of the African continent and diaspora;
3. The need for political and community organizing within the African American community;
4. The positive pedagogical implications of the indigenous language, African American English (Delain, Pearson, & Anderson, 1985; Gee, 1989; Heath, 1989; Labov, 1972; Smitherman, 1977);
5. Child development principles that are relevant to the positive and productive growth of African American children (Hale, 1986; Warfield-Coppock, 1990; Wilson, 1978);
6. African contributions in science, mathematics, literature, the arts, and societal organization;
7. Teaching techniques that are socially interactive, holistic and positively affective (Hale-Benson, 1986; Warfield-Coppock, 1990; Willis, 1989);
8. The need for continuous personal study [and critical thinking];
9. The African principle that "children are the reward of life";
10. The African principle of reciprocity (Armah, 2000; Mbiti, 1970/1989; Nobles, 1980); that is, a teacher sees his or her own future symbiotically linked to the development of students. (pp. 52–53)

Further, to embody such principles in one's teaching, a teacher must be well-read in a "Black Classic Education." Madhubuti (1990) has offered an excellent reference list of 200 books that he believes "conscientious" Black people should read. To expect teachers to be such well-read individuals may appear demanding and unrealistic, yet the liberatory objectives of African-centered education demand that teachers, students, and parents alike must learn to be more than they think possible. Teachers grounded in African-centered pedagogy must also be well-read in contemporary theories of learning and prepared to view such theories critically. In the early years of NCDC's history, when both teachers and students were learning, it was not unusual for the staff to read Piaget and attempt to replicate some of his classic developmental tasks with children at the same time that they were studying and implementing innovations in educational practice from Tanzania, Cuba, and the People's Republic of China.

The question of cultural infusion is fraught with debate. This is particularly the case in the domains of science and mathematics. Here again, the principles of cultural infusion in IBIs can serve as models for multicultural curriculum development in public schools. Some have argued that teaching American schoolchildren about numeration systems from other parts of the world is a waste of valuable instructional time because they will not be required to use such notation systems in today's world (Ravitch, 1990). Others contend that adapting mathematics to multicultural contexts can have positive intellectual consequences (Zaslavsky, 1990). African-centered schools maintain that considering why different groups of people at different time periods developed distinct counting systems, for example, helps students to understand that mathematics serves real-world functions and is not an artifact of the classroom, and that it is not a finite or static science. Over the years, NCDC students have learned to count and use the notational systems of both the ancient Egyptians and the Yoruba of Nigeria as well as the base-10 Arabic notational system to which we in the West are accustomed. Primary instruction is, of course, given in the latter system. However, exposure to the Egyptian system reinforces the students' understanding that the base-10 system involves regroupings of sets and multiples of 10, a concept more visually evident in the Egyptian system. This also helps distinguish the amount or quantity from the notation used to represent the quantity. Further, teaching students to do long multiplication or division using both the traditional algorithm and Egyptian methods helps to solidify the underlying mathematical concepts behind these operations.

Games such as the Shango networks and the Dware games of West Africa have also been incorporated into the NCDC curriculum, as have mathematical games from many other cultures around the world. As Zaslavsky (1990) has noted: "Games of strategy help children to acquire skills in logical inference and decision making, important training for solving problems in the technological society of the future" (p. 16).

In schools such as NCDC, the linking of cultural knowledge to traditional school subject matters is only one part of a comprehensive environment. Cultural studies are not restricted solely to review of historical events nor exclusively to the continent of Africa. For example, at the third-grade level, social studies and reading instruction have been merged in a unit that addresses a critical issue in Black life today: family responsibilities and expectations. Using the CIBI (1990) social studies curriculum, the children are guided to read trade books about Black families of various configurations to extrapolate for themselves a set of criteria that defines a "good" family. They are then asked to use these criteria to think about and discuss their own families. In another instance, classroom discussion of a text from the fourth-grade basal reading series asks students to examine the diary of the Puritan explorer John Smith and look for any evidence of bias in his observations about the Native Americans with whom he and other White settlers came into contact. Smith's encounter is then contrasted with an account from *Wounded Knee* (Brown, 1974), a children's version of a Native American–eye view of the clash of cultures between Whites and indigenous peoples during the colonization of America. Without any lecture on the part of the teacher, the children are asked to compare and contrast the two perspectives. The purpose of these lessons is to challenge the children to think and to help them develop a questioning stance toward the traditional story of the founding of America that they can expect to receive when they move on to the public schools.

THE CREATION OF COMMUNITY IN AFRICAN-CENTERED SCHOOLS

As parents, educators, and citizens, proponents of the independent African-centered school movement have institutionalized Armah's (1979) conclusion:

> There is no beauty but in relationships. Nothing cut off by itself is beautiful. Never can things in destructive relationships be beautiful. All beauty is in the creative purpose of our relationships. . . . The mind that knows this, the destroyers will set traps for it, but the destroyers' traps will never hold that mind. (p. 321)

Within independent African-centered schools, the distinctions between family and community are often blurred. At NCDC, for example, all teachers and staff are referred to by the title of *Mama* or *Baba* (Kiswahili for "mother" or "father") and their first names. Both students and parents refer to teachers and staff by these titles. This practice makes the public statement that teachers serve an *en loco parentis* function for the children. NCDC teachers are required to assume responsibility for the character development and academic achievement of their students. They also strive to ensure that families become and remain supportive of their children's physical, social, and moral development, as well as their educational development. These expected social relations are made clear to parents when they enroll their children in the school. Indeed, teachers at NCDC have been known to "call parents on the carpet" for not fulfilling their parental educational responsibilities, and, to this day, young adults who attended NCDC 35 years ago still address me as "Mama," although there is clearly no social requirement that they do so. Such precedents are not unknown in the African American community, particularly during the period before widespread integration when middle-class and working-class families lived in the same neighborhood and it was not uncommon for teachers to be students' neighbors.

At NCDC, simply producing scholars is insufficient. Our students are encouraged to try hard, to achieve meaningful levels of mastery of academic concepts, and to share their knowledge with others. We seek to help shape whole human beings who recognize the beauty of their Blackness and their culture, who are kind and responsive to one another, and who can contribute not only to their own families and communities but to the "forward flow of human progress and civilization" (Karenga, 1990).

Although some may view our goals at NCDC as idyllic and impossible in the face of the grave crises that challenge African Americans today, such goals must be seen as basic requirements for survival. The heroic efforts of African Americans to obtain an education during the slavery and post-Reconstruction eras provide ample evidence that what seems impossible can be achieved. Many narrative accounts tell of enslaved Africans hiding books and struggling to read in the dark of night under the threat of horrendous physical punishment and even death. The widespread growth of Sabbath Schools among African American churches and some 1,500 community-based schools started by African Americans in the South and of reading clubs in cities in the North (Anderson, 1988; Harding, 1981; Bennett, 1964) provide further historical testimony to inspire and undergird NCDC's belief in the power of community-based, culturally responsive, and politically conscious efforts to educate Black people in America.

IMPLICATIONS FOR PUBLIC EDUCATION

To suggest that the independent African-centered school movement is without problems would be to give a false impression. The national support network for the independent African-centered school movement, the Council of Independent Black Institutions, is underfunded and, as a result, has not been able to provide the level of support that its member institutions desperately need. At the same time, the stability of its National Teacher Training Institutes and its national science fairs for students in CIBI schools has been a source of continuity and reinforcement for independent schools. Its expansion of teacher training services for public school teachers and its publication of a social studies curriculum guide represent significant growth.

Many IBIs have fallen by the wayside. The reasons for their demise include lack of adequate funding, centralizing leadership in a "star" individual or elite group, inadequate in-service training for staff, and narrow ideological foci with little grounding in or support from the communities being served. Some of the surviving schools do not provide developmentally appropriate instruction; others require young children to master meaningless rote material. Still other schools are not broad enough in their base to attract children other than the biological children of their organizational members, nor do they attract families who are not explicitly political Pan-Africanists or those from poor and working-class backgrounds.

Likewise disturbing is the lack of formal presence of educators from IBIs among the national, publicly visible leadership in the movement to include African-centered education in the nation's public schools. Much of the leadership in this drive give only lip service to the contributions that the independent school movement has made to shaping the current national discourse, yet IBIs can provide real direction to efforts at the local levels to implement African-centered curriculum in public schools. They also provide tangible examples of African-centered education as more than merely teaching children to recite African proverbs; wave red, black, and green flags; and recognize Black heroes and heroines on a wall. Indeed, IBIs represent the "laboratory" schools for the development of pedagogy and projects that reflect African worldviews and interests. Their experienced staff have developed comprehensive, classroom-tested unit plans and curricula that do not depend on commercial basal series or Eurocentrically biased textbooks; and they have engaged as professionals in extensive, ongoing study. They and their institutions have learned how, as the old folks say, to "make a way out of no way."

The question, then, is whether schools such as NCDC and other CIBI schools represent bastions of narrow, separatist, anti-American instruction or whether they offer some promise of hope for public education. The answer lies in the old saying, "The proof is in the pudding." The achievements of IBI graduates speak the most powerful truth. They are decidedly not among the gang members, dope dealers, and high school dropouts that plague our communities. Alumni from NCDC and its sister institution Betty Shabazz International Charter Schools have graduated from, or are currently enrolled in, some of the most prestigious public schools and gifted programs in the Chicago school system. Even NCDC graduates identified as having learning disabilities have been found to hold their own in public schools. Public school principals have enthusiastically welcomed NCDC graduates because they have come to expect these children to enjoy reading, patiently engage in mathematical and scientific problem solving, think critically about social issues, be well-rounded in their creative interests and talents, and behave well. After 35 years, NCDC alumni have graduated from historically Black colleges and universities as well an array of mainstream universities, including Stanford, Northwestern, and Princeton, among others. Betty Shabazz International Charter School has been identified as a school of distinction within the Chicago Public Schools. Ratteray (1989), in a survey of results on standardized achievement tests of students from a cross-section of independent schools (not all CIBI schools, but including NCDC), found that, on average, children from these schools achieved at or above grade level. These figures stand in stark contrast to the generally disparaging figures and forecasts of achievement for so-called minority and poor children in public education.

In making these comparisons, however, it is important to note some important distinctions between independent African-centered schools and public schools. Class size in the former is generally smaller, although research suggests that smaller class size in itself is not a determining factor in student achievement. This point is especially evident in the class sizes of countries like Japan. More important, enrollment in independent schools is based on a selective rather than an open admission process, and, unlike public schools, IBIs are not bound by union contracts that force them to retain teachers who fail to perform. Yet, in its 35-year history NCDC has accepted every student who has registered to attend, and only two children have ever been asked to leave the school. In the primary grades, NCDC has actually tended to accept more students who have not had success in public school. As a charter school, its sister institution, Betty Shabazz International Charter Schools, have open enrollment, using a lottery when there are more applicants than available spots. A majority of children in each of the three charter schools is on free or reduced-price lunch.

The achievements of NCDC, other independent schools, and African-centered charter schools cannot be attributed to an influx of money or simply to the commitment of its staff; nor can they be attributed to the mere inclusion of African American and African history in its curriculum. This is not to suggest that money is not required to address the ills of public education in the United States; rather, the issue is to what ends money should be directed. NCDC's survival, expansion, and maturation can be attributed to four reasons:

1. the long-term commitment of most of its founders;
2. the implementation of strategic planning to expand leadership capabilities and responsibilities among staff;
3. the governing board's adoption of a realistic attitude about the financial, ideological, and professional needs of its staff; and
4. an unwavering belief on the part of school personnel that African American culture is both a lifeline to Africa and a buoy to keep Black people, and Black children in particular, afloat amid widespread societal confusion and danger.

Many will argue that these expectations are not realistic for public education. Perhaps so. But, as has been noted, there are a number of public African-centered schools, typically charter schools, in most urban school districts. However, the problems faced by African Americans as a group, and especially by poor African Americans, are so monumental that only monumental solutions will correct them. The quality of our collective future depends on reclaiming the minds of our children, who are far too often lost to the streets. Whether it is realistic to expect a majority of public schools, even those that serve completely African American populations, to adopt an African-centered pedagogy is questionable. However, we have clear and convincing evidence that African-centered education can be incorporated into public education. The principles that have inspired the pedagogy and cultural environment of NCDC, other independent Black schools, and African-centered charter schools are human and humane, stimulating and inspirational, a worthy model for others to follow. There is much that efforts to expand the multicultural content of curriculum and orientation of increasingly diverse public schools have to learn from the African-centered school movement (Lee, 2007).

CHAPTER 19

Rebel Musics
African Diaspora Popular Culture and Critical Literacies

Ernest Morrell

The acquisition of literacy has been a central issue throughout the entire history of Africans in the American diaspora. For centuries it was illegal to teach Black slaves to read or write for fear of the revolutionary potential of literate slaves (DuBois, 1903/1982; James, 1962). More recently, these same populations have been subjected to racist and colonialist educational systems where rigorous academic literacy instruction has been largely denied. Regardless of the tactic, the consequences are the same: the prevention of a highly literate African diaspora population. At the same time, however, educators and communities have resisted these systems and found ways to impart powerful literacies to African American populations (Perry, 2003). This article will attempt to analyze the radical curricular and pedagogical potential of literacy practices associated with participation in popular culture among African diaspora youth in the United States and the Caribbean.

African diaspora students and their families have often been characterized by educational policymakers as unskilled or unmotivated, and proposed solutions have often proceeded along the lines of remedying cultural deficits or licensing a "banking education" where teachers feel charged to fill the empty receptacles that are students' minds with relevant (dominant) cultural knowledge (Freire, 1970/1993). Under the colonizing educational systems of the West, this process is even more sinister; often, teachers see it as their responsibility to empty or expunge adulterated cultural knowledge and replace it with elite (Western) knowledge. Nowhere is this more prevalent than in language and literacy education (Freire & Macedo, 1987).

Schools have not validated the nonschool linguistic, literate, and cultural lives of African diaspora students; many administrators, educators, and policymakers have seen no reason to learn from these populations or to develop curricula and pedagogies that honor and make connections to their lived experiences. Rather than develop curricula and pedagogies of access and connection, we instead produce curricula and pedagogies of remediation and alienation. The result of this crisis is the academic underachievement of marginalized populations in both the United States and the Caribbean. More than 50% of secondary students who take the Caribbean Examination Council (CXC) Exam in English fail. Black Caribbean students in classrooms in the United Kingdom trail their White counterparts on relevant assessments of academic achievement; African American and Latino students in U.S. schools consistently manifest lower standardized test scores, lower enrollment in college-track courses, lower college-going rates, and higher dropout rates than their White peers (Darling-Hammond, 1998; USDE, 2005).

We know that even those students who are achieving in classes are usually only acquiring *functional literacies* that may put them at odds with home and community, and even nation. While the acquisition of literacies of power must be placed at a premium in education, it is important to acknowledge that literacies transmitted through academic instruction are not always empowering. And, although they are important to the quality of social and economic life, functional literacies without critical consciousness can be extremely problematic; when promoted to the exclusion of *critical literacies*, they contribute to the production of literate yet docile and complicit workers and citizens with a limited ability to navigate an imperialist Western capitalist hegemony.

In order to work toward critical literacies, educators need an understanding of the ways that African diaspora youth already use literacies in their everyday lives as they participate in sociocultural activity (Barton & Hamilton, 2001). Young people engage in rich, vibrant, and sophisticated language and literacy practices via their participation in youth popular culture (Morrell, 2002). Carol Lee's work and some of my own draw upon the language and literacy practices of African American and other marginalized youth in nonschool settings to scaffold academic literacies. Lee (1993), for instance, has utilized African American discourse genres to scaffold the language of literary interpretation. Specifically, Lee identified the sophisticated cognitive and linguistic practices associated with the prevalent African American discourse practice of signifying; she then drew parallels between this practice and the practice of literary interpretation, and developed and taught a unit to impoverished African American students where she used their ability to signify to develop complex literary interpretations of college-level texts.

In past research, I have looked across film, music, and digital media production, but, for the purposes of this article, I focus specifically on popular cultural musical forms that have been developed and propagated by young Africans in the American diaspora, particularly reggae and hip-hop. Furthermore, I have identified specific traditions within reggae and hip-hop: roots reggae and critical hip-hop, which provide opportunities for educators to make connections to youth-diaspora literacies that function as social critiques and as discourses of youth empowerment and resistance. For this purpose, I and others have identified them as "rebel musics." If we think of them as pedagogical models, they offer promising ways of developing both functional and critical literacies among African diaspora youth in the United States and the Caribbean. As I will endeavor to demonstrate throughout this article, the language, literacy, and cultural practices of African diaspora youth often transcend national boundaries; it is no secret, for instance, that hip-hop and reggae are international discourses of critique that resonate with Africans and other populations under siege around the globe (Spady, Alim, & Meghelli, 2006).

HIP-HOP CULTURE

Most adults view hip-hop as a problematic genre of music filled with images of violence, misogyny, and conspicuous consumption rather than as a complex culture of resistance, celebration, and social critique. However, most marginal or nonparticipants in the culture are only exposed to the music of top 40 hits played on the radio or seen on MTV, and the only news they hear about hip-hop is negative, pathologizing, and regulated by conservative, mainstream news media. This huge misconception on the part of the larger public is attributable to the co-optation of rap music by the corporate executives of the culture industries to the exclusion of hip-hop's other elements. Those who experience hip-hop via MTV and the evening news miss out on the sophisticated, sometimes contradictory, and multifaceted nature of the culture. Hip-hop, first and foremost, is a culture of urban youth production that emerged in urban America only a generation ago, yet has become an international force that is ascendant among musical genres (Farley, 1999). Hip-hop is also a vibrant culture practiced in many activities that extend beyond rap music. Before we go any further, it is important to retheorize and reclaim this term and explicate the culture that produces and exists alongside the music.

Hip-hop is a worldwide phenomenon with extensive influence over youth in the United States and the Caribbean, particularly urban and African diaspora youth. Old-school artist and founder of the Temple of Hip-hop KRS One asserts:

> Hip-hop is a collective consciousness. It is generally expressed through the unique elements of Breakin, Emceein, Graffiti Art, Deejayin, Beatboxin, Street Fashion, Street Language, Street Knowledge, and Street Entrepreneurialism (Hip-

hop's nine elements). . . . Hip-hop is practiced as an alternative behavior capable of transforming subjects and objects in an attempt to manifest a collective consciousness. Hip-hop is a state of mind. (KRS One, 2005)

There is no question that the proliferation of hip-hop music and culture is a mixed bag. While more people than ever are attracted to the music and culture, they have also been co-opted and marketed by mainstream corporate interests that have highlighted the gangsta image, the objectification of women, and, of course, the ideals of capitalist consumption. It is also important to note, however, that this critique is levied as strongly by some artists on the inside as it is by adults and conservatives on the outside of the culture. These artists, along with prominent hip-hop historians (Alim, 2006; George, 1998; Light, 1999) insist that, at its core, hip-hop is a social commentary, a call to action, and a celebration of urban youth culture; what I have termed a *critical hip-hop*. From these histories and countercritiques emerge important components that qualify critical hip-hop as a rebel music.

First, critical hip-hop originated, at least in part, as a critique of post-industrialism, lamenting and resisting the economic and structural conditions that have strained life and limited financial opportunities for those who hail from inner-city ghettos. Critical hip-hop further recognizes and acknowledges that hip-hop culture has stood as a righteous voice of resistance against poverty, injustice, racism, police brutality, and an inequitable educational system, to name a few (George, 1998).

Those who see themselves as producers of critical hip-hop also view their charge as a pedagogical one. KRS One's 1990 album entitled *Edutainment* serves as a model for critical hip-hop artists who view themselves as public entertainers and as public pedagogues. Classic artists such as X-Clan (*To the East, Blackwards*) and contemporary artists such as Lauryn Hill send messages pertaining to closer ties with an African homeland or positive messages about young Black girls learning to love and re-educate themselves (*Miseducation of Lauryn Hill*).

There is also an element of critical hip-hop that is concerned with social activism. Throughout hip-hop's 30-year history, hip-hop artists have been using lyrics to promote political messages and even political action. Public Enemy's role in the late 1980s of consciousness-raising transformed rap into a political tour de force. KRS One's "Free Mumia" and Lauryn Hill's "Rebel" are good examples of how hip-hop artists and songs have fostered social activism, encouraging listeners to see themselves as agents of change who can fight against injustice and oppression in the world.

A close analysis of hip-hop discourses reveals a number of salient themes, including violence and crime in urban ghettos, urban poverty, Black Power movements, corruption and greed in American government, racism in American society, connections with an African "motherland," the importance of acquiring a critical consciousness, indoctrination via school and the media, youth resistance, the history of hip-hop, and the continual struggle for the heart and soul of hip-hop culture. Many of these themes, for example, are found in the following verse from a popular hip-hop track:

> The subconscious psychology that you use against me,
> If I lose control will send me to the penitentiary.
> Such as Alcatraz, or shot up like al Hajj Malik Shabazz.
> High class get bypassed while my ass gets harassed.
> And the fuzz treat bruh's like they manhood never was.
> And if you too powerful, you get bugged like Peter Tosh and Marley was.
> And my word does nothing against the feds,
> So my eyes stay red as I chase crazy bald heads,
> WORD UP. (Refugee Camp, "The Beast")

The analysis offered by the artists is consistent with a Gramscian analysis of dominant hegemony, what the artists refer to here as "subconscious psychology" proliferated via media and educational discourses. The artists also make an explicit link between these dominant discourses and the actions of contemporary urban residents, many of whom (more than a million in the United States alone) find themselves incarcerated. Explanations for the actors and the system of incarceration are subjects of complex sociological analysis, making connections between structural inequalities, dominant discourses, and the everyday actions of marginalized populations, many of whom have voluntarily committed criminal acts. Gramsci (1971) asks how majority populations in Western democracies submit to conditions that disserve their self-interests without resorting to revolution; the Refugee Camp (1996) takes a similar line in asking how a million African Americans have submitted to a set of conditions that have led to their incarceration.

Next, the Refugee Camp artists link the struggles and violence of their contemporaries with those of the Black Power movement, specifically the (government-sponsored?) assassination of Malcolm X (an African American with Caribbean roots). They then transition to the inequitable treatment of the urban poor, while staying with the theme of the United States as a repressive police state. Here, their work provides a critique of the social theory of Gramsci, who contended that hegemony had replaced forced coercion of the police state. From history and the actions of CIA and FBI, we know that these activities happen in tandem; Refugee Camp's urban sociological analyses are more accurate than Gramsci's. The verse concludes with a more explicit critique of the way that the American intelligence community handles those who have become "too powerful" (read: too critical). It is interesting that these hip-hop artists cite two roots reggae artists, Peter Tosh and Bob Marley, as primary targets of U.S. surveillance. In one succinct, hard-hitting verse, these young artists have demonstrated the complex and poignant social critiques that are frequently disseminated through critical hip-hop, yet are rarely acknowledged or valued by larger publics who consistently and categorically denigrate the entire genre and its practitioners.

REGGAE MUSIC AND CULTURE

[S]*laves were uprooted, detribalized, denamed, dehumanized. . . . Through it all music was the one means through which the slave held onto the past and endured the present. Any discussion of the blues, the calypso, the reggae must begin at this point. . . . Of them all, reggae is the most explicitly revolutionary. It is commentary; satirical at times; often cruel; but its troubadours are not afraid to speak of love, of hope, of ideals, of justice, of new things and new forms. It is this assertion of revolutionary possibility that sets reggae apart.* (Manley, 2004, pp. 218–219)

As with hip-hop music and culture, reggae music is a worldwide phenomenon with tremendous influence in the Caribbean and the United States. The roots of Jamaica's modern music are in rebellion and independence (Bradley, 2001). Reggae music specifically is a genre born, in part, out of a combination of the rising influence of the Rastafarian religion, the economic and civil unrest in the postindependence period, and the intense pride in separation from a colonial power (Britain). It is, therefore, a (chronologically) postcolonial and (ideologically) anticolonial musical form. It is also an explicitly pedagogical musical form whose artists know how to combine lyrical mastery and satirical social commentary with a brilliant defiance that is both entertaining and pedagogical (Cooper, 2004).

Within the reggae tradition, I focus on the specific tradition of roots reggae, which took hold of the genre in the late 1960s and early 1970s. The radical social climate of the 1960s internationally and the election in Jamaica of the leftist People's National Party created a climate for the production of a more explicitly spiritual and political reggae music (Bradley, 2001), most notably spread through the lyrics of international spokesperson and reggae ambassador Bob Marley, hailed by Jacobson (2005) as:

one of the most eloquent artists of social unrest in the second half of the 20th century. Marley became an icon in what used to be called the Third World through his exhortation to "Get up, stand up" and his across-the-board condemnation of "de downpressers." (p. 209)

Other important artists of the initial "Roots and Culture" phase include Burning Spear, The Mighty Diamonds, and DJ Lee Perry.

The 21st century has witnessed a return to roots reggae in Jamaica through contemporary artists such as Buju Banton, Cappleton, Cocoa Tea, and Luciano. There are at least five tenets of roots reggae past and present that lead me to classify it as a rebel music: its roots are in rebellion and independence; it is both a postcolonial and anticolonial musical form; it is an explicitly pedagogical musical form; it is an explicitly spiritual musical form; and it is an explicitly political musical form.

An in-depth analysis of roots reggae discourse reveals a number of salient critical themes, including the Black Holocaust (also known as slavery), the Rastafarian religion, African heritage, colonization/decolonization of the mind, emancipation, economic injustice, revolution, Black heroes and heroines, African/diaspora history and culture, cultural pride, urban decay, and the revolutionary potential of roots reggae music. Many of these themes are exemplified in this passage from a popular roots reggae text:

> The whole of the nation
> Living in these tenements,
> Crying and applying to their council
> For assistance every day
> Now that their tribulation so sad
> Now that their environment so bad
> High rise concrete
> No back yard for their children to play
> African children
> I wonder do they know where you're coming from,
> African children
> In a concrete situation. (Aswad, "African-Children")

What stands out immediately is that the artists refer to Jamaican urban residents as African children, a population that ostensibly has been relocated in the Americas for 4 centuries. Time, for these artists, does not diminish the spiritual and cultural connections to an African homeland that are fostered through the Rastafarian religion and reggae music. Next, the penultimate phrase poses a question to the listeners in the African diaspora: Do you know where you're coming from? The critique is clearly one of separation on many levels. Most obviously, there is a geographical separation of several thousand miles and a chronological separation of 400 years. More significantly, though, the artists are identifying an ideological separation as they link the lack of knowledge about African histories and cultures to current conditions on the island (and, indeed, the region). The remainder of the passage entails a sociological critique of contemporary conditions of urban decay that define the "situations" of many urban Jamaicans—situations caused by the physical, historical, and ideological separation from cultural roots. The remedy is clear: Learn about the history and reestablish these vital links for the future of African diaspora peoples. The musical text is poignant, yet pedagogical and inspirational, where reggae artists are positioned as intellectuals, teachers, sociologists, and cultural historians.

With that background and insight into hip-hop and reggae music and culture, I would like to transition into a brief consideration of how these African diaspora musical genres might contribute to empowering literacy pedagogy and practice across content areas and educational levels.

MUSICAL PRODUCTION AND CONSUMPTION AS LITERACY PRACTICES

Hip-hop and reggae artists and others who imagine themselves as cultural producers are involved in a wide range of complex, cognitively demanding literacy practices that can be drawn upon in academic literacy education. Many of these artists begin young, as early as the primary grades, developing their craft. No doubt literacy educators at all levels will have numerous students who self-identify as current or future producers in these genres. First and foremost, artists and other producers of reggae and hip-hop are involved in "reading" past and present musical genres (i.e., jazz, blues, soul, folk music, funk, rock and roll, rhythm and blues, ska, rock steady, and so forth); serious study is an important component of developing as artists. This reading includes listening to hours of tapes, albums, and CDs, but also reading biographies of legendary artists, reading historical texts, and scouring all the latest periodicals for musical reviews, information on record sales, and upcoming performances. The development of hip-hop and reggae artists also involves reading a variety of historical and contemporary texts in preparation for writing lyrics; this is evidenced in the many allusions to classic and contemporary texts and historical events in musical lyrics. Finally, would-be artists read as part of their ongoing research; this involves checking the websites of record labels, researching the hottest A&Rs (i.e., talent scouts for major record labels), and borrowing innovative strategies from their predecessors to make a name for themselves and their music.

Composing musical texts employs many facets of the same writing process that is promoted in primary, secondary, and collegiate courses. Any lyrical production inevitably begins with a critical "reading" of the world in search of ideas for texts. Many artists immediately transcribe these ideas into notebooks that they carry with them wherever they go, including into the very literacy classrooms where they are labeled as nonwriters. The next stage normally involves mining the lyrics from these notebooks and "composing" drafts as written texts or freestyles to be performed. This process also involves "workshopping" (in the streets or in the studio) and a constant revision of texts in the studio or via public performances.

Finally, a large amount of reading and writing accompanies the marketing and distribution of musical texts especially for teen and preteen independent artists who are in charge of their own operations. Activities include researching exemplars, designing websites, and creating promotional materials to send to record labels or club owners. For those lucky enough to experience a measure of success, there are numerous literacies associated with complicated aspects of the business side of the culture, such as negotiating deals, keeping track of sales (even sales made out of the car trunk), booking concert dates, paying employees, and so on.

I would be remiss to end this section without a brief clarification of what I mean by *reading* and *writing*. The broader view of literacy invoked here, which extends beyond merely decoding and transcribing, is important in the shift from functional toward critical literacy. Reading includes understanding the meanings of texts and interpreting the world through a critical lens. Much of the decoding reading is preceded by these critical readings of the world. At the very least, they operate in a dialectic relationship, where they inform and inspire one another. It should be abundantly clear, however, that a plethora of traditional literacies are involved with being artists and producers within the reggae and hip-hop cultures.

Of course, not all participants are producers in the sense of being artists or performers, but even those who identify themselves primarily as consumers of these cultures (and almost all students do, at some level) are involved in a number of parallel literacy practices that have potential connections to academic and critical literacies. First, these peripheral yet legitimate participants are engaged in reading hip-hop and reggae core texts, which include CDs, music videos, and CD liner notes. This activity includes reading in the traditional sense. CDs, for instance, contain a great deal of printed text; some even come with small booklets. The reading also includes "reading" in the sense of critically interpreting media aurally and visually. For example, students will research artists via the Internet and even create websites and My Space pages that are tributes to their favorite musical artists. Musical consumption promotes a rereading of the world through the lens of critical hip-hop or reggae music.

TOWARD A CRITICAL PEDAGOGY OF POPULAR MUSIC WITH DIASPORA YOUTH IN THE AMERICAS

A legitimate case has been made for teaching popular music forms such as hip-hop and reggae in English language, English literature, and social studies classes at primary and secondary levels. However, functional literacies do not necessarily equate to freedom or empowerment for historically marginalized and alienated citizens. Functional literacies are significant, but only to the degree that they are augmented by critical literacies, those "literacies involving the consumption, production, and distribution of print and new media texts by, with, and on behalf of marginalized populations in the interests of naming, exposing, and destabilizing power relations; and promoting individual freedom and expression" (Morrell, 2004, p. 54). These revolutionary literacies encompass all of the relevant reading, writing, and reasoning skills associated with functional literacy, but also contain an understanding of the ideological nature of literacy. Critical literacy can also illuminate the power relationships in society and teach those who are critically literate to participate in and use literacy to change dominant power structures to liberate those who are oppressed by them (Freire & Macedo, 1987). Critical literacy is our best tool and our best hope for enabling dispossessed populations to work to liberate themselves and to work to make the world a more equitable and humane place. This is the literacy for freedom that has been part and parcel of the African diaspora narrative from Toussaint L'Ouverture to Frederick Douglass to Harriett Jacobs, and that continues into the present day (Douglass, 2001; James, 1962; Perry, Steele, & Hilliard, 2003).

To date, the work with hip-hop and reggae music has taken many forms, including close textual analyses of hip-hop and reggae lyrics (Quintero & Cooks, 2003; Morrell & Duncan-Andrade, 2002), writing and sharing student-generated lyrics via performance and publishable texts (Fisher, 2007; Jocson, 2006), and encouraging students to conduct research and write reports on the critical themes addressed in the music. Students, for instance, have investigated the potential of hip-hop music and culture to intersect with the goals of English curricula (Morrell, 2004); they have also analyzed the problematic corporate influences on the contemporary production of hip-hop culture (Camangian, 2006). These research studies have made direct links between the teaching of hip-hop music and culture and the academic literacy development of African diaspora youth.

In social studies classes, teachers have been encouraged to teach about African and African diaspora history, culture, and geography through the lens of hip-hop and reggae texts. Dagbovie (2005), for example, argues that hip-hop is a powerful yet underutilized tool for teaching about African

American history. In a classroom where I am currently working (in 2007), students are conducting documentaries that explore the relationships between popular music and youth resistance in their communities. This particular class has taken a historical approach to the study of popular music that includes folk, blues, rock, funk, reggae, hip-hop, and punk.

In my own work (Morrell, 2004), for example, I have investigated the empowering literacies associated with apprenticing youth as critical researchers of the language and literacy practices that occur within their communities and cultures. Starting in 1999, I began codirecting a seminar for urban teens in southern California. The 5-week seminar brings together students, teachers, and parents from urban schools and communities to design and carry out critical qualitative and quantitative research projects on issues of immediate concern to these schools and communities. The students work in groups of four or five on research teams that are led by a teacher in the local schools. Two primary goals are (1) to use the seminar space to help students acquire the literacies and tools they need to function within the academy, and (2) to engage teachers, students, and parents as collaborators in community-based praxis-oriented research.

Over the 8 years of the research project, I have documented the various ways that students have tapped into their own nonschool literacies to investigate the language and literacy practices of urban schools and communities. For example, students have investigated the language practices of students of color in urban schools, they have researched the language and literacy practices associated with popular culture, and they have investigated the language that the mainstream media use to construct youth of color.

The students demonstrated powerful academic literacies, both in the process of critical research and in the work products that emanate from the seminar. For example, in a recent seminar, students averaged more than 100 pages of notes each in their composition notebooks. These pages consisted of lecture notes, discussion notes, reading summaries, drafts of research protocols, field notes, interview transcriptions, analytic memos, and preliminary data analyses. These students also produced 1,500-word critical memoirs that encouraged them to reflect on their own personal experiences as they related to the research process, and to make connections between their changing identities as critical researchers and their plans for the future. The students also produced 3- to 5-minute iMovies that reported some aspect of the groups' research findings; 20-minute PowerPoint presentations that were prepared for an audience of university faculty and public officials; and 30-page collaboratively written research reports that contained introductions, literature reviews, a methods section, a discussion of findings, and implications for policy, research, and social action. These students have also translated this research into presentations and publications at the national peer-review level, as well as into changes in practice and policy at the local school level (Morrell, 2005). Thus, students are, in fact, doing high-quality academic work, but using rebel musics to frame that work allows them, in the spirit of Gramsci (1991), simultaneously to become better critical consumers (of dominant culture) and producers (of proletarian culture).

These research projects are contributing toward a grounded theory of African diaspora popular cultural literacy pedagogy in that they show that youth who appear unmotivated to the casual observer are motivated to engage rebel music inside and outside of their classrooms. Further, the projects document the sophisticated literacy practices and social analyses that accompany consumption and production of these texts. Nevertheless, we are only at the threshold of the truly meaningful work that needs to happen in critical education.

For example, what we know about African diaspora youth and popular culture warrants the introduction of media education and ethnic studies as stand-alone courses or extended units of study at primary and secondary levels. More than the occasional unit or lesson within traditionally defined disciplines, such as English or social studies, new ways of knowing and communicating, and the cultural turn in social sciences and philosophy, necessitates conversations about innovative disciplines in primary and secondary education. Great Britain and Canada, for instance, have already instituted compulsory media education into their primary and secondary curricula. Ethnic studies faces more of an uphill battle, though courses and programs in the United States date back to the late 1960s. Media education and ethnic studies courses are ideal spaces to feature reggae and hip-hop pedagogies and curricula to develop literacy skills and more critical approaches to media discourses and discourses about race and ethnicity.

As scholars, activists, and educators, we need to theorize literacy education as encompassing more than primary and secondary language arts and literature instruction. Incorporating critical hip-hop and reggae pedagogy across humanities and social sciences at the postsecondary level is an essential component of any comprehensive model of critical literacy education. There are immediate and powerful connections to be made within existing majors of linguistics, anthropology, sociology, education, English, literature, cultural studies, communication, women's studies, history, philosophy, political science, and African diaspora studies.

What is needed, then, is a movement toward a universal critical literacy that includes a critical literacy education across the disciplines, across the life span, and across contexts. If this movement is to be truly transformational, it must be cross-age, cross-discipline, and transnational; it will also require diligent efforts in schools (primary, secondary, and postsecondary) and in nonschool settings (homes, community centers, the workplace, and independent media).

We are all challenged to contemplate our roles and to develop innovative strategies, such as the inclusion of the study and production of rebel musics in our curricula and pedagogies, which facilitate the acquisition and development of empowering literacies for African diaspora students attending American and Caribbean schools.

UNESCO has declared 2003–2012 the decade of "literacy." This is an important and worthwhile goal, given the significance of acquiring literacies of power for academic advancement and professional membership. It becomes even more important if we understand "literacy" to include critical literacy. Systems of privilege are not immutable, as Gramsci (1991) noted, but changing them requires the development of citizens who are capable of "reading" systems of domination. We know enough to know that, across the diaspora, rebel musics can play a crucial role in the development of that citizenry.

Afterword

Carol Sills Strickland

What does it mean to "teach freedom" in the 21st century? How does the African American educational tradition inspire young people's innovation and liberation? Share the glimpse I had recently of what that possibility looks like.

It's a calm, sunny August afternoon in Washington, DC. I walk past the pool filled with frolicking boys and girls, their brown bodies shiny wet from the heat and water, and enter the coolness of the air-conditioned community center next door.

Here, another group of young people, about 20 teens of the Washington Enrichment and Cultural Arts Network's (WE CAN) "Reach-One-To-Teach-One" Academy, busily make final preparations backstage for their summer performance showcase. There's a friendly buzz in the room as parents, siblings, neighbors, relatives, and friends wait expectantly for the show to begin. As children settle on laps and conversations quiet, the founders of WE CAN, Mayfair residents Johnice Galloway Miller and Thandor Miller, welcome the audience warmly and create a feeling of community support for the young people who are about to show us their talents and creations. Then, their 5-year-old grandson, Kibwe, announces, "Let the show begin."

Among the performances are an original positive rap and a song called "You don't know my name," both of which point out how youth are so often judged by adults who know nothing about them. In dance vignettes, confident young women thoughtfully and gracefully express the challenges of making choices when peers and conscience pull in opposing directions. A play poignantly expresses a single mother's triumphs—sharing her oldest daughter's acceptance to college—and struggles—trying to help her younger daughter understand and resist the dangers of the streets. The final scene is a church service in which the young minister asks, "Why do we always ask 'What's wrong with the youth today?' Why don't we ask what we can do to help our youth help themselves?" The finale includes an original song about intergenerational caring, sung in harmony by adults and youth.

The audience's standing ovation shows genuine appreciation for the performers' talented presentations, which defy the negative media images, low expectations, and pervasive violence so often associated with urban young people. Reflecting on this performance of 21st-century youth, I realize that I am witnessing the unfolding of what we earlier called a "counternarrative for the current generation."

WE CAN is but one example of a program where strong and caring intergenerational relationships and a chance to participate creatively provide, as David Levine puts it in Chapter 3, a "radical affirmation of students' dignity." The program, like many other high-quality programs across the nation, gives young people the support, opportunities, and experiences that will help them challenge themselves and their friends to develop the best aspects of themselves and their communities. When we adults listen to what youth need, give them opportunities to shine, provide the supports that will help them to succeed, and encourage them to critically read their world, we are teaching freedom. Although the soundtrack and style may be different, the outcome is very similar to what Septima Clark and Ella Baker and their kindred sisters and brothers were striving to achieve—education for liberation.

References

About the Council of Independent Black Institutions (CIBI). Retrieved November 27, 2007 from www/cibi.org/about.htm

Adams, F., & Horton. M. (1975). *Unearthing seeds of fire: The idea of Highlander.* Charlotte, NC: John F. Blair.

Adickes, S. (2005). *Legacy of a freedom school.* New York: Palgrave Macmillan.

Agbasgebe, B. (1987). Family life on Wadmalaw Island. In P. Jones-Jackson (Ed.), *When roots die: Endangered traditions on the Sea Islands* (pp. 57–58). Athens: The University of Georgia Press.

Akbar, N. (1998). *Know thyself.* Tallahassee, FL: Mind Productions.

Alim, H. S. (2006). *Roc the mic: The language of hip-hop.* New York: Routledge.

Anderson, J. D. (1988). *The education of Blacks in the South, 1860–1935.* Chapel Hill: University of North Carolina Press.

Ani, M. (1994). *Yurugu: An African-centered critique of European cultural thought and behavior.* Trenton, NJ: Africa World Press.

Anyon, J. (2005). *Radical possibilities: Public policy, urban education, and a new social movement.* New York: Routledge.

Armah, A. (2000). *Two thousand seasons.* Popenguine, Senegal: Per Ankh.

Arroyo, C. G., & Zigler, E. (1995). Racial identity, academic achievement, and the psychological well-being of economically disadvantaged adolescents. *Journal of Personality and Social Psychology, 69*(5), 903–914.

Ayers, R. (2000). Social justice and small schools: Why we bother, why it matters. In W. Ayers, M. Klonsky, & G. Lyon (Eds.), *A simple justice: The challenge of small schools* (pp. 95–109). New York: Teachers College Press.

Baker, E. (1992). Developing community leadership. In G. Lerner (Ed.), *Black women in white America* (pp. 345–351). New York: Vintage Books.

Baldwin, J. (1996). A talk to teachers. In W. Ayers & P. Ford (Ed.), *City kids, city teachers: Reports from the front row* (pp. 219–227). New York: New Press.

Banks, J. (1992). African American scholarship and the evolution of multicultural education. *Journal of Negro Education, 61,* 273–286.

Barton, D., & Hamilton, M. (1998). *Local literacies: Reading and writing in one community.* London: Routledge.

Belfage, S. (1965). *Freedom summer.* New York: Viking Press.

Belgrave, F. Z., Van Oss Marin, B., & Chambers, D. B. (2000). Culture, contextual, and interpersonal predictors of risky sexual attitudes among urban African American girls in early adolescence. *Cultural Diversity and Ethnic Minority Psychology, 6*(3), 309–322.

Bennett, L. (1964). *Before the Mayflower: A history of the Negro in America*. Chicago: Johnson Publishing.

Black Community Crusade for Children. (1993, July 16–25). Summary of the Black Community Crusade for Children regional offices and constituency group meetings, Sante Fe, NM.

Black Panther. (1969a, June 25). Liberation means freedom, p. 13.

Black Panther. (1969b, June 21). Chairman's press conference at Safeway boycott, p. 14.

Black Panther. (1969c, August 2). San Francisco liberation school, p. 14.

Black Panther. (1971a, March 27). Educate to liberate, p. 1.

Black Panther. (1971b, November 11). A talk with the students of the Huey P. Newton Intercommunal Youth Institute, p. 4.

Black Panther. (1973a, Sept. 15). Youth institute opens, p. 4.

Black Panther. (1973b, October 27). Bobby Seale dedicates new youth institute and Son of Man Temple to community, p. 3.

Black Panther. (1973c, November 3). The world is their classroom: Interview with Brenda Bay, Director of the Intercommunal Youth Institute, p. 4.

Black Panther. (1974a, January 5). Youth institute's environmental studies project: An educational experience, p. 5.

Black Panther. (1974b, February 2). Youth institute succeeding where public schools failed: Interview with school's director Erika Huggins, p. 4.

Black Panther. (1974c, February 9). Youth institute teachers have "great love and understanding": Interview with Erika Huggins, director of model school, p. 4.

Black Panther. (1974d, February 16). Student's interests stressed in learning center's music program: Interview with Director Charles Moffett, p. 4.

Black Panther. (1974e, April 13). Group 4: Language arts with novelty, p. 4.

Black Panther. (1974f, April 20). I love freedom, I love community, p. 9.

Black Panther. (1974g, April 27). Group 6: Motivation is no problem, p. 4.

Black Panther. (1974h, May 4). Group 7: Method is very important, p. 4.

Black Panther. (1974i, May 18). Art in service of the people.

Black Panther. (1974j, June 22). Address of Deborah Williams at First Intercommunal Youth Institute graduation exercise, p. 2.

Black Panther. (1974k, June 22). Youth institute band wins west region FESTAL '74, p. 4.

Black Panther. (1974l, June 6). Youth committee develops independence and discipline, p. 4.

Black Panther. (1975a, February 1). Youth Institute carnival FUN! FUN! FUN!, p. 4.

Black Panther. (1975b, March 1). February in black people's history: Intercommunal Youth Institute honors Huey P. Newton in play, p. 14.

Black Panther. (1975c, August 18). Interview with Steve McCutchen, Director of the community learning center martial arts program, p. 23.

Black Panther. (1975d, October 18). Oakland community school: Education put into action.

Black Panther. (1975e, December 27). "Mighty Panthers" drill team highlights O.C.S. "December Festival", p. 4.

Black Panther. (1976a, January 3). 1976—The year of the Youth-In-Review, p. 14.

Black Panther. (1976b, October 16). Oakland Community School: A history of serving the youth, body and soul, p. 4.

Black Panther. (1977a, February 5). A brighter tomorrow: Courageous students join common bond.

Black Panther. (1977b, April 2). Come to me, let's be friends.

Black Panther. (1977c, April 2). Oakland Community School SOS: Win $1,000 in Support Our $chool donation drive.

Black Panther. (1977d, June 18). 11 graduate from Oakland Community School: "We want to set examples for our little children," p. 14.

Black Panther. (1977e, August 27). State award, radiothon boost community school and O.C.L.C. programs, pp. 1, 13.

Black Panther. (1977f, August 27). Text of resolution, p. 13.

Black Panther. (1977g, December 10). Oakland Community School—A model in action: Mathematics program, Part 2, p. 4.

Black Panther. (1977h, December 17). OCS donation drive raffle, p. 5.

Black Student Leadership Network. (1994, May 12–15). Black Student Leadership Network's Midwest Academy training sessions, prepared by the Ella Baker Child Policy Training Institute, Washington, DC.

Black Student Leadership Network. (1996). 1996 Black Student Leadership Network conference debriefing report.

Black theater groups: A directory. (1968). *Drama Review, 12,* 173.

Bolster, P. D. (1972). Civil rights movements in twentieth century Georgia. Ph.D. Dissertation, University of Georgia.

Bond, H. (1935). The curriculum and the Negro child. *Journal of Negro Education, 4,* 159–168.

Bond, J. (1995). Preface. In P. Foner (Ed.), *The Black Panthers speak* (p. xix). New York: Da Capo.

Bowman, P., & Howard, C. (1985). Race related socialization, motivation, and academic achievement: A study of black youths in three-generation families. *Journal of the American Academy of Child Psychiatry, 24,* 134–141.

Boyce, J. (1990, July 26). Grass-roots quest: More blacks embrace self-help programs to fight urban ills. *Wall Street Journal.*

Boykin, A. W. (1986). The triple quandary and the schooling of Afro-American children. In U. Neisser (Ed.), *The school achievement of minority children: New perspectives* (pp. 57–92). Hillsdale, NJ: Erlbaum.

Bradley, L. (2001). *This is reggae music: the story of Jamaica's music.* New York Grove Press.

Branch, T. (1988). *Parting the waters: America in the King years, 1954–1963.* New York: Simon and Schuster.

Brown, C. (1986). *Ready from within: Septima Clark and the civil rights movement.* Navarro, CA: Wild Trees Press.

Brown, D. (1974). *Wounded Knee* [Adapted for young readers by A. Ehrlich from D. Brown's *Bury my heart at Wounded Knee*]. New York: Holt, Rinehart and Winston.

Brown, E. (1992). *A taste of power: A Black woman's story.* New York: Pantheon.

Brown-Nagin, T. (1999). The transformation of a social movement into law? The SCLC and NAACP's campaigns for civil rights reconsidered in light of the educational activism of Septima Clark. *Women's History Review, 8*, 81–138.

Budge, W. (Trans.). (1967). *The Egyptian book of the dead.* New York: Dover Publications.

Bulhan, H. A. (1985). *Frantz Fanon and the psychology of oppression.* New York: Plenum.

Burrowes, N. (2000, May 2). Interview by Sekou Franklin.

Bushwick School for Social Justice. (2003). Available at http://www.bssj.net/ OurMission.asp.

Butler, K. D. (2000). From black history to diasporan history: Brazilian abolition in Afro-Atlantic context. *African Studies Review, 43*(1), 125–139.

Camangian, P. (2006). Real talk: Critical pedagogy in an urban English classroom. A paper presented at the annual meeting of the American Educational Research Association, San Francisco.

Canada, G. (2001, January 4). Interview by Sekou Franklin.

Cantarow, E., with O'Malley, S. G., & Strom, S. H. (1980). *Moving the mountain: Women working for social change.* Old Westbury, NY: Feminist Press.

Carawan, G. (n.d.). "Report of Guy Carawan's work with the adult school program—South Carolina Sea Islands 1960–1961," Box 37, Folder 11, Highlander Collection, Wisconsin State Historical Society.

Carawan, G., & Carawan, C. (1994). *Ain't you got a right to the tree of life? The people of Johns Island, South Carolina—Their faces, their words, and their songs.* Athens and London: University of Georgia Press.

Carmichael, S. (1971a). Free Huey (17 Feb. 1968). In *Stokely speaks* (pp. 113–121). New York: Random House.

Carmichael, S. (1971b). Pan-Africanism (Apr. 1970). In *Stokely speaks* (pp. 185–190). New York: Random House.

Carson, C. (1981). *In struggle: SNCC and the Black awakening of the 1960's.* Cambridge: Harvard University Press.

Carson, C. (1995). Foreword. In P. Foner (Ed.), *The Black Panthers speak* (pp. ix–xviii). New York: Da Capo.

Castle, M. A., & Arella, L. R. (2003). *The Brotherhood/Sister Sol survey evaluation report.* New York: Organizational Research & Development Associates.

Chatmon, K. (2000, August 17). Interview by Sekou Franklin.

Children's Defense Fund. (1991a, March 1, 1990–December, 1990). *Children's Defense Fund interim report to the Van Ameringen Foundation, Inc., Black community leadership training.* Washington, DC: Author.

Children's Defense Fund. (1991b). *Biographical sketches of black student leadership meeting participants.* Washington, DC: Author.

Children's Defense Fund. (2006). *CDF Freedom Schools® orientation and training manual.* Washington, DC: Author.

Children's Defense Fund. (n.d.). *Our program and why it works.* Washington, DC: Author. Available at http://www.freedomschools.org/program/default.aspx.

Clark, S. (1990). *Ready from within: Septima Clark and the civil rights movement.* Trenton, NJ: Africa World Press.

Clark, S., & Blythe, L. (1962). *Echo in my soul.* New York: E. P. Dutton Company.

Clark, S., with Brown, C. (1986). *Ready from within: Septima Clark and the civil rights movement.* Navarro, CA: Wild Trees Press.

Cobb, C. (1981). A summer freedom school in Mississippi (14 Jan. 1964). In *Student Nonviolent Coordinating Committee Papers, 1959–1972*, A=VIII=122. Sanford, NC: Microfilming Corporation of America.

Cobb, C. (1991). Prospectus for a Summer Freedom School Program. *Radical Teacher, 40,* 36.

Cobb, C. (1999). Organizing freedom schools. In S. Erenrich (Ed.), *Freedom is a constant struggle: An anthology of the Mississippi civil rights movement* (pp. 134–137). Montgomery, AL: Black Belt Press.

Cochran-Smith, M. (2004). *Walking the road: Race, diversity, and social justice in teacher education.* New York: Teachers College Press.

Cohen, E., & Lotan, R. (Eds.). (1997). *Working for equity in heterogeneous classrooms: Sociological theory in practice.* New York: Teachers College Press.

Collins, J. (2000, February). Brother Floyd. *Mays News, 1*(2), page numbers p. 1.

Cooper, C. (2004). *Sound clash: Jamaican dancehall culture at large.* New York: Palgrave Macmillan.

Council of Independent Black Institutions. (1990). *Positive Afrikan images for children: Social studies curriculum.* Trenton, NJ: Red Sea Press.

Countryman, M. (1988, March 26). Lessons of the divestment movement. *Nation,* pp. 406–409.

Countryman, M. (1991, July 24). Letter to Marian Wright Edelman.

Countryman, M. (2000, September 13). Interview by Sekou Franklin.

Cross, W. (1985). Black identity: Rediscovering the distinction between personal identity and reference group orientation. In M. B. Spencer, G. K. Brookins, & W. R. Allen (Eds.), *Beginnings: The social and affective development of Black children* (pp. 155–172). Hillsdale, NJ: Lawrence Erlbaum Associates.

Cruse, H. (1967). *The crisis of the Negro intellectual.* New York: William Morrow.

Curry, C. (1995). *Silver rights.* Chapel Hill, NC: Algonquin Books.

Curtis, L. (1990). *Literacy for social change.* Syracuse, NY: New Readers Press.

Dagbovie, P. (2005). Of all our studies, history is best qualified to reward our research: Black history's relevance to the hip hop generation. *Journal of African-American History, 90*(3), 299–323.

Darling-Hammond, L. (1998). New standards, old inequalities: The current challenge for African-American education. In *The state of Black America report.* Chicago: National Urban League.

Davis, J. (1969, August 2). The Liberation School. *Black Panther,* p. 14.

Delain, M., Pearson, P. D., & Anderson, R. (1985). Reading comprehension and creativity in Black language use: You stand to gain by playing the sounding game. *American Educational Research Journal, 22,* 155–173.

Delpit, L. (1986). Skills and other dilemmas of a progressive Black educator. *Harvard Educational Review, 56,* 379–385.

Delpit, L. (1988). The silenced dialogue: Power and pedagogy in educating other people's children. *Harvard Educational Review, 58,* 280–298.

Dewey, J. (1990). *The school and society.* Chicago: University of Chicago Press.

Dittmer, J. (1994). *Local people: The struggle for civil rights in Mississippi.* Urbana: University of Illinois Press.

Douglas, V. (1969, August 2). The youth make the revolution. *Black Panther,* p. 2.

Douglass, F. (2001). *Narrative of the life of an American slave, Frederick Douglass: Written by himself.* New Haven, CT: Yale University Press

DuBois, W.E.B. (1973). The revelation of Saint Ogrne the Damned (1938). In *The education of Black people: Ten critiques, 1906–1960* (pp. 103–126). New York: Monthly Review.

DuBois, W.E.B. (1982). *The souls of Black folk.* New York: Signet. (Original work published 1903).

Durlak, J. A., & Wells, A. M. (1997). Primary prevention mental health programs for children and adolescents: A meta-analytic review. *American Journal of Community Psychology, 25*(2), 115–135.

Fairclough, A. (2001). *Teaching equality: Black schools in the age of Jim Crow.* Athens: University of Georgia Press.

Farley, C. (1999). Hip-hop nation: There's more to rap than just rhythms and rhymes. After two decades, it has transformed the culture of America. *Time, 153*(5), 55–65.

Fifth annual spring conference of the Student Nonviolent Coordinating Committee. (1964). 1981. In *Student Nonviolent Coordinating Committee Papers, 1959–1972* (reel 18, 0929). Sanford, NC: Microfilming Corporation of America.

Fine, M. (1991). *Framing dropouts: Notes on the politics of an urban public high school.* Albany: State University of New York Press.

Finnegan, W. (1990, September 10). A reporter at large: Out there—I. *New Yorker,* pp. 51–86.

Fisher, M. (2007). *Writing in rhythm: Spoken word poetry in urban classrooms.* New York: Teachers College Press.

Foner, P. (1970). Liberation schools. In P. Foner (Ed.), *The Black Panthers speak* (pp. 170–171). Philadelphia: Lippincott.

Fraser, C. (1989). *Charleston! Charleston! The history of a southern city.* Columbia: University of South Carolina Press.

Freedom school curriculum—1964. (1991). *Radical Teacher, 40,* 6–34.

Freire, P. (1993). *Pedagogy of the oppressed.* New York: Continuum. (Original work published 1970).

Freire, P. (1998). *Education for a critical consciousness.* New York: Continuum. (Original work published 1973).

Freire, P., & Macedo, D. (1987). *Literacy: Reading the word and the world.* New York: Bergin and Garvey.

Freire, P., & Shor, I. (1987). *Pedagogy of liberation.* New York: Bergin and Garvey.

Garrett, J. (1968). And we own the night: A play of Blackness. *Drama Review, 12,* 61–69.

Garrett, J. (1969, April 16). Black Power and Black education. *Washington Free Press,* p. 8.

Garrett, J. (1981). The why of freedom schools (c. 1965). In *Student Nonviolent Coordinating Committee Papers, 1959–1972* [C=I=74]. Sanford, NC: Microfilming Corporation of America.

Garrett, J. (1998–1999). Black/Africana/pan African studies: From radical to reactionary to reform. *Journal of Pan African Studies*, *1*, 150–179.

Gavins, R. (2000, April 18). Interview by Sekou Franklin.

Gee, J. P. (1989). The narrativization of experience in the oral style. *Journal of Education, 171*, 75–96.

George, N. (1998). *Hiphopamerica*. New York: Penguin.

Giles, H. (1998). *ERIC Digest: Parent engagement as a reform strategy*. New York: ERIC Clearinghouse on Urban Education.

Glen, J. M. (1996). *Highlander: No ordinary school*. Knoxville: University of Tennessee Press.

Gonzalez, F. (2004). Graduation address. Retrieved February 21, 2007, from http://www.elpuente.us/academy/index.htm.

Goodwyn, L. (1976). *Democratic promise: The populist moment in America*. New York: Oxford University Press.

Gordon, B. M. (1995). African American cultural knowledge and liberatory education: Dilemmas, problems, and potentials in postmodern American Society. In Shujaa, M. J. (Ed.), *Too much schooling, too little education: A paradox of Black life in White societies* (pp. 57–80). Trenton, NJ: Africa World Press.

Gordon, D. M. (2000). *Mentoring urban Black male students: Implications for academic achievement, ethnic/racial identity development, racial socialization, and academic disidentification*. Ph.D. Dissertation, University of South Dakota.

Gramsci, A. (1971). *Selections from the prison notebooks*. New York: International.

Gramsci, A. (1991). *Selections from cultural writings*. Cambridge, MA: Harvard University Press.

Grant, J. (Director). (1981). *Fundi: The story of Ella Baker*. New York: New Day Films.

Grant, J. (1998). *Ella Baker: Freedom bound*. New York: Wiley.

Greene, S. (2000, April 11). Interview by Sekou Franklin.

Gurwitt, R. (1990, February). A younger generation of black politicians challenges its leaders. *Governing the states and localities*, 29–33.

Hahn, S. (2003). *A nation under our feet: Black political struggles in the rural south from slavery to the Great Migration*. Cambridge, MA: Harvard University Press.

Hale-Benson, J. (1986). *Black children: Their roots, culture and learning styles* (Rev. Ed.). Baltimore: The Johns Hopkins University Press.

Hanson, P. D. (1975). *The dawn of apocalyptic*. Philadelphia: Fortress Press.

Harding, R. (1998). Biography, democracy, and spirit: An interview with Vincent Harding. *Callaloo* (Summer), 682–698.

Harding, V. (1981). *There is a river: The Black struggle for freedom in America*. New York: Harcourt Brace Jovanovich.

Hayden, C. (2003). Ella Baker as I knew her: She trusted youth! *Social Policy*, 34(2), 101–103.

Hayes, F. W., & Kiene, F. A. (1998). All power to the people: The political thought of Huey P. Newton and the Black Panther Party. In C. E. Jones (Ed.), *The Black Panther party reconsidered* (pp. 157–176). Baltimore: Black Classic Press.

Heath, G. (1976). *Off the pigs! The history and literature of the Black Panther Party*. Metuchen, NJ: Scarecrow Press.

Heath, S. B. (1989). Oral and literate traditions among Black Americans living in poverty. *American Psychologist, 44*, 367–373.

Henry, A., & Curry, C. (2000). *Aaron Henry: The fire ever burning.* Jackson: University Press of Mississippi.

Highlander Reports. (1954, October 1). Highlander Library. Highlander Research and Education Center Collection, New Market, Tennessee.

Hill, P. (2004). Passages: Birth, initiation, marriage and death. In J. Gordon (Ed.), *The African presence in Black America.* Trenton, NJ: Africa World Press.

Hilliard, A. G. (1998). *SBA: The reawakening of the African mind.* Gainesville, FL: Makare.

Hilliard, A. G., Williams, L., & Damali, N. (1987). *The teachings of Ptahhotep: The oldest book in the world.* Atlanta, GA: Blackwood.

Hilliard, D., & Cole, L. (2001). *This side of glory: The autobiography of David Hilliard and the story of the Black Panther Party.* Chicago: Lawrence Hill (Original work published 1993).

Hine, D. (1992). The Black studies movement: Afrocentric-traditionalist-feminist paradigms for the next stage. *Black Scholar, 23*, 11–18.

Hoffman, F. (1968, August 30). Stokely teaches in Watts. *Los Angeles Free Press*, pp. 8, 18.

Hoffman, J. (1975, June 30). Reading, writing and fighting in the Oakland ghetto. *Black Panther*, pp. 23–24.

hooks, b. (2004). *We real cool: Black men and masculinity.* London: Routledge.

Horton, A. I. (1989). *The Highlander Folk School: A history of its major programs, 1932–1961.* Brooklyn, NY: Carlson.

Horton, M. (1990). *The long haul: An autobiography.* New York: Doubleday.

Howe, F. (1984). Mississippi's freedom schools. In F. Howe (Ed.), *Myths of coeducation: Selected essays* (pp. 1–17). Bloomington: Indiana University Press.

Howlett, C. (1993). *Brookwood Labor College and the struggle for peace and social justice in America.* Lewiston, NY: Edwin Mellen Press.

Hoy, D. (1996). BSLN history project.

Hoy, D. (2000, September 9). Interview by Sekou Franklin.

Hoy, D., Gavins, R. T., & Walker, N. (1995, April). *One thousand by two thousand: Training, organizing, and galvanizing a new generation of African Americans for power in the twenty-first century* [Position paper] (pp. 1–10).

Huggins, E. (1978, April 17). Weekly report, Re: Collective parents meeting from Ericka to Huey.

Huggins, E. (1993, March 18). Interview with Charles Jones.

Hunter, C. (1969 August 18). Panthers indoctrinate the young. *New York Times*, p. 31.

Jacobson, M. (2005). Bob Marley live: Reggae, rasta, and Jamaica fourteen years after Marley's death. In H. Bordowitz and R. Steffens (Eds.), *Every little thing gonna be alright: The Bob Marley Reader.* Cambridge, MA: Da Capo Press.

James, C.L.R. (1962). *The Black Jacobins: Toussaint L' Ouverture and the Santo Domingo revolution.* New York: Vintage.

James, T. (1999, August 15). Interview by Sekou Franklin.

Jennings, R. (1998). Why I joined the Party: An Africana womanist reflection. In

C. E. Jones (Ed.), *The Black Panther Party Reconsidered* (pp. 257–266). Baltimore: Black Classic Press.

Jocson, K. (2006). Bob Dylan and hip hop: Intersecting literacy practices in youth poetry communities. *Written Communication, 23*(3), 231–259.

Johnson, D., & Hoy, D. (1994). Freedom schools feed children and empower parents. *We speak! A voice of African American youth, 1*(3), 1.

Jones, C. E., & Jeffries, J. L. (1998). Don't believe the hype: Debunking the panther mythology. In C. E. Jones (Ed.), *The Black Panther party reconsidered* (pp. 22–55). Baltimore: Black Classic Press.

Jones, J. M. (1991). Racism: A cultural analysis of the problem. In R. L. Jones (Ed.), *Black psychology* (3rd ed., pp. 609–636). Berkeley, CA: Cobb and Henry.

Jones, K. (1991, July 29). Memo to black leadership meeting participants, meeting follow-up.

Jones, K. (2000, June 17). Interview by Sekou Franklin.

Jones-Jackson, P. (1987). When roots die. In *When roots die: Endangered traditions on the Sea Island Root* (pp. 22–55). Athens: University of Georgia Press.

Karenga, M. (1989). *The African American holiday of Kwanzaa: A celebration of family, community and culture*. Los Angeles: University of Sankore Press.

Karenga, M. (Trans. & commentator). (1990). *The book of coming forth by day: The ethics of the declarations of innocence*. Los Angeles: University of Sankore Press.

Kelly, R. (2002). *Freedom dreams: The Black radical imagination*. Boston: Beacon Press.

Kennedy, T. (n.d.). About Esau Jenkins and the Sea Islands of South Carolina. Folder 10, Box 55, The Highlander Research and Education Center Collection, The State Historical Society of Wisconsin, Madison.

King, Jr., M. (1985). Letter from Birmingham Jail—April 16, 1963. In M. Sernett (Ed.), *Afro-American religious history: A documentary witness* (pp. 430–445). Durham, NC: Duke University Press.

KRS One. (2005). The elements of hip-hop. Retrieved May 25, 2005, from http://www.templeofhiphop.org.

Labov, W. (1972). *Language in the inner city*. Philadelphia: University of Pennsylvania Press.

LaCocque, A. (1979). *The book of Daniel*. D. Pellauer (Trans.). Atlanta: John Knox Press.

LaCocque, A. (1988). *Daniel in his time*. Columbia: University of South Carolina Press.

Ladson-Billings, G. (1995). Toward a theory of culturally relevant pedagogy. *American Educational Research Journal, 32*, 465–491.

Lawson, S. F., & Payne, C. (2006). *Debating the civil rights movement, 1945–1968*. Lanham, MD: Rowman and Littlefield.

Lazarre-White, K. (Ed.), *Voices of the brotherhood/sister sol*. New York: The Brotherhood/Sister Sol, 2001.

Leblanc-Ernest, A. (1998). The most qualified person to handle the job: Black Panther women. In C. E. Jones (Ed.), *The Black Panther Party reconsidered* (pp. 305–334). Baltimore: Black Classic Press.

Lee, C. D. (1993). *Signifying as a scaffold for literary interpretation: The pedagogical implications of an African American discourse genre.* Washington, DC: National Council of Teachers of English.

Lee, C. D. (2007). *Culture, literacy and learning: Blooming in the midst of the whirlwind.* New York: Teachers College Press.

Lee, C., Lomotey, K., & Shujaa, M. (1990). How shall we sing our sacred song in a strange land? The dilemma of double consciousness and the complexities of an African-centered pedagogy. *Journal of Education, 172,* 45–61.

Lee, C. K. (1999). *For freedom's sake: The life of Fannie Lou Hamer.* Urbana: University of Illinois Press.

Levine, D. P. (1999). *Citizenship schools.* Ph.D. Dissertation, University of Wisconsin-Madison.

Levine, D. P. (2004). The birth of the citizenship schools: entwining the struggles of literacy and freedom. *History of Education Quarterly, 44*(3), 388–414.

Levine, L. (1977). *Black culture and black consciousness: Afro-American folk thought from slavery to freedom.* New York: Oxford University Press.

Levine, M. (1998). Prevention and community. *American Journal of Community Psychology, 26*(2), 189–200.

Light, A. (1999). *The vibe history of hip-hop.* New York: Three Rivers Press.

Lorde, A. (1981). The master's tools will never dismantle the master's house. In C. Moraga and G. Anzaldúa (Eds.), *This bridge called my back: Writings by radical women of color* (pp. 98–101). Watertown, MA: Persephone Press.

Lucas, B. (1976, February 5). East Oakland ghetto blooms with growth of Black Panther school. *Jet,* p. 15.

Lydia, M. (1999, November 2). Interview by Sekou Franklin.

Madhubuti, H. R. (1979). *From plan to planet.* Chicago: Third World Press.

Madhubuti, H. (1990). *Black men: Single, obsolete, dangerous?* Chicago: Third World Press.

Major, R. (1971). *A Panther is a black cat.* New York: William Morrow.

Make the Road by Walking. (2002, October 10). As Bloomberg and NYC Schools Chancellor Joel Klein push for "200 new schools"' parents, students, teachers, say: "You must consult with us!" [Press release].

Make the Road by Walking. (2004). Annual report: Building community strength. New York: Author.

Manley, M. (2004). Reggae and the revolutionary faith: The role of Bob Marley. In H. Bordowitz (Ed.), *Every little thing gonna be alright: The Bob Marley reader* (pp. 216–224). Cambridge, MA: De Capo Press.

Mann, H. (1844). *Reply to the "remarks" of thirty-one Boston schoolmasters on the Seventh Annual Report of the Secretary of the Massachusetts Board of Education.* Boston: Fowle and N. Capen.

Marable, M. (1991). *Race, reform, and rebellion: The second reconstruction in Black America, 1945–1990* (2nd ed.). Jackson: University Press of Mississippi.

Martín-Baró, I. (1994). *Writings for a liberation psychology.* Cambridge, MA: Harvard University Press.

Mason, C. A., Cauce, A. M., Robinson, L., & Harper, G. W. (1999). Introduction:

Adolescent risk behavior: Linking theory with action; A community psychology agenda. *American Journal of Community Psychology, 27*(2), 107–115.

Matthews, T. (1998). "No one ever asks what a man's place in the revolution is": Gender and the politics of the Black Panther Party, 1966–1971. In C. E. Jones (Ed.), *The Black Panther Party reconsidered* (pp. 277–278). Baltimore: Black Classic Press.

Matthews, V. R. (1998). Mays and racial justice. In L. E. Carter Sr. (Ed.), *Walking integrity: Benjamin Elijah Mays, mentor to Martin Luther King, Jr* (pp. 263–288). Macon, GA: Mercer University Press.

Mbiti, J. (1989). *African religions and philosophy.* London: Heinemann. (Original work published 1970)

McCutchen, S. (1992, May). Interview with Charles Jones.

Mediratta, K., & Fruchter, N. (2003). *From school governance to community accountability: Building relationships that make schools work.* New York: The Institute for Education and Social Policy, New York University

Milstein, S. (1985, April 12). Ex-panther Newton accused of embezzling school funds. *San Francisco Chronicle.*

Moraga, C. (1981). La güera. In C. Moraga and G. Anzaldúa (Eds.), *This bridge called my back, Writings by radical women of color* (p. 100). Watertown, MA: Persephone Press.

Morgan, J. (2000, February). Back to our roots. *Mays News, 1*(2).

Morrell, E. (2002). Toward a critical pedagogy of popular culture: Literacy development among urban youth. *Journal of Adolescent and Adult Literacy, 46*(1), 72–77.

Morrell, E. (2004). *Becoming critical researchers: Literacy and empowerment for urban youth.* New York: Peter Lang.

Morrell, E. (2005). Critical English education. *English Education, 37*(4), 312–322.

Morrell, E., & Duncan-Andrade, J. (2002). Toward a critical classroom discourse: Promoting academic literacy through engaging hip-hop culture with urban youth. *English Journal, 91*, 6, 88–94.

Morris, A. (1984). *The origins of the civil rights movement: Black communities organizing for change.* New York: Macmillan.

Morris, R. C. (1981). *Reading, 'riting, and reconstruction: The education of freedmen in the South, 1861–1870* (pp. 174–181). Chicago: University of Chicago Press.

Moses, R., & Cobb, C., Jr. (2001). *Radical equations: Math literacy and civil rights.* Boston: Beacon Press.

Mueller, C. (1990). Ella Baker and the origins of "participatory democracy." In V. Crawford, J. Rouse, & B. Woods (Eds.), *Women in the civil rights movement: Trailblazers and torchbearers, 1941–1965* (pp. 51–70). New York: Carlson.

Murrell, P. C. (1997). Digging again the family wells: A Freirian literacy framework as emancipatory pedagogy for African-American children. In P. Freire (Ed.), *Mentoring the mentor: A critical dialogue with Paulo Freire* (pp. 19–55). New York: Peter Lang.

Murrell, P. C. (2001). *The community teacher.* New York: Teachers College Press.

Newton, H. (1972). *To die for the People: The writings of Huey P. Newton.* New York: Vintage.

Newton, H. (1974). Intercommunal Youth Institute. *Co-Evolution Quarterly: Supplement to the Whole Earth Catalog, 3*(3), 9.

Newton, H. (1996). *War against the Panthers: A study of repression in America.* New York: Harlem River Press.

Newton, H. (n.d.a). Memoir: Each one teach one champagne sip. In *Huey P. Newton Foundation Papers* (Series 2, Box 16, Folder 11). Stanford University.

Newton, H. (n.d.b). Oakland community school handbook. Vol. Series 2, *Huey P. Newton Foundation Papers* (Series 2, Box 17, Folder 1). Stanford University.

Newton, H. (n.d.c). Oakland community school structure. In *Huey P. Newton Foundation Papers* (Series 2, Box 16, Folder 15). Stanford University.

New York City Board of Education. (2001). *Bushwick High School annual school report.* New York: New York City Board of Education.

New York City Department of Education. (2005). *Bushwick High School annual school report.* New York: New York City Department of Education. Available at http://schools.nyc.gov/daa/SchoolReports/05asr/332480.PDF.

New York City Housing and Neighborhood Information System (NYCHANIS). (2000). Available at http://www.nychanis.com

Njeri, A. (1991). *My life with the Black Panther Party.* Oakland: Burning Spear Publications.

Nobles, W. (1980). African philosophy: Foundations for Black psychology. In R. Jones (Ed.), *Black psychology* (pp. 23–36). New York: Harper and Row.

OLS Weekly Report. (1978, March 19). Huey Newton Foundation Papers (Series 2, Box 16, Folder 4): Stanford University, Stanford CA.

Oldendorf, S. (1990). The South Carolina Sea Islands citizenship schools, 1957–1961. In V. L. Crawford, J. A. Rouse, & B. Woods (Eds.), *Women in the civil rights movement: Trailblazers and torchbearers, 1941–1965* (pp. 169–182). Bloomington: Indiana University Press.

Oldendorf, S. (1998, April). *The Sea-Island citizenship schools: Pedagogy of the disenfranchised.* Paper delivered at the annual meeting of the American Educational Research Association, San Francisco.

Orrick, Jr., W. (1969). *Shut it down! A college in crisis, San Francisco State College, October 1968–April 1969.* Washington, DC: National Commission on the Causes and Prevention of Violence.

Payne, A. (1996, April 8–9). One step forward. *City limits.* New York: City Futures, Inc.

Payne, C. (1989). Ella Baker and models of social change. *Signs: Journal of Women in Culture and Society, 14*(4), G885–899.

Payne, C. (1995). *I've got the light of freedom: The organizing tradition and the Mississippi freedom struggle.* Berkeley: University of California Press.

Payne, C. (2000). Education for activism: Mississippi's freedom schools in the 1960s. In W. Ayers, M. Klonsky, & G. Lyon (Eds.), *A simple justice: the challenge of small schools* (pp. 67–77). New York: Teachers College Press.

Payne, C. (2003, September). More than a symbol of freedom: Education for liberation and democracy. *Phi Delta Kappan,* 22–29.

Payne, C., & Green, A. (2003). *Time longer than rope: A century of African American activism, 1850–1950.* New York: New York University Press.

Peck, C. (2000, Oct.). *From guns to grammar: Education and change in the Black Panther Party.* Paper presented at the annual meeting of the History of Education Society, San Antonio.

Perlstein, D. (1990). Teaching freedom: SNCC and the creation of the Mississippi freedom schools. *History of Education Quarterly, 30,* 297–324.

Perlstein, D. (2004). *Justice, justice: School politics and the eclipse of liberalism.* New York: Peter Lang.

Perry, T. (2003). Up from the parched earth: Toward a theory of African-American achievement. In T. Perry, C. Steele, & A. Hilliard III (Eds.), *Young, gifted, and Black: Promoting high achievement among African-American students* (pp. 1–10). Boston: Beacon Press.

Perry, T., Steele, C., & Hilliard III, A. (Eds.). (2003). *Young, gifted, and Black: Promoting high achievement among African-American students.* Boston: Beacon.

Phinney, J. S. (1992). The Multi-Group Ethnic Identity Measure: A new scale for use with diverse groups. *Journal of Adolescent Research, 7*(2), 156–176.

Prilleltensky, I., & Fox, D. (1997). Introducing critical psychology: Values, assumptions, and the status quo. In D. Fox & I. Prilleltensky (Eds.), *Critical psychology: An introduction* (pp. 3–20). Thousand Oaks, CA: Sage.

Quintero, K., & Cooks, J. (2003). Hip hop as authentic poetry. *Voices from the Middle, 10*(2), 56–57.

Ramanathan, G. (1965). *Educational planning and national integration.* New York: Asia Publishing House.

Ransby, B. (2003). *Ella Baker and the black freedom movement: A radical democratic vision.* Chapel Hill: University of North Carolina Press.

Ratteray, J. D. (1989). *What's in a norm? How African-Americans score on achievement tests.* Washington, DC: Institute for Independent Education.

Ravitch, D. (1990, Summer). Multiculturalism: E. pluribus plures. *American Scholar, 59*(3), 337–354.

The Refugee Camp. (1996). *The score* [compact disc]. New York: Ruffhouse/Columbia Records.

Reports on Washington DC Liberation School. (1981). In *Student Nonviolent Coordinating Committee papers, 1959–1972,* I=C=74. Sanford, NC: Microfilming Corporation of America.

Reyes, M. (1991a, April). *The "one size fits all" approach to literacy.* Paper presented at the annual meeting of the American Educational Research Association, Chicago.

Reyes, M. (1991b). A process approach to literacy instruction for Spanish-speaking students: In search of a best fit. In E. H. Hiebert (Ed.), *Literacy for a diverse society: Perspectives, practices and policies* (pp. 157–171). New York: Teachers College Press.

Richards, J. (1987). *The Southern Negro Youth Congress: A history.* Ph.D. dissertation, University of Cincinnati.

Richardson, J. (1981a). Memo to SNCC executive committee RE: Residential freedom school (6 Sept. 1964). In *Student Nonviolent Coordinating Committee Papers, 1959–1972*, A=II=4. Sanford, NC: Microfilming Corporation of America.

Richardson, J. (1981b). Residential freedom school report (Aug. 1965). In *Student Nonviolent Coordinating Committee Papers, 1959–1972*, 20, 0101. Sanford, NC: Microfilming Corporation of America.

Robinson, J. (1991, July 23). Black college student group proposal, submitted by the working committee to the Children's Defense Fund.

Rothschild, M. (1982). *A case of Black and White: Northern volunteers and the southern freedom summers, 1964–1965*. Westport, CT: Greenwood Press.

San Francisco Chronicle. (1967, May 26). An angry benefit for S.F. Black Panthers, p. 2.

Seale, B. (1969, March 3). Chairman Bobby Seale: From the March 1969 Issue of the Movement. *Black Panther*, p. ??.

Seale, B. (1970). *Seize the time: The story of the Black Panther party*. New York: Random Books.

Shaw, S. (1996). *What a woman ought to be and do: Black professional women workers during the Jim Crow era*. Chicago: University of Chicago Press.

Sheets, R. H. (1999). Relating competence in an urban classroom to ethnic identity development. In R. H. Sheets & E. R. Hollins (Eds.), *Racial and ethnic identity in school practices: Aspects of human development* (pp. 157–178). Mahwah, NJ: Erlbaum.

Shirley, D. (1997). *Community organizing for urban school reform*. Austin: University of Texas Press.

Smith, E. P., Walker, K., Fields, L., Brookins, C., & Seay, R. C. (1999). Ethnic identity and its relationship to self-esteem, perceived efficacy and prosocial attitudes in early adolescence. *Journal of Adolescence*, 22(6), 867–880.

Smith, R., Axen, R., & Pentony, D. (1970). *By any means necessary: The revolutionary struggle at San Francisco State*. San Francisco: Jossey-Bass.

Smitherman, G. (1977). *Talkin and testifyin: The language of Black America*. Boston: Houghton Mifflin.

Spady, J., Alim, S., & Meghelli, S. (2006). *The global cipha: Hip hop culture and consciousness*. Philadelphia: Black History Museum Press.

Spencer, M. B. (1988). Self-concept development. In D. T. Slaughter (Ed.), *Black children and poverty* (pp. 59–72). San Francisco: Jossey-Bass.

Stembridge, J. (n.d.). *Freedom school notes*. Boston: New England Free Press.

Stembridge, Jane. (n.d.). *Notes on Teaching in Mississippi*. Retrieved December 14, 2007, from http://educationanddemocracy.org/FSCfiles/B_10_NotesOnTeaching InMS.htm.

Stevenson, H. (1994). Validation of the Scale of Racial Socialization for African American adolescents: Steps toward multidimensionality. *Journal of Black Psychology*, 20(4), 445–468.

Stevenson, H. (1995). Relationship of adolescent perceptions of racial socialization to racial identity. *Journal of Black Psychology*, 21(1), 49–70.

Sullivan, L. (2000, May 3). Interview by Sekou Franklin.

Sutherland, E. (1965). *Letters from Mississippi*. New York: McGraw-Hill.

Taaffe, C. (1999, April 24). Interview by Sekou Franklin.

Tate, G. (2005, January 5–11). Hiphop turns 30, Whatcha celebratin' for? *Village Voice*, p. 32.

Thelwell, M. (1969). Black studies: A political perspective. *Massachusetts Review*, 10, 701–712.

Tjerandsen, C. (1980). *Education for citizenship: A foundation's experience*. Santa Cruz, CA: Schwarzhaupt Foundation.

Townsend, T. G., & Belgrave, F. Z. (2000). The impact of personal identity and racial identity on drug attitudes and use among African American children. *Journal of Black Psychology*, 26(4), 421–436.

Tuck, S.G.N. (1995). A city too dignified to hate: Civic pride, civil rights, and Savannah in comparative perspective. *Georgia Historical Quarterly, 79*, 539–559.

Tuck, S.G.N. (2001). *Beyond Atlanta: The struggle for racial equality in Georgia, 1940–1980*. Athens: University of Georgia Press.

U.S. Bureau of the Census. (1963). *Census of Population and Housing*, 34, 39; Bureau of the Census, Census of the Population: 1960-Volume 1. Characteristics of the Population, Part 42. Bureau of the Census, South Carolina.

United States Department of Education (2005). *National assessment of educational progress' the nation's report card: reading 2005*. Jessup, MD: EdPubs.

View, J. (1996, February). *Citizenship 2000: A civic curriculum for mobilizing communities trainers' guide*.

Walker, J. (2000, March 16). Interview by Sekou Franklin.

Ward, S. (2001). Scholarship in the context of struggle: Activist intellectuals, the Institute of the Black World and the contours of black power radicalism. *Black Scholar, 31*, 42–54.

Warfield-Coppock, N. (1990). *Adolescent rites of passage*. Vol. 1 of *Afrocentric theory and applications*. Washington, DC: Baobab Associates.

Warren, M. 2005. Communities and schools: A new view of urban education reform. *Harvard Educational Review, 75*(2):133–173.

Waugh, J. (1969, May 6). Angry young Black changed all that. *Christian Science Monitor*, p. 6.

White, S. (2000, March 3). Interview by Sekou Franklin.

White, S., Sullivan, L., & Countryman, M. (1992–1993). Building a cross-class, multigenerational movement for black children. *We speak! A voice of African-American youth, 1*(2), 1, 6–7.

Williams, C. (1987). *The destruction of Black civilization*. Chicago: Third World Press. (Original work published 1974)

Williams, L. (1982, April 2). State probes panther school funding. *Oakland Tribune*.

Williams, L., & Ayres, G. (1982, November 7). School aid says he warned official of misused funds. *Oakland Tribune*.

Williamson, J. (2000, April). *Educate to liberate! SNCC, Panthers, and emancipatory education*. Paper presented at the annual meeting of the American Educational Research Association, New Orleans.

Willis, M. (1989). Learning styles of African-American children: A review of the literature and interventions. *Journal of Black Psychology, 16*, 47–65.

Wilmore, G. S. (1984, November 4–7). *Spirituality and social transformation*. Lecture delivered during The Howard Thurman Consultation at Northwestern University, Evanston, Illinois.

Wilson, A. (1978). *The developmental psychology of the Black child.* New York: Africana Research Publications.

Winnicott, D. W. (1960). Ego distortion in terms of true and false self. In The maturational processes and the facilitating environment (1965, pp. 140–152). New York: International Universities Press.

Woodruff, N. (1984). *Esau Jenkins: A retrospective view of the man and his times.* Charleston, SC: Avery Institute of Afro-American History and Culture.

Woodson, C. G. (1933). *Mis-education of the Negro.* Washington, DC: Associated Publishers.

Zaslavsky, C. (1990, October–November). Bringing the world into the math class. *Rethinking Schools, An Urban Educational Journal, 5,* 5. [Reprinted from *Curriculm Review,* 1985 (January–February), 24].

About the Editors
and the Contributors

Chris Myers Asch taught elementary and middle school for 3 years in Sunflower, Mississippi, as part of Teach for America/AmeriCorps. He cofounded the Sunflower County Freedom Project in 1998 and launched the U.S. Public Service Academy initiative in 2006.

William Ayers is Distinguished Professor of Education and Senior University Scholar at the University of Illinois at Chicago (UIC), and founder of both the Small Schools Workshop and the Center for Youth and Society. He teaches courses in interpretive and qualitative research, urban school change, and teaching and the modern predicament. Ayers has written extensively about social justice, democracy and education, the political and cultural contexts of schooling, and the meaning-making and ethical purposes of students and families and teachers.

Charles E. Cobb, Jr. is senior writer and diplomatic correspondent for allAfrica .com, the world's largest electronic provider of news and information from Africa, and a visiting professor at Brown University. After entering Howard University in 1961, Cobb left a year later to work as a field secretary for the Student Nonviolent Coordinating Committee in the Mississippi Delta. He accompanied Mrs. Fannie Lou Hamer on her first attempt to register to vote in 1962. Cobb is coauthor, with Robert P. Moses, of the book *Radical Equations, Civil Rights from Mississippi to the Algebra Project.* His latest book is *On the Road to Freedom, a Guided Tour of the Civil Rights Trail* (2008).

Sekou Franklin teaches in the Department of Political Science at Middle Tennessee State University. From 1993 to 1996, he served as a teaching intern/organizer in Oakland, California, for the Black Student Leadership Network's Summer Freedom School Program. In the late 1990s, he also worked as a teaching intern/organizer for LISTEN Inc.'s Mason-Butler-Hobson Freedom School Program in Washington, DC. His research areas are African American politics, social movements, civil rights, and municipal politics. Currently, he is completing a book that examines social movement activism among the post–civil rights generation.

Jonathan Gayles, Assistant Professor of African American Studies at Georgia State University, has published widely in the areas of the cultural context of educational outcomes and educational policy analysis.

Hollyce C. Giles is an Associate Professor of Community and Justice Studies at Guilford College, in Greensboro, North Carolina. Her research and publications focus on the group dynamics of community-school relations, particularly partnerships between community organizing groups and public schools.

Deanna M. Gillespie is a Ph.D. candidate in the History Department at the State University of New York–Binghamton. Her dissertation traces the history of the Citizenship Education Program through case studies of the South Carolina Sea Islands, southeastern Georgia, and the Mississippi Delta.

Steven Hahn is the Roy F. and Jeannette P. Nichols Professor of History at the University of Pennsylvania. His books include *The Roots of Southern Populism: Yeoman Farmers and the Transformation of the Georgia Upcountry, 1850–1890* and *A Nation Under our Feet: Black Political Struggles in the Rural South from Slavery to the Great Migration,* which won the Pulitzer Prize in History, the Bancroft Prize in American History, and the Merle Curti Prize in Social History of the Organization of American Historians.

Michael G. Hayes is a minister and educational activist concerned with the moral and spiritual development of youth. In addition to his work in churches, he was a member of a group of educators, activists, and parents who launched the Chicago Algebra Project, an innovative mathematics curriculum that helps children transition from arithmetic to algebra.

Charles E. Jones is an Associate Professor in, and founding Chair of, the Department of African American Studies at Georgia State University. He has published extensively in scholarly journals and anthologies on African American politics and African American studies and is the editor of *The Black Panther Party Reconsidered.* He is the current president of the National Council for Black Studies.

Carol D. Lee is Professor of Education and Social Policy at Northwestern University and a member of the National Academy of Education. Her most recent book, *Culture, Literacy, and Learning: Taking Bloom in the Midst of the Whirlwind* demonstrates how learning outcomes for traditionally under-served students can be improved when teachers draw on the knowledge that students bring to school with them. She taught in both public and private schools before assuming a university career and is a cofounder of two African-centered schools.

David Levine is an Assistant Professor in the School of Education at the University of North Carolina–Chapel Hill and serves on the editorial board of the urban education journal *Rethinking Schools*. His research interests include parent organizing in urban contexts and the role of radical pedagogy in the civil rights movement. Prior to his academic career, he spent several years teaching and working in educational change groups in Milwaukee, Wisconsin.

Ernest Morrell is an Associate Professor in Urban Schooling and Associate Director for Youth Research at the Institute for Democracy, Education, and Access (IDEA) at the University of California at Los Angeles. Morrell is the author of *Linking Literacy and Popular Culture: Finding Connections for Lifelong Learning, Becoming Critical Researchers: Literacy and Empowerment for Urban Youth*, and *Critical Literacy and Urban Youth: Pedagogies of Access, Dissent, and Liberation.*

Robert Charles Morris taught history at the University of Maryland, Rutgers University, and Teachers College before joining the National Archives and Records Administration in 1987 as director of the Northeast Region. *Reading, Writing and Reconstruction* was nominated for the Pulitzer Prize in History.

Charles M. Payne is the Frank P. Hixon Distinguished Service Professor in the School of Social Service Administration at the University of Chicago. His books include the award-winning *I've Got the Light of Freedom: The Organizing Tradition and the Mississippi Freedom Struggle* and the forthcoming *So Much Reform, So Little Change: The Persistence of Failure in Urban School Systems* (Harvard Education Publishing Group). Along with Randolph Potts and Charles Jones, he is a cofounder of the Education for Liberation Network (www.edliberation.org).

Daniel Perlstein is a historian who has written widely on the interplay of democratic aspirations and social inequalities in American education. His works include *Justice, Justice: School Politics and the Eclipse of Liberalism*. He teaches in the Graduate School of Education at Berkeley.

Randolph Potts is a licensed psychologist in Memphis, Tennessee. He was a member of the Council of Directors of the Benjamin E. Mays Institute in

Hartford while on faculty at Holy Cross College, and developed a rites of passage program at a medium-security prison in Connecticut. He has published articles on topics including emancipatory education, rites of passage, and the relationship between spirituality and illness.

Fannie Theresa Rushing is Associate Professor of History at Benedictine University. Rushing organized the first chapter of the Friends of the Student Nonviolent Coordinating Committee (SNCC) at the University of Illinois/Chicago and became the director of the Chicago office of SNCC. She now works on the Chicago SNCC History Project, collecting oral histories of the civil rights movement.

Gale Seiler teaches science education as well as sociocultural theory as an Associate Professor at McGill University in Montreal. Her current work employs theories from cultural sociology, Black psychology, and cultural studies to explore the teaching and learning of science among urban, African American high school students. She was a founder of the Baltimore Freedom School.

Carol Sills Strickland, Ed.D., studies how urban students benefit from after-school and summer programs that integrate culturally competent youth development principles into education. She has served as associate editor for the journal *New Schools, New Communities*, on the editorial board of the *Harvard Educational Review*, and on the editorial board of *Afterschool Matters*. She currently serves as director of research and evaluation for the DC Children and Youth Investment Trust Corporation in Washington, DC.

Susan Wilcox is a coexecutive director of The Brotherhood/Sister Sol (BHSS) a Harlem-based comprehensive youth organization. Since 1987, Susan has coordinated and led education and development programs in Africa, Latin America, and the Caribbean with BHSS, IYLI, and Operation Crossroads Africa, Inc. She earned an Ed.D. in Curriculum and Teaching at Teachers College/Columbia University and an Ed.M. in Educational Technology at Harvard Graduate School of Education.

Index